IMAGES
of America

MICHIGAN CITY MARINAS

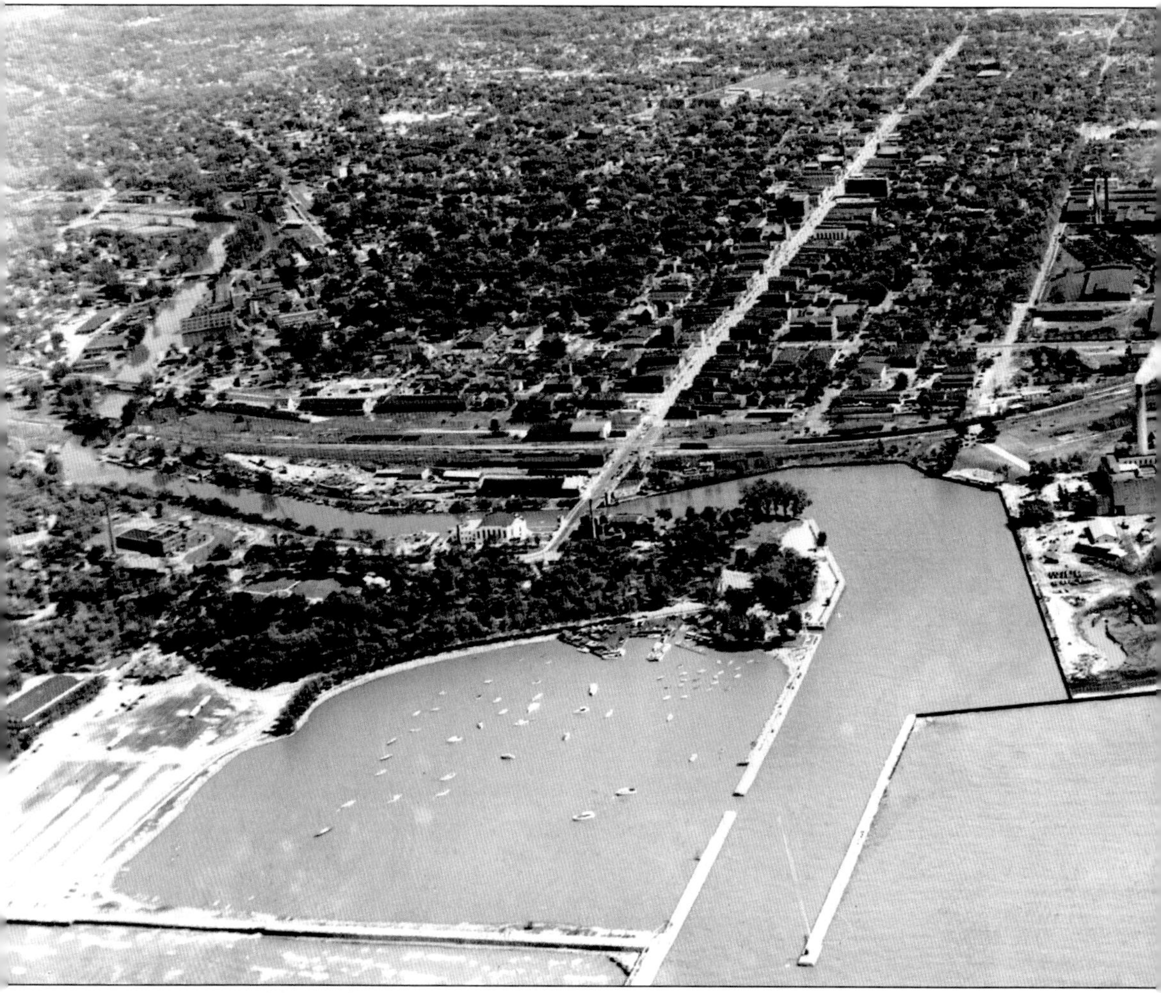

Here is an aerial view of Michigan City's harbor in 1949, 10 years before the Michigan City Port Authority was created. The boats in the basin are moored by "cans" scattered throughout the area. The boating community in Michigan City was worried whether these meager facilities were enough to accommodate the growing popularity of boating in the area. Also shown here is the Trail Creek channel getting narrower and shallower as it winds into the city. By 1959, residents were able to walk across the creek upstream, although the factories were faced with the problem of docking without water. (Michigan City News Dispatch.)

On the cover: Photographer Bill Swedenberg captures a boat parade in July 1960. The boating community turned out in force each year to attend the parade sponsored by the Michigan City Yacht Club. The club was the only advocate for pleasure boating in the area until the Michigan City Port Authority came along in 1959. Thereafter the two collaborated to sponsor many activities at the lakefront. (Bill Swedenberg.)

IMAGES
of America

MICHIGAN CITY MARINAS

Jonita Davis
for the Michigan City Port Authority

ARCADIA
PUBLISHING

ISBN 978-0-7385-6126-4

Published by Arcadia Publishing
Charleston SC, Chicago IL, Portsmouth NH, San Francisco CA

Printed in the United States of America

Library of Congress Catalog Card Number: 2008929033

For all general information contact Arcadia Publishing at:
Telephone 843-853-2070
Fax 843-853-0044
E-mail sales@arcadiapublishing.com
For customer service and orders:
Toll-Free 1-888-313-2665

Visit us on the Internet at www.arcadiapublishing.com

This book is dedicated to all the boaters, harbor enthusiasts, and Michigan City Port Authority advocates who have fought long and hard to create Michigan City's marinas.

CONTENTS

ACKNOWLEDGMENTS

I would like to thank those who helped my quest for photographs, including Anthony Lambre at the *Michigan City News Dispatch*; Bill Swedenberg, who has captured Michigan City on film for decades; John Haynes; and everyone else who did not shy away from a photograph for the history books. Unless otherwise indicated, all images are courtesy of the Michigan City Port Authority.

INTRODUCTION

From the early 1800s, the point where Trail Creek spilled into Lake Michigan was an area coveted as a perfect location for a port. While the area was naturally desirable, the funds required to improve the small harbor that sprang up were hard to come by. A sandbar at the mouth of the harbor reduced depth to only one foot in some spots. Lake Michigan winds kicked up violent waves, which prevented many ships from getting close enough to dock. Residents tried to garner federal attention. In the meantime, Michigan City sprang up on the lakeside.

On July 4, 1837, news arrived that the town would get funds to improve its harbor—a sum of $20,000. That same day, a lumber schooner named the *Sea Serpent* reached the harbor with a load destined for one of the lumber companies that emerged on the banks of Trail Creek. Brave ships like the *Sea Serpent* usually docked just outside the harbor, ready to "cut and run" if high winds or thieves were to strike. That day, however, residents crowded the dock in celebration of their windfall and decided that the *Sea Serpent* would dock. The town residents gathered to pull the ship over the sandbar at the mouth of the harbor, using only ropes and their bare hands. After the grueling task, barrels of whiskey were tapped, and another celebration began at the docks. The port at Michigan City was officially open.

After that first cash payment, the federal government clearly stated that it would fund only one major commercial port on Lake Michigan. A stiff competition erupted between Chicago and Michigan City. Millions of federal dollars were at stake to the winning city. Michigan City residents wanted those funds; they were not the only ones, however. The Indiana state government also wanted it; the state decided to give the town a hand. Roads in and around Michigan City were paved. Other small improvements were made in and around the lakefront to capture the federal government's attention as well as its money.

Soon the promise of millions and the title of the commercial port on Lake Michigan had faded away. Chicago was picked to be the major commercial port on Lake Michigan. The people of Michigan City felt slighted. Their city had the most hospitable harbor, frequented by what they saw as a bigger host of commercial clients than Chicago. The townsfolk were livid as they watched millions of dollars pour into the town across the lake. At the same time, ships and small boats that ventured into Michigan City's harbor tried their best to navigate the slowly filling channel.

By 1864, the city's harbor was in a crisis. The crumbling facilities had begun to deter business. Several downtown businessmen decided to do something before the shipping activity dried up altogether. These men formed the Michigan City Harbor Company, which would continue the work that was started but abandoned by the federal government. The company sold bonds to Michigan City residents, raising $100,000 to get the channel and harbor dredged. In two years, the company found that its harbor needed more than a dredge. The needed improvements required more money that the shareholders did not have. The company was liquidated, and the debt was absorbed by the city. City officials resumed their lobby for federal development funds.

Twenty years passed before the federal government finally turned its attention back to Michigan City's harbor. Money was allocated to repair and expand the meager, deteriorating harbor facilities. Eastern and western piers were constructed to extend Trail Creek. The breakwater in the outer harbor was also constructed at this time. Its purpose was to provide safety to boaters for the days when the Lake Michigan winds kicked up destructive waves. To finish these projects, city tax money was used. There were no objections from the public, however. Everyone had been waiting to have the harbor built; a few extra taxes seemed a small compromise. When the work was done, Michigan City had a new 30-acre yacht basin that could accommodate pleasure boaters as well as new dock facilities for the commercial ships. Traffic increased tremendously.

Michigan City's shipping boom lasted until the start of the 20th century when once again the harbor fell into disrepair. The government funds for dredging and maintenance had dried up like the channel. The result was a swift decline in commercial shipping. The revenues at the lakefront declined with the shipping. Seeing this, local officials, business leaders, and city residents rallied once again for federal support. They were successful, gaining only a partial dredge of the harbor, but more was needed. Businesses along Trail Creek folded, and traffic slowed even more. Silt filtered into the harbor, making the trip up the channel challenging once again. The piers, bulkheads, and even the breakwater began to deteriorate. The yacht basin was swallowed up in silt and weeds.

After a long fight and no success, the city residents began to turn a blind eye toward the lakefront. They moved on to other issues that pressed the city. By 1920, the basin was the site of an unofficial landfill. The mayor, in an attempt to get rid of the eyesore, tried to have the entire area filled in. Afterward, he planned to put in a baseball diamond with a parking lot. The yacht basin would be no longer.

According to *Our Heritage: Michigan City, IN*, by the Michigan City News Dispatch, two men, dubbed "two of the city's earliest pleasure boating enthusiasts," stepped between the city and the basin. Pop Heisman and E. G. "Babe" Browne took the city to court to obtain a cease and desist order for the trash dumping as well as the planned ball field. To Heisman and Browne's dismay, however, the damage had already been done. The immense pleasure boating mooring area—the yacht basin—had been reduced to a third of its original size. Today's yacht basin is smaller than that.

The entire harbor area was still in dire need of maintenance and improvement. Like the Michigan City Harbor Company 57 years before, a group of boaters and businessmen organized to fight for the harbor. However, unlike their earlier counterparts, these men were focused only on attracting the pleasure-boating industry back to Michigan City. The industrial heyday that the harbor saw in the late 1800s was long gone. Led by a man named Harry Frey, they had no desire to revive it. Instead, Frey and his group felt that pleasure boating would bring in the economic windfall that the city once saw from commercial shipping. They organized in 1933, forming the Michigan City Yacht Club, which was born in the naval armory's mess hall. With Frey as its commodore, the group organized a massive cleanup effort for the basin, the docks, and the surrounding areas. Yacht clubbers also successfully petitioned the federal government for a much-needed dredge.

The pleasure-boating industry soon dominated the lakefront. By 1958, there was a recorded 2,000 boats moored in the yacht basin. Despite the growth in popularity of pleasure boating, the facilities soon fell into disarray once again. Another dredge was sorely needed, and a massive expansion was in order to accommodate the boaters who flocked to the area each season. By the late 1950s, commercial boating had decreased even more, with only a few shipments trickling into to the harbor each year. This time, try as they might, the men of the yacht club could not get the funds or the attention needed to maintain the harbor. Another group of pleasure boaters organized—the Northern Indiana Boating Association (NIBA)—and tried to rally support. According to the *Michigan City News Dispatch*, at the group's first meeting, boater Bill Udell foreshadowed the future of the harbor if something was not done. "Michigan City this summer will face a critical shortage of boat mooring facilities [without] municipal help, either in money or in acting."

Later in the meeting, NIBA members acknowledged that a group of citizens could only get so far. A new group was needed, a government agency that had the power to get things done. The NIBA joined the yacht club and city officials, and together they brought that agency into being.

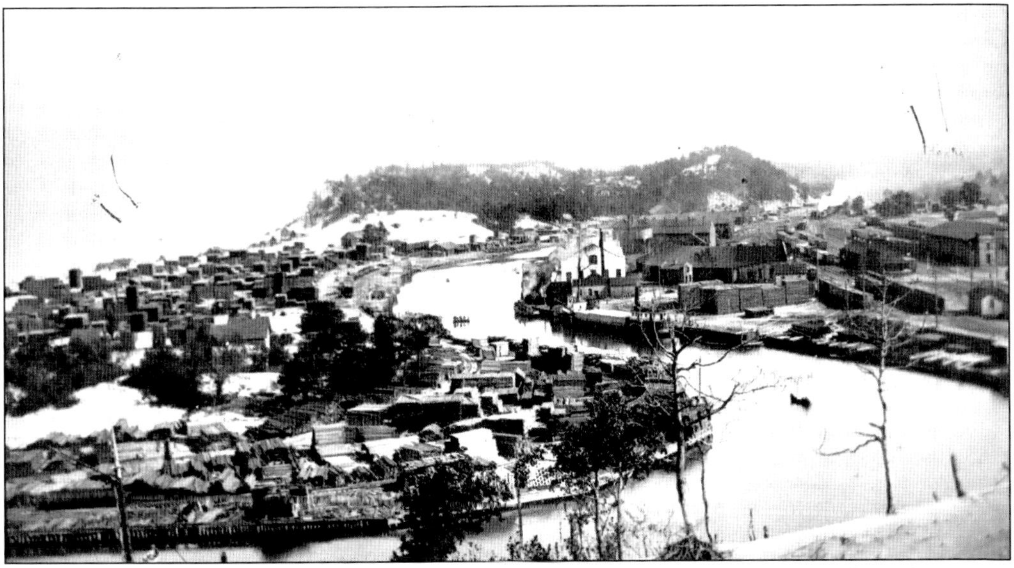

The height of shipping in Michigan City took place in the 19th century. One of the first major exports was lumber, seen here stacked along Trail Creek. Soon commercial fisheries opened and factories grew up along the channel as well. By the turn of the century, in 1900, however, commercial shipping was declining. (Bill Swedenberg.)

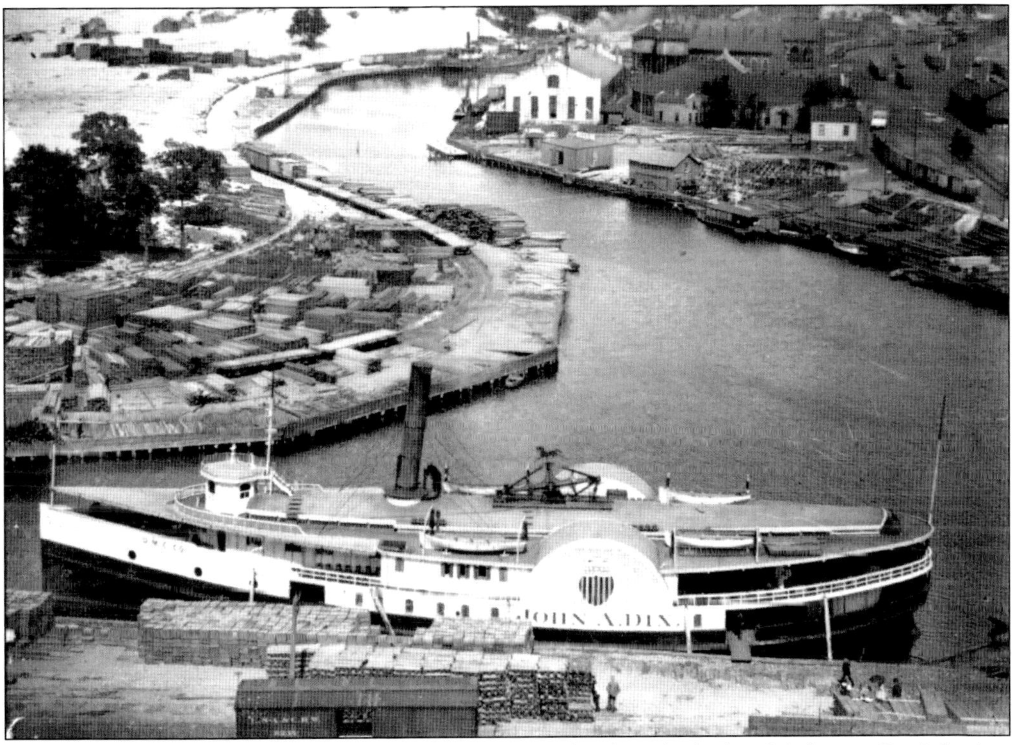

Large boats such as the *John A. Dix* in the photograph often docked in Michigan City's harbor in the late 1800s. Michigan City officials had trouble maintaining the docks that accommodate ships like this one and those much larger. Despite the sometimes deteriorating facilities, many ships continued to come to Michigan City each year to conduct business. (Bill Swedenberg.)

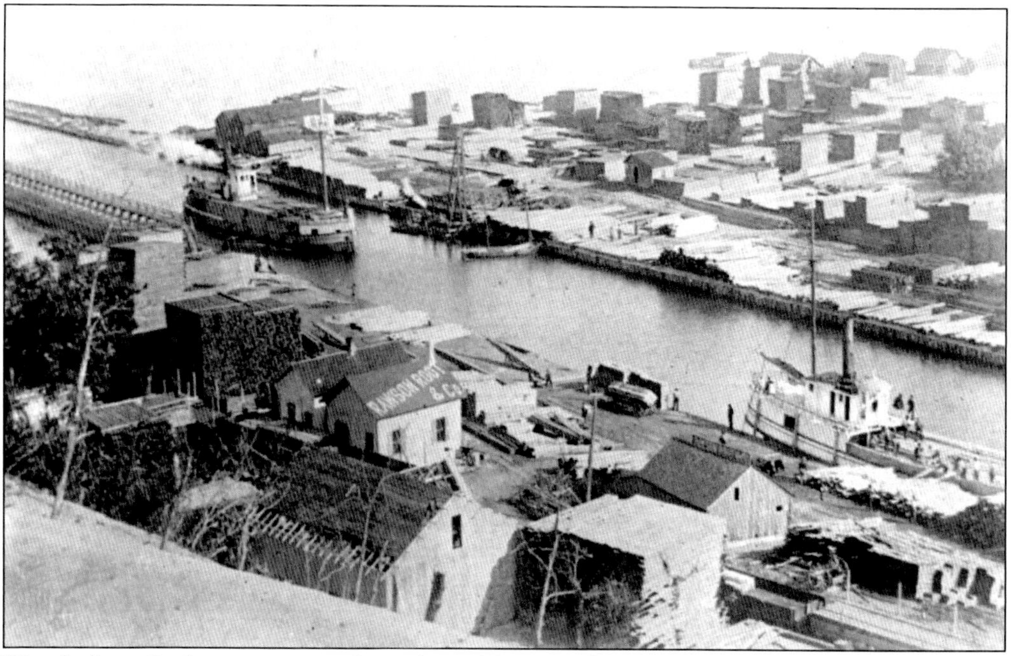

The docking facilities were not the only problems at that time. Navigating the channel into and out of the harbor was also risky at times. City residents continuously requested funds to dredge or remove sand and silt buildup from the harbor. These requests were often denied. (Bill Swedenberg.)

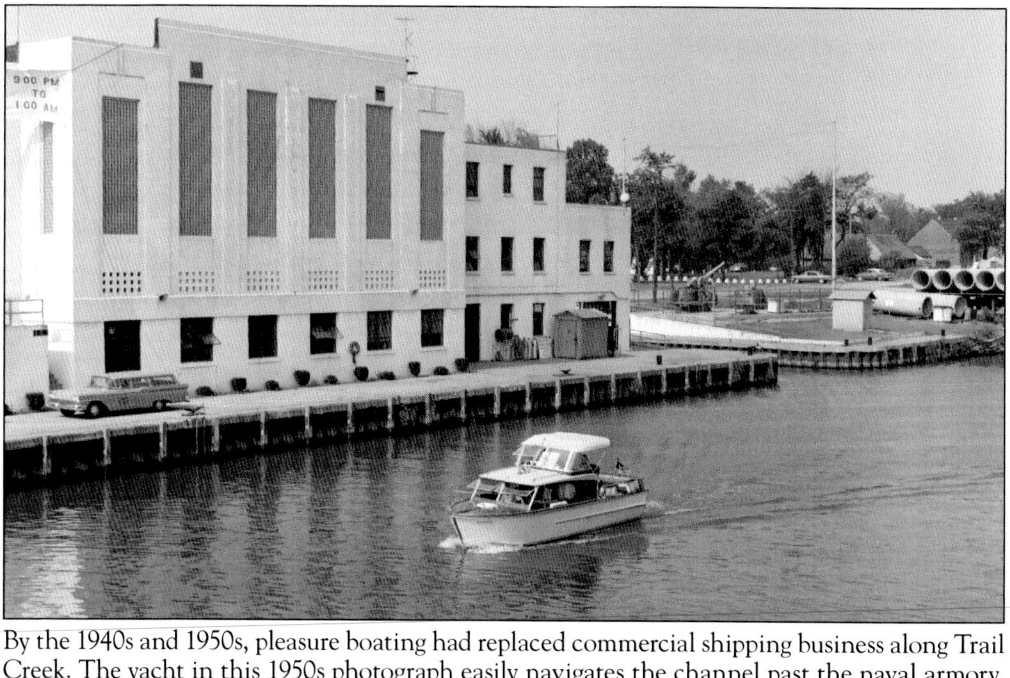

By the 1940s and 1950s, pleasure boating had replaced commercial shipping business along Trail Creek. The yacht in this 1950s photograph easily navigates the channel past the naval armory. At the time, the only large ships that frequented the channel past the Franklin Street Bridge were naval ships docking at the armory, scenic cruise ships, and soon the occasional salt boat. (Michigan City News Dispatch.)

One

Birth of the Port Authority

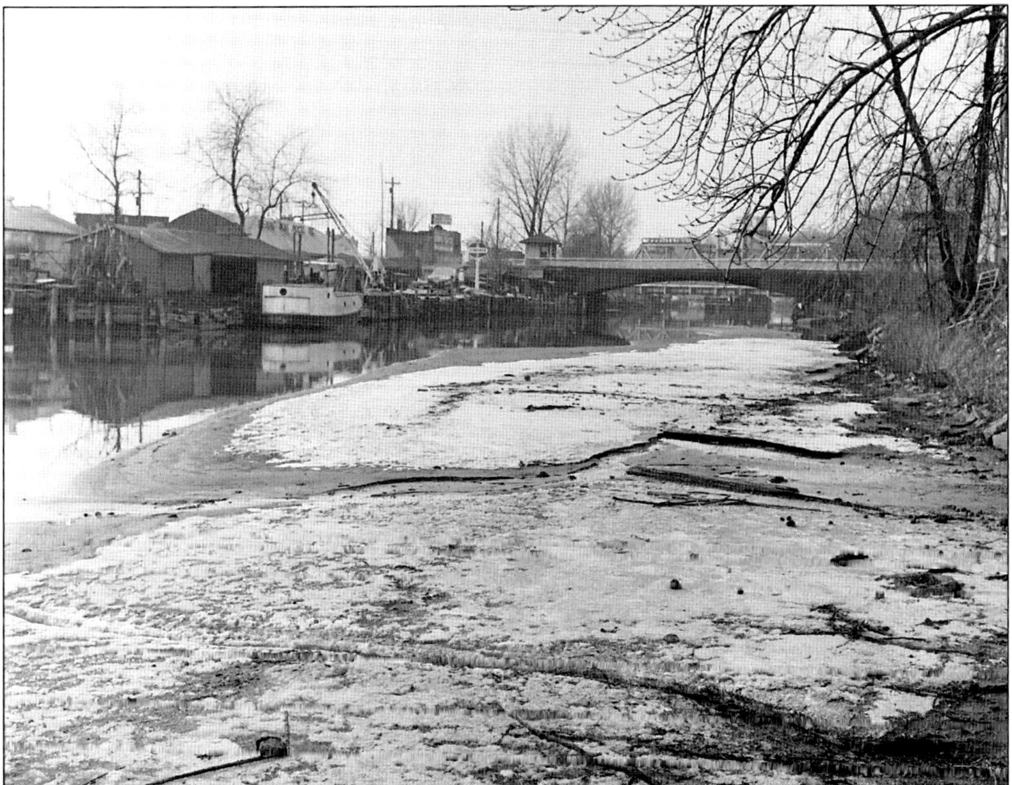

This description appeared in *Our Heritage: Michigan City, IN*, published in 1976: "The harbor channel southeastward from the New York Central Railroad Bridge looks more like a dirt lane after a rainstorm than the healthy, flowing waterway it ought to be. The turning basin adjacent to the Blocksom Company, where lumber schooners once maneuvered, is a vast mud flat . . . Birds land mid-harbor without getting a feather wet." (Michigan City News Dispatch.)

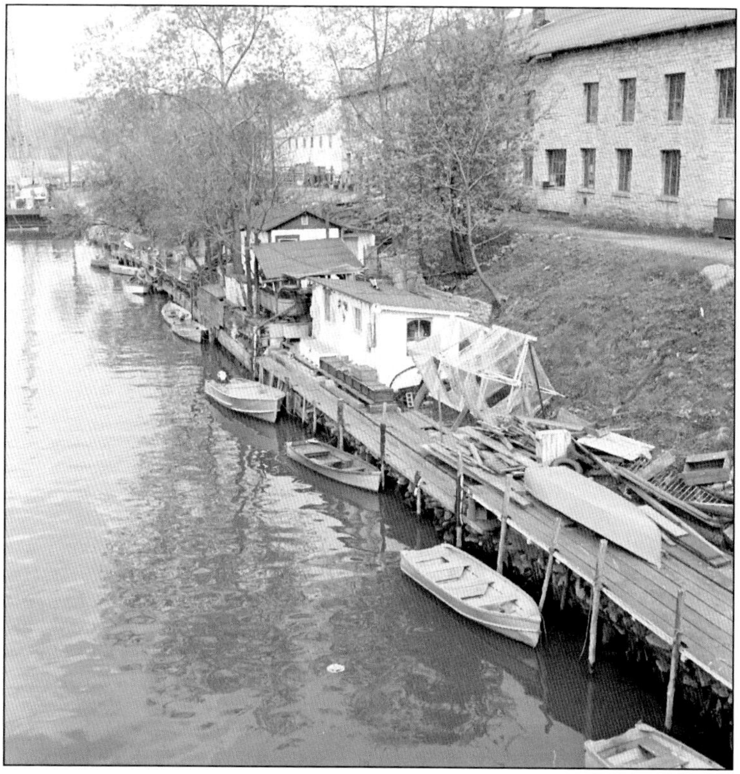

In this photograph, boats sit a few feet below dock on low water in Trail Creek. Tugboat operator Fred "Butch" Ritter described a ditch that he and other businesses created so that they could navigate the channel. According to a Bob Kaser article from the *Michigan City News Dispatch*, "That hole's all we've got now, and we have to try to stay in it." (Michigan City News Dispatch.)

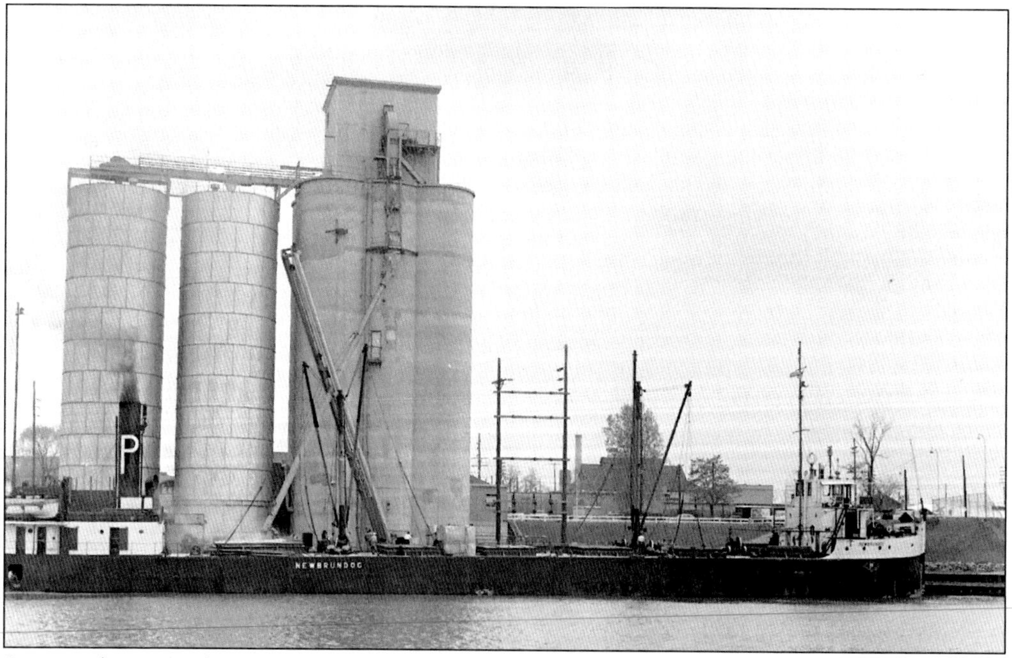

Seen in this 1959 photograph, even the Cargill Grain Elevator had trouble getting ships in and out of the harbor despite its position near the mouth of Trail Creek. However, the commercial traffic generated by the Cargill Grain Elevator and others proved beneficial to obtaining a dredge, but they had to wait a few years. (Michigan City News Dispatch.)

Mayor Francis Fedder and the city council, upon hearing the news, appointed the Michigan City Harbor Advisory Commission to come up with a plan of action. Mark "Mr. Harbor" Moorman (pictured), who was the township assessor and a former Michigan City Yacht Club (MCYC) commodore, headed the group. Moorman's nickname came from his dedication to advancing pleasure boating in Michigan City.

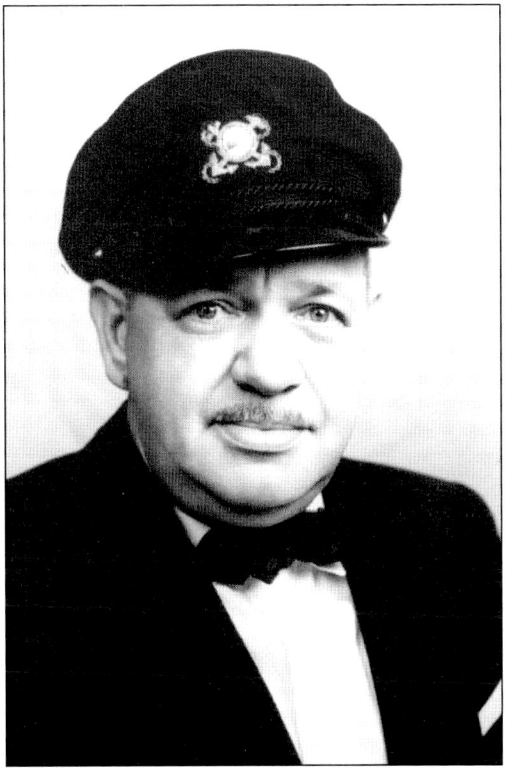

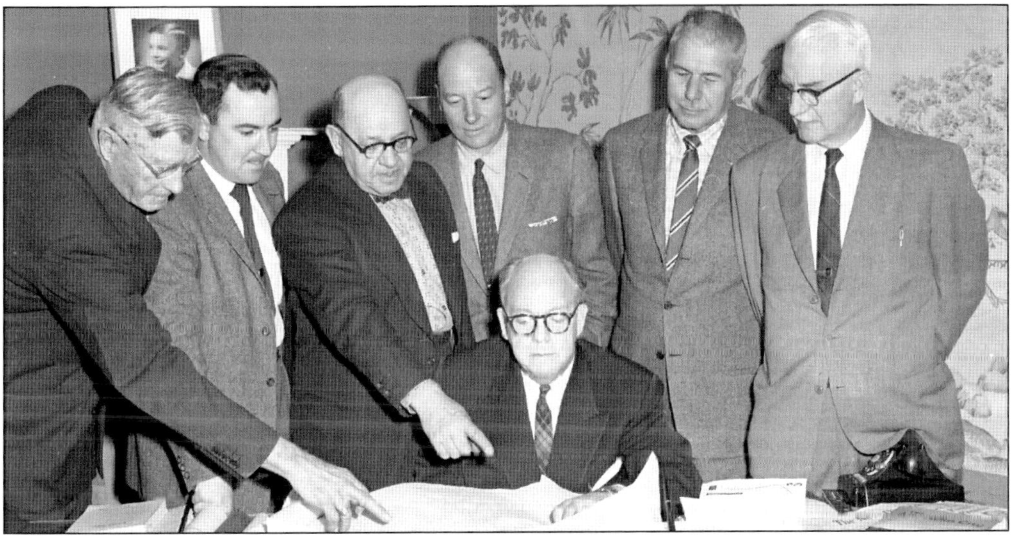

Joining Moorman were others with interests in the lakefront, including city engineer and harbormaster John Kelley and Paul Jackson, who was city attorney. The Michigan City Harbor Advisory Commission (shown here), along with Northern Indiana Boating Association (NIBA) and the MCYC, eventually drafted a resolution that formed a new government agency. That agency had the power to operate and maintain Trail Creek, the yacht basin, and all other port facilities. In this photograph are Mayor Francis Fedder (sitting) with, from far left to right, William Blank, Roger McKee, Mark Moorman, Harry Frey, Paul Jackson, and John Kelley. (Michigan City News Dispatch.)

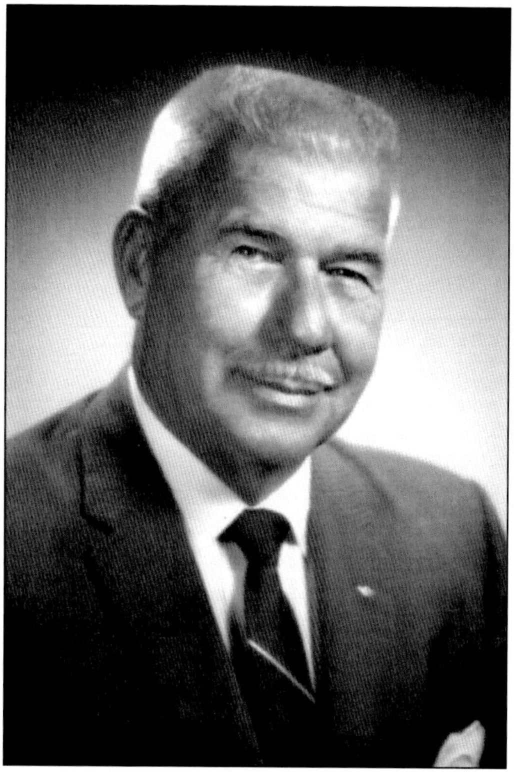

Paul Jackson (pictured) drafted the resulting bill, which was sent to Indiana state representative Henry "Bud" Kintzele. Jackson was the first of many Michigan City Port Authority (MCPA) members to write the agency's own bills and then recruit a legislator to submit it to the state senate or house of representatives. Representative Kintzele pushed the bill through the house as the Michigan City Harbor Advisory Commission continued planning.

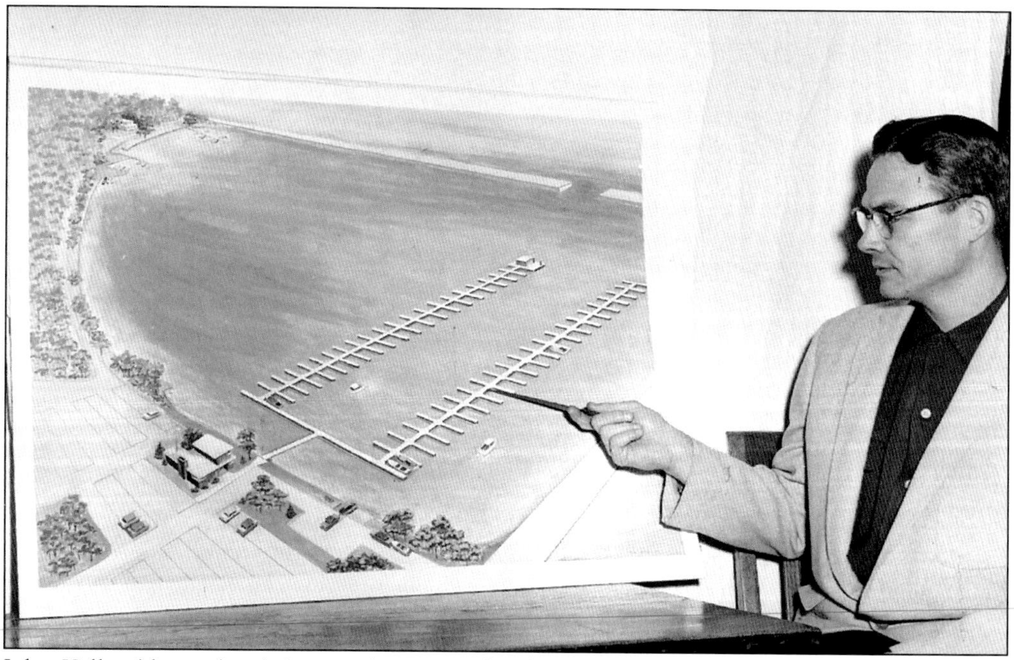

John Kelley (shown here) drew up his vision for the harbor, using ideas submitted by everyone involved in planning. His draft included slips lining the entire basin and docks that cut through, horizontally, from east to west. Kelley's plans also included the few slips already in the basin, a comfort station, a parking lot, and other facilities. (Michigan City News Dispatch.)

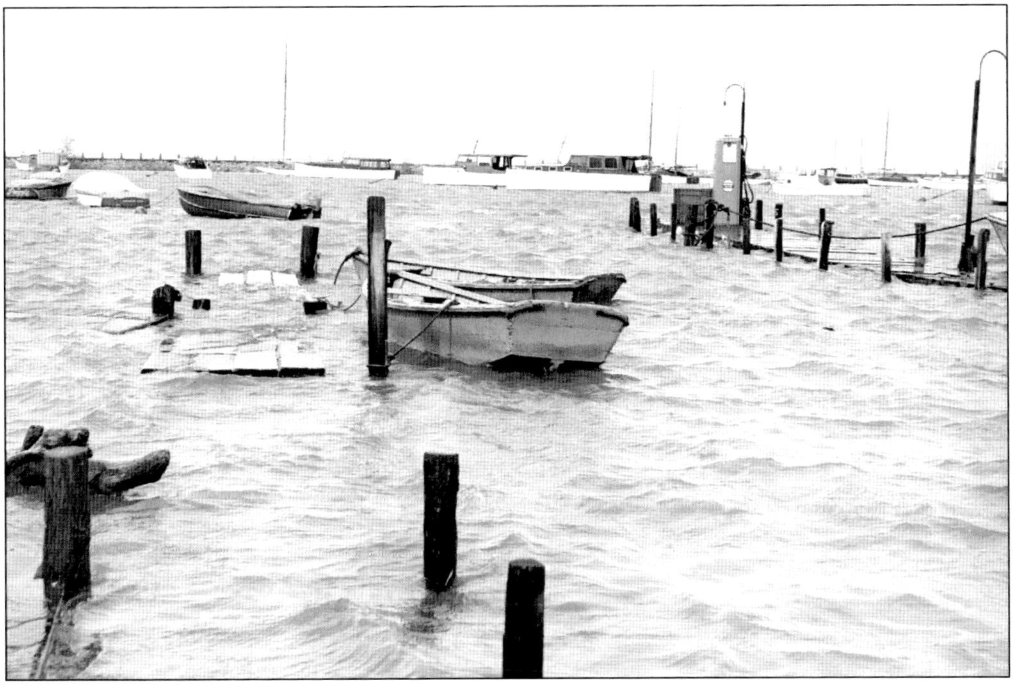

The service businesses operating in these facilities were owned by Matt Goerg. Goerg rented the land from the city to run his boat maintenance and slip-rental business situated at the south side of the basin. He also gave tours in his boat throughout the basin. (Bill Swedenberg.)

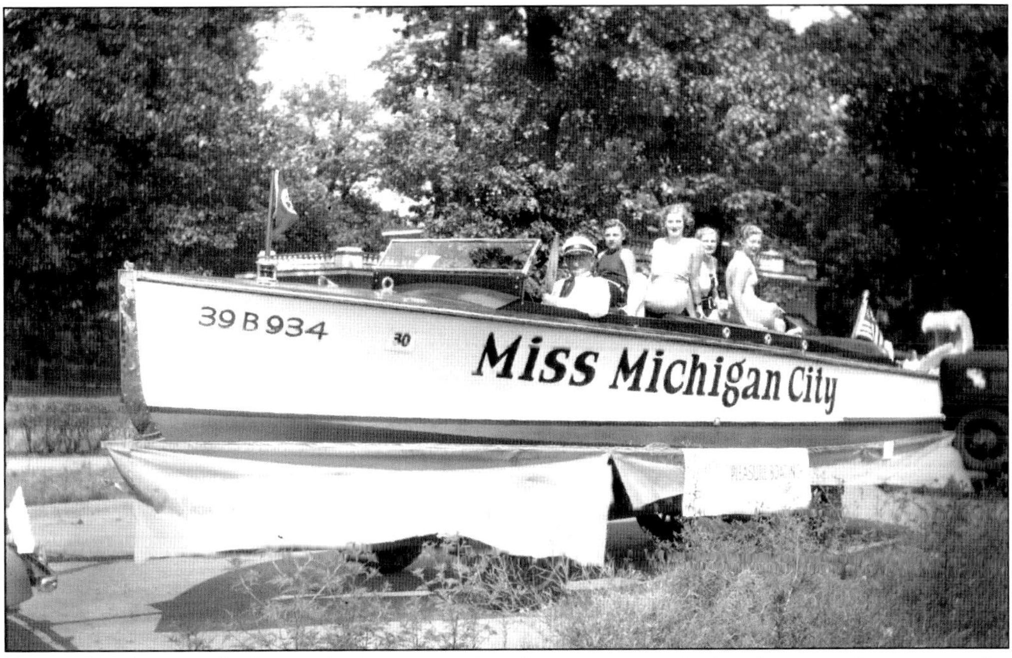

Because his lease with the city had yet to expire, the new agency had to figure out how to acquire and develop the property without endangering Goerg's business. It needed to tear down the existing facilities to make room for a new building and docks. The commission liked Kelley's draft enough to present it to the public. (Bill Swedenberg.)

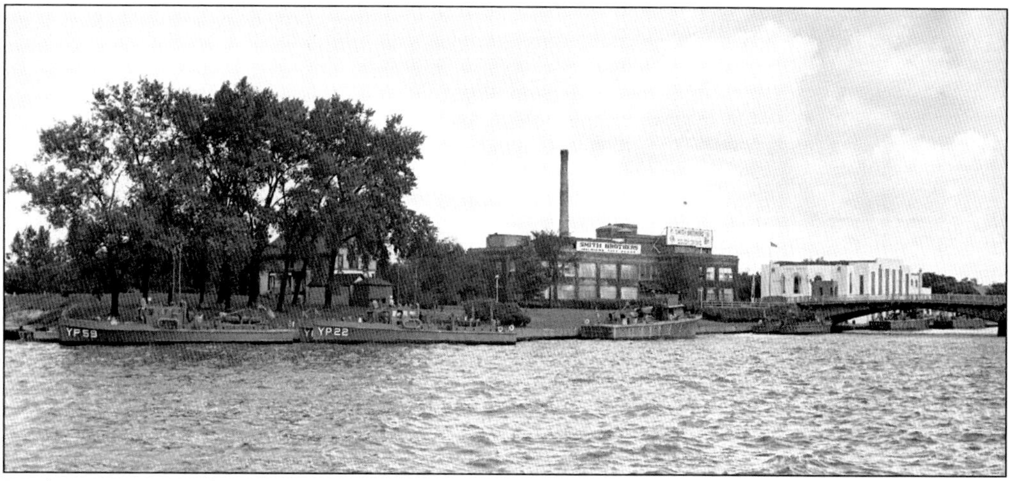

In the meantime, the Port Authority Enabling Act was signed into law on March 13, 1959. According to the *Michigan City News Dispatch*, Gov. Harold W. Handley enthusiastically supported the bill, "enabling a port authority set up by the city to operate and expand port facilities . . . The authority would be able to levy its own taxes or float revenue bonds to finance it operations." (Michigan City News Dispatch.)

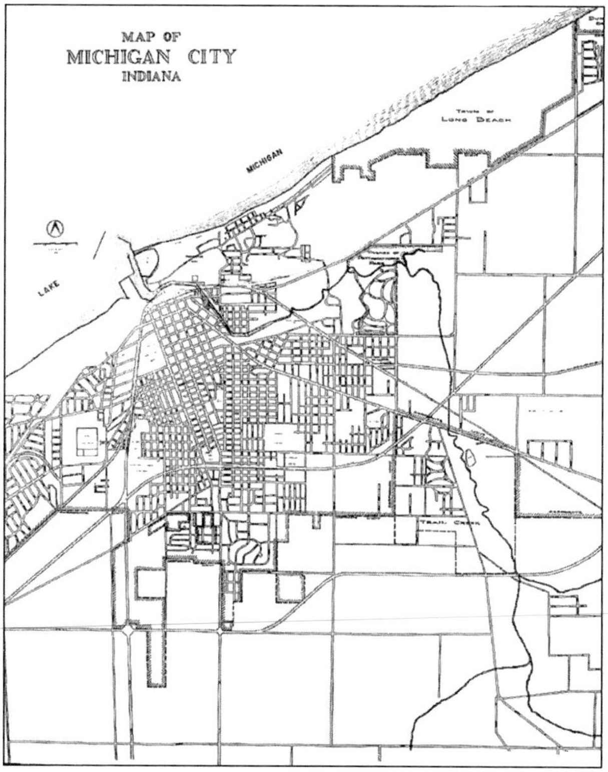

The bill required that the Michigan City Common Council draft an ordinance to officially create a port authority of its own. This new agency was to have jurisdiction over the harbor and channel, what some saw as the pride of the north end of Michigan City, seen in this 1959 map. The town was built up around the harbor but had begun to pull away, growing southward. (Michigan City News Dispatch.)

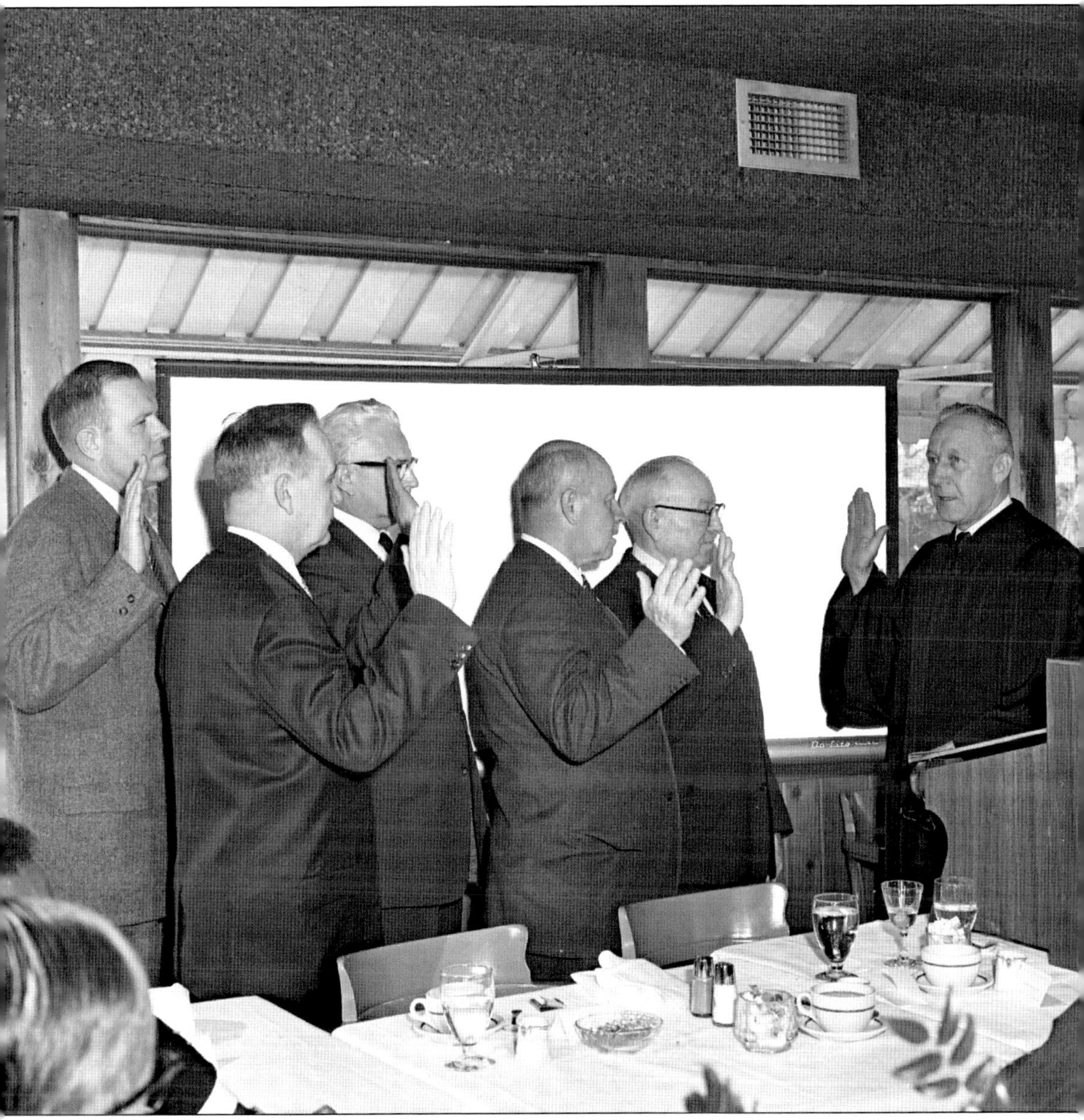

Each member's term was staggered, ranging from three to five years, and the mayor made each appointment. Chosen from the Michigan City Harbor Advisory Commission were Mark Moorman and John Kelley. Mayor Francis Fedder also appointed Hartley Job, Jaymar Ruby executive and MCYC commodore. Because Michigan City was retroactively merging with Lakeland Township, the Lakeland Town Board chose the other two members: Paul Jackson, from the harbor commission, and city council representative Roger McKee. (Michigan City News Dispatch.)

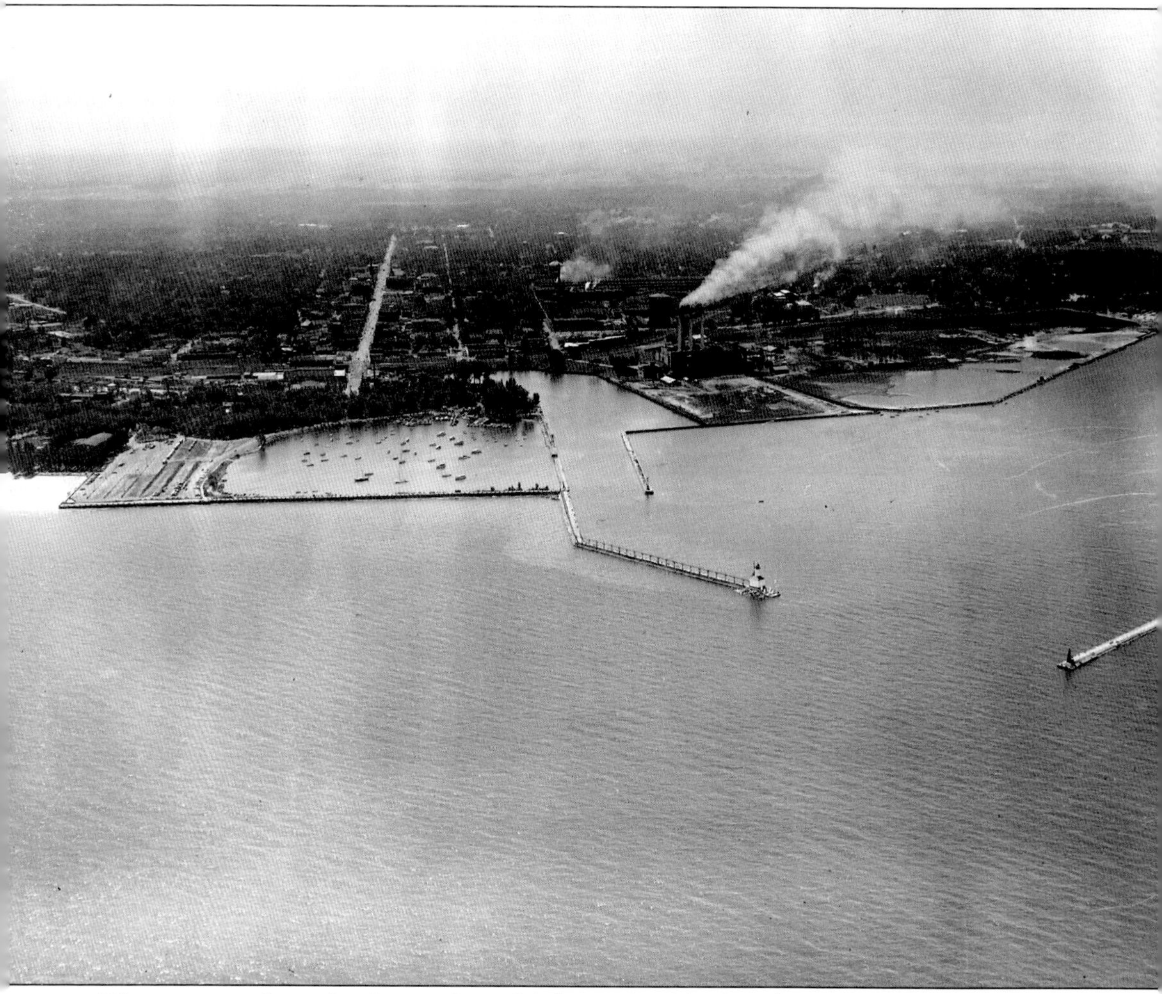

The men were charged with revitalizing Michigan City's harbor, shown in this 1940s photograph, a task that many before them have attempted unsuccessfully. Later Michigan City's marinas served as a model for other municipalities from Canada to as far south as Galveston, Texas. (Michigan City News Dispatch.)

Hartley Job, standing on the left in this 1958 photograph, is preparing a boat for the yacht club's Venetian Night. Job served as commodore to the MCYC for two years. Although many of the MCPA's biggest supporters were MCYC members, the organization still had issues that were aired during that first meeting. The city that so struggled for a harbor also questioned the fledgling agency's projects, many of which were an extension of the city's harbor commission plans. These issues and more arose before the first documented MCPA board meeting was scheduled. A larger challenge was also brewing, courtesy of the MCPA's neighbor, the Michigan City Park Department. (Michigan City News Dispatch.)

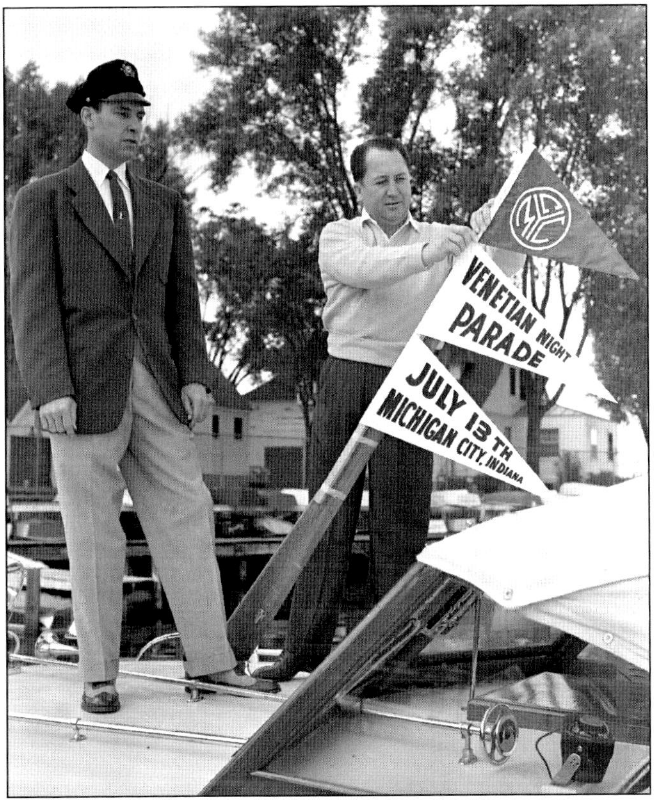

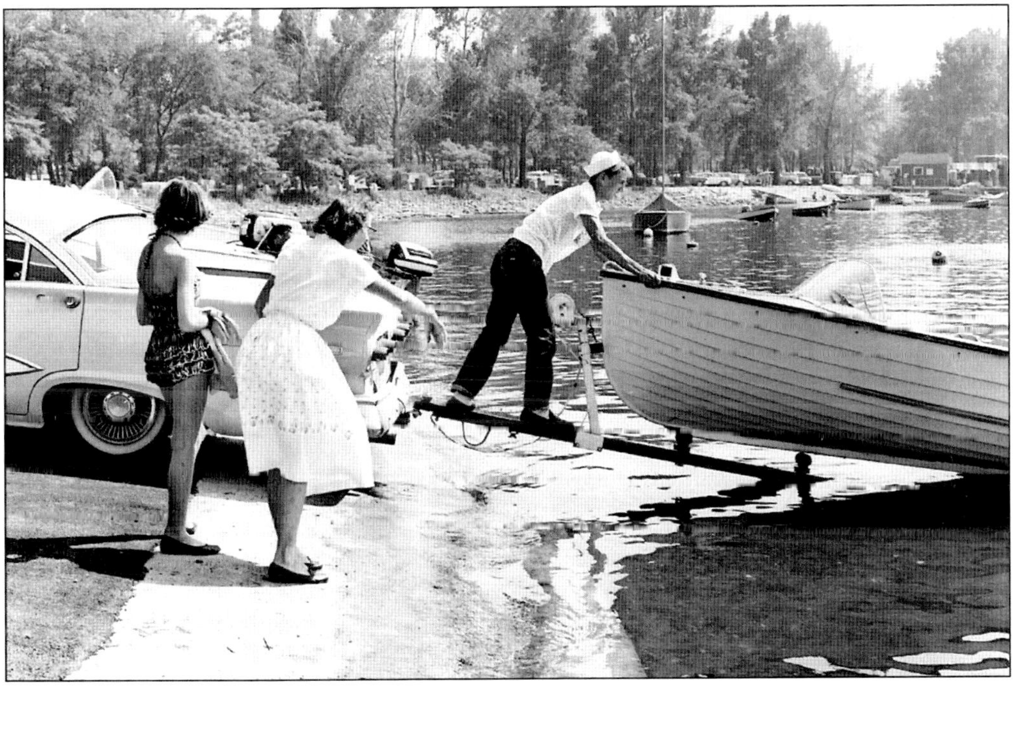

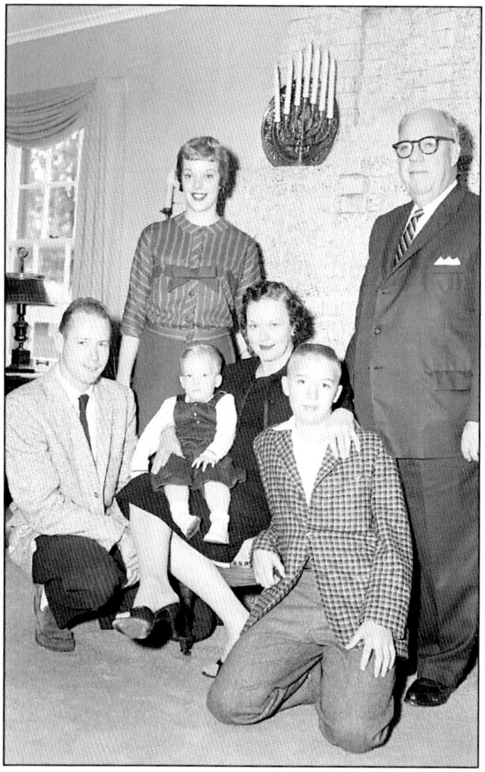

Both complainants bypassed the board, taking their problems to Mayor Francis Fedder, shown here with his family. These complaints prompted that first meeting of the MCPA Board of Directors. "Various complaints had been turned in to the Mayor regarding actions of the Port Authority," read the minutes of that June 15, 1959, meeting. "The purpose of the meeting was to discuss these various points with the Mayor, to explain what has actually transpired." (Michigan City News Dispatch.)

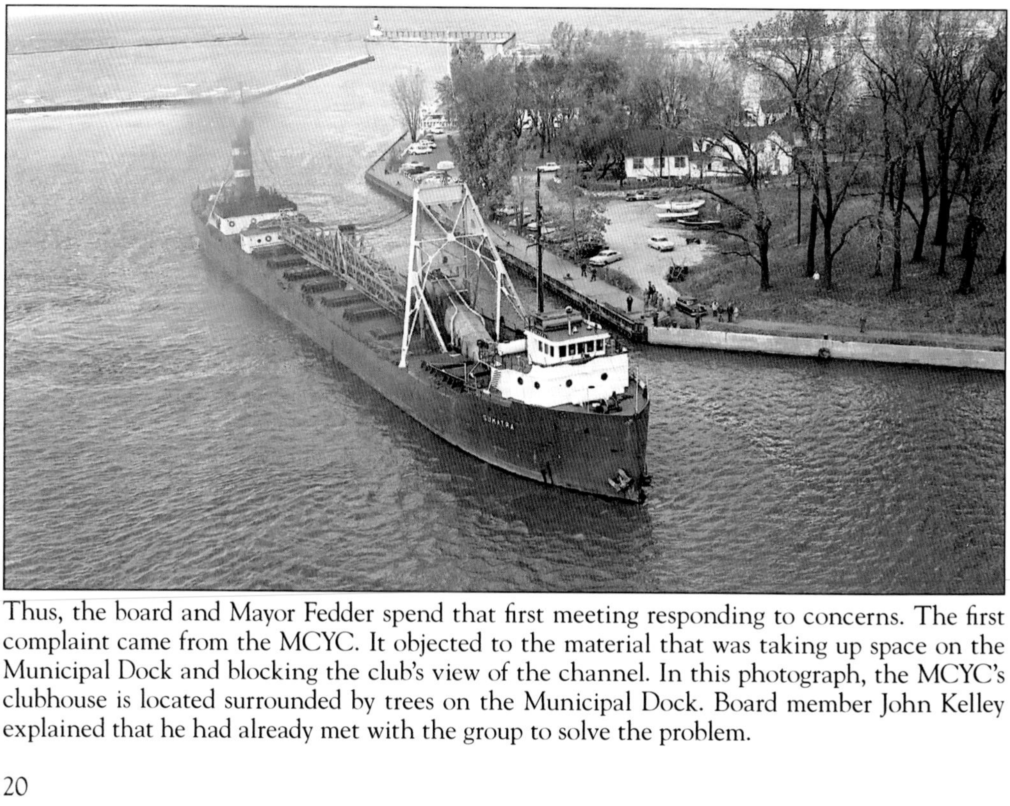

Thus, the board and Mayor Fedder spend that first meeting responding to concerns. The first complaint came from the MCYC. It objected to the material that was taking up space on the Municipal Dock and blocking the club's view of the channel. In this photograph, the MCYC's clubhouse is located surrounded by trees on the Municipal Dock. Board member John Kelley explained that he had already met with the group to solve the problem.

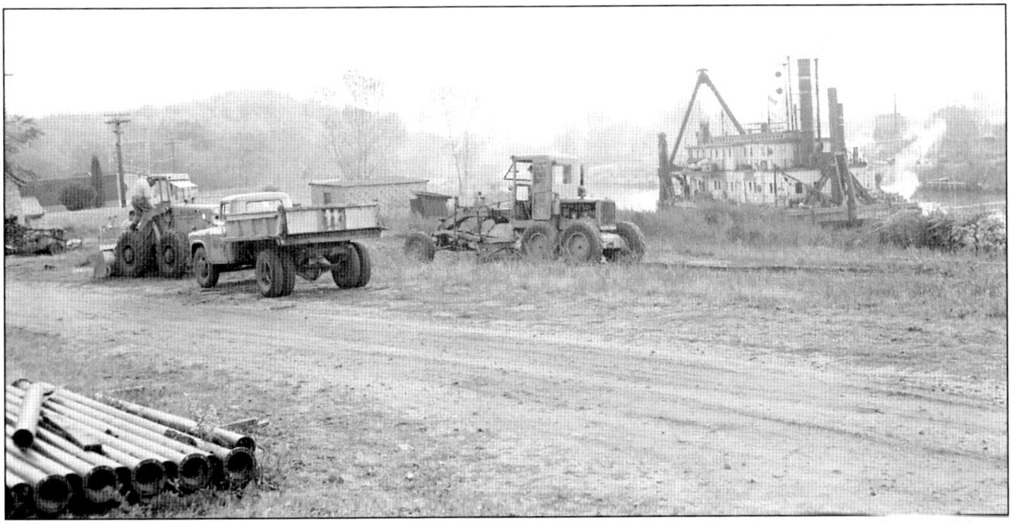

The Michigan City Water Department's project on the Municipal Dock was the problem. Kelley gave contractor Luedke Engineering permission to build a temporary extension to move the material away from the MCYC clubhouse. Kelley explained that there was not a quicker way to solve the problem. As stated in the *Minutes of the Michigan City Port Authority I*, he explained, "This was the only place available in Michigan City accessible to both truck and barge." (Michigan City News Dispatch.)

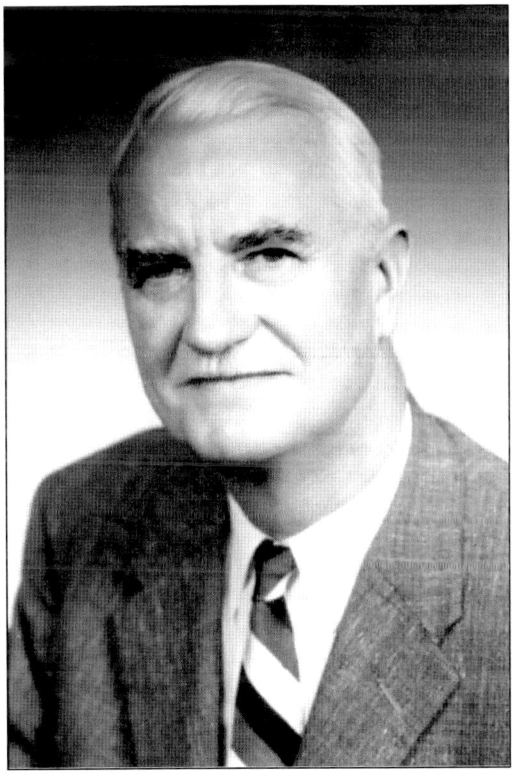

Next the MCYC and city residents believed that the board was destroying the area around the Municipal Dock, using the Michigan City Sanitary District's equipment and workers to do so. It was really a tree and brush removal project on the land alongside the dock. Kelley (pictured here) explained, reiterating the speech he gave the MCYC only days earlier, the MCPA was trying to beautify the area not destroy it.

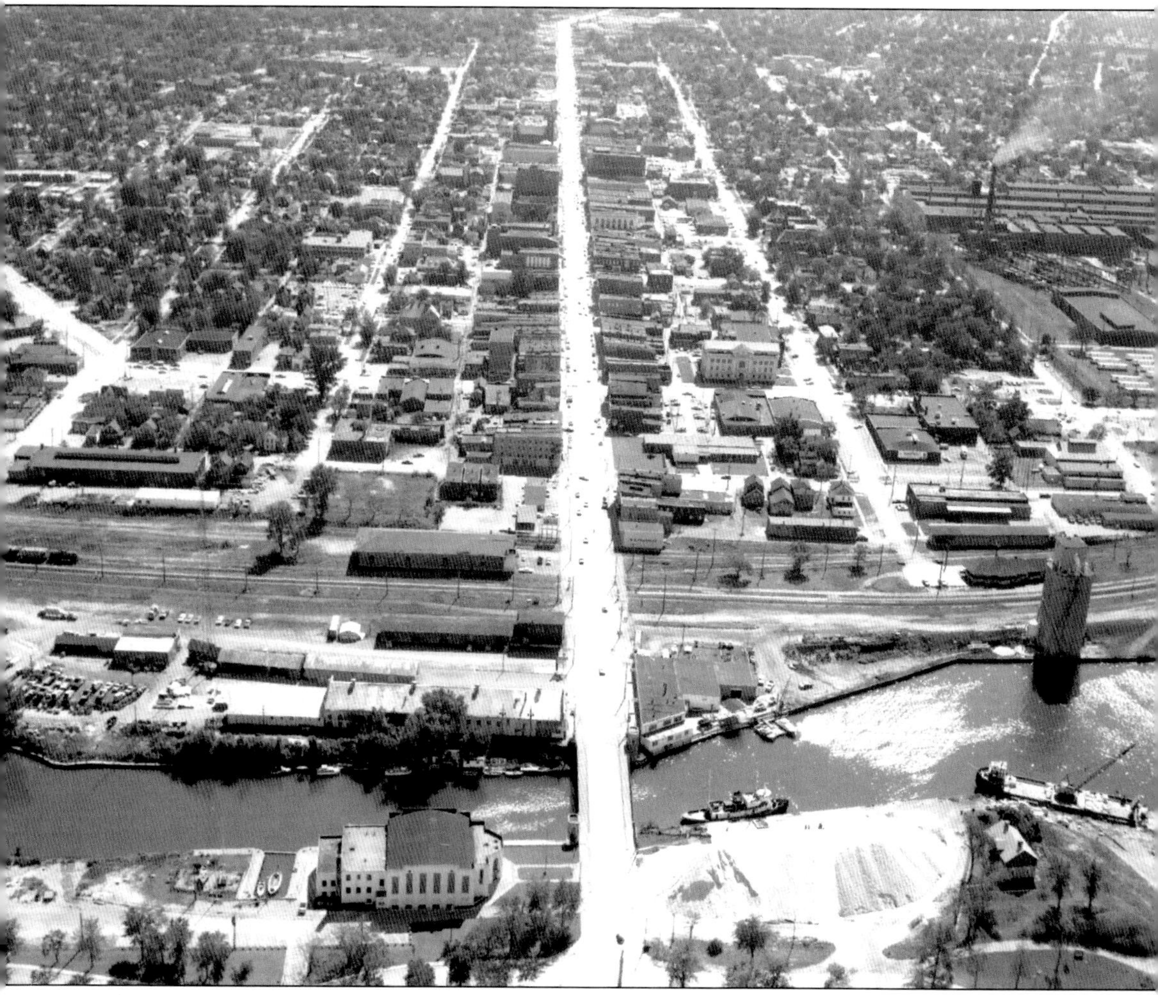

The mayor's own complaint was next. Morton Salt Company brought road salt to store in Michigan City for use in the winter. The city terminated the lease in early 1959, because the potential costs to the city seemed to outweigh the benefits. However, the MCPA saw a source of income. It allowed Morton to store its salt on the Municipal Dock; in return, Morton would pay the MCPA 50¢ per ton of salt stored. (Bill Swedenberg.)

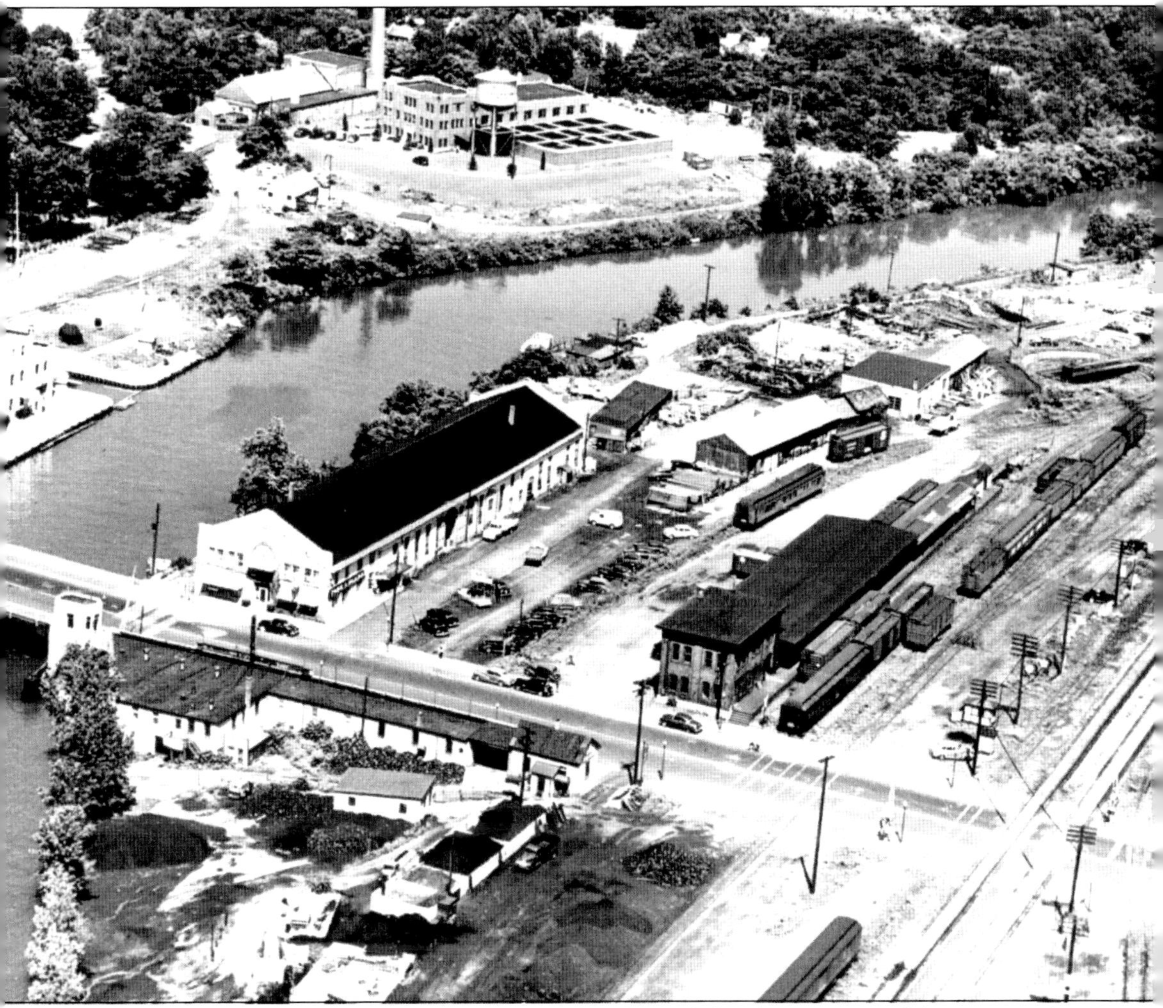

This view shows businesses on the other side of the channel that have a view of the mammoth salt pile (seen on page 22). Many business owners were worried about how the salt boat traffic would affect the businesses across from it. (Bill Swedenberg.)

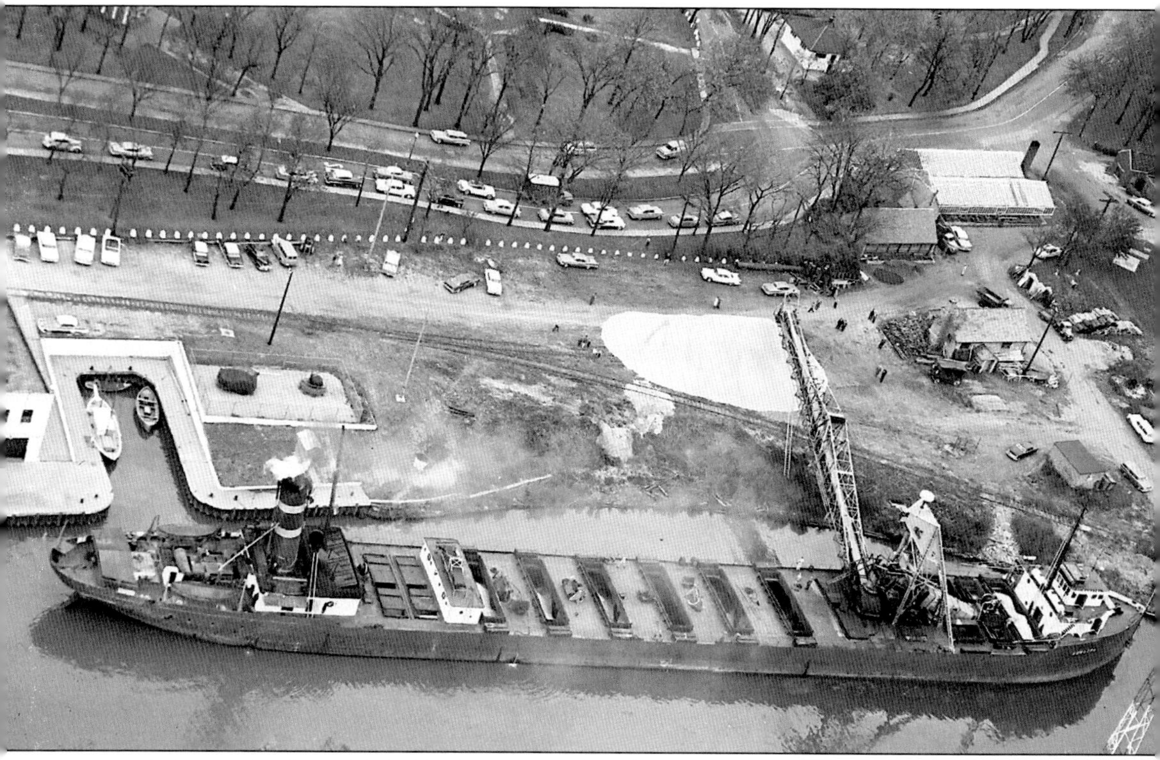

A salt boat unloads in 1968. The MCPA needed the funds from the salt storage, for when the common council created the agency, it was unanimous in not wanting it to operate on tax funds. The agency had no other income. Mayor Francis Fedder did try to describe his difficult task of selling the MCPA's plans to the public. Mark Moorman and the rest were indifferent; their only mission was to save the harbor. (Michigan City News Dispatch.)

Two

BATTLE TO BUILD A MARINA

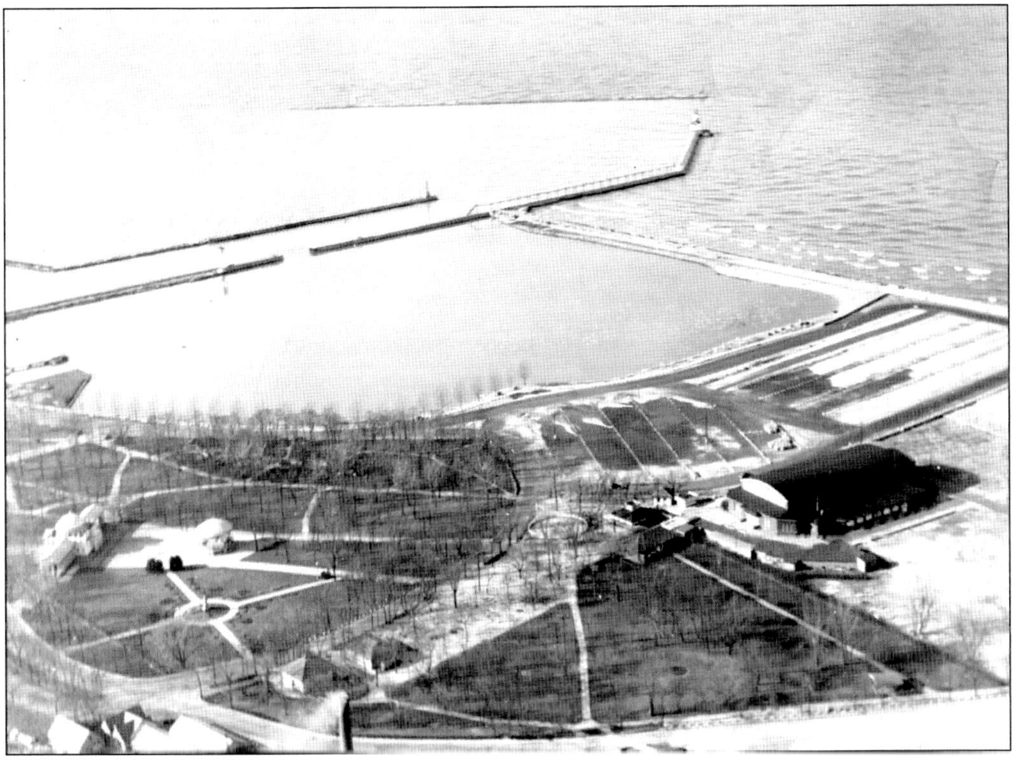

The large building in this view of the yacht basin and adjacent to Washington Park is the Oasis Dancing Pavilion, demolished in 1962. The basin was hot property at the time. Before the MCPA formed in 1958, there were already over 2,000 boaters using the basin. Trouble began when the park board announced its intent to build a marina in 1959. Regarding concerns that it was taking over MCPA property, the park board stated in the March 6, 1959, *News Dispatch* article "Park Board to Hire Expert on Development of Basin," "The Port Authority will pertain only to the harbor while [the park board] were only concerned with the basin." (Bill Swedenberg.)

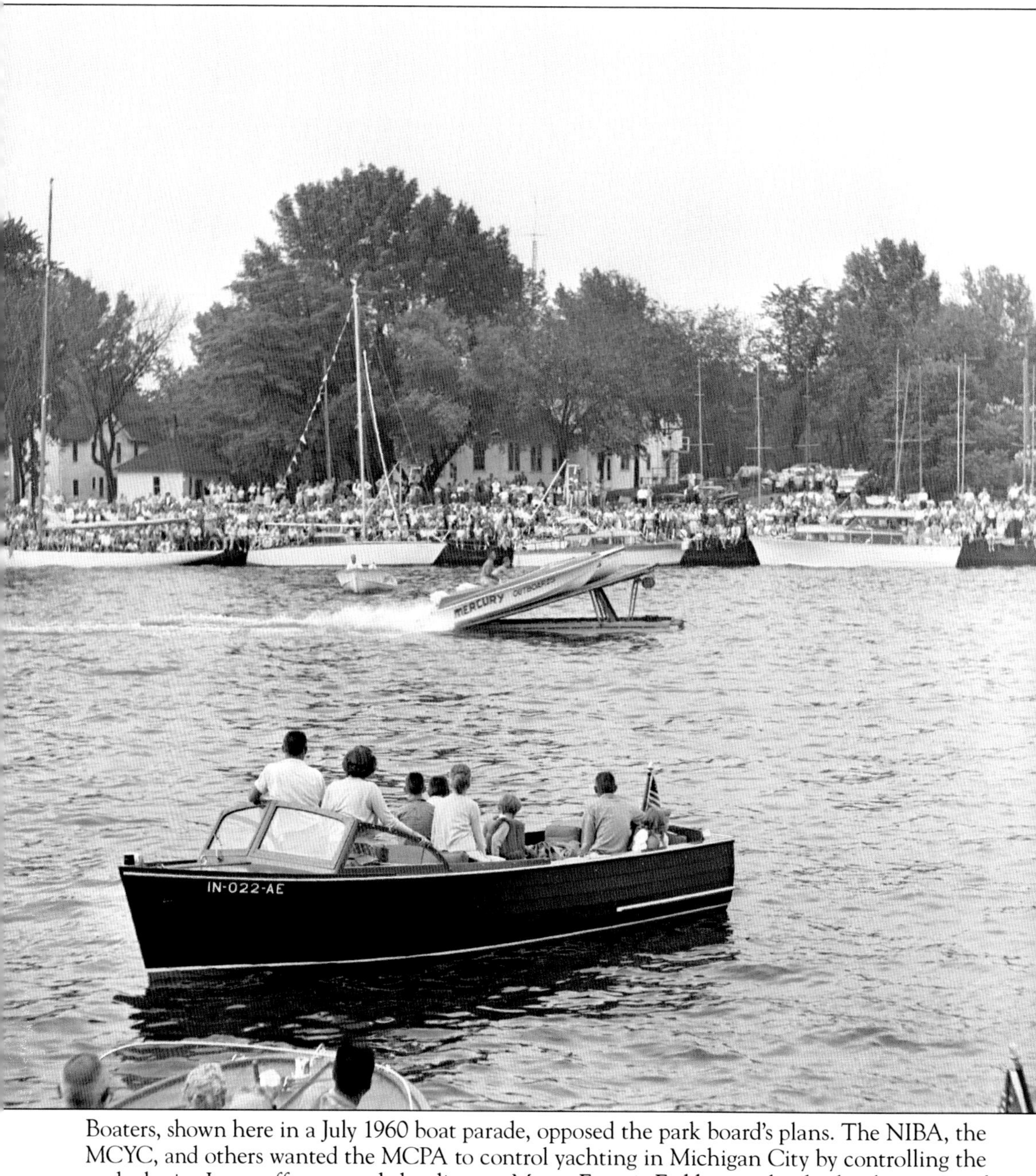

Boaters, shown here in a July 1960 boat parade, opposed the park board's plans. The NIBA, the MCYC, and others wanted the MCPA to control yachting in Michigan City by controlling the yacht basin. In an effort to end the dispute, Mayor Francis Fedder sought the legal opinion of city attorney James P. Gleason. Gleason officially sided with the park department. (Michigan City News Dispatch.)

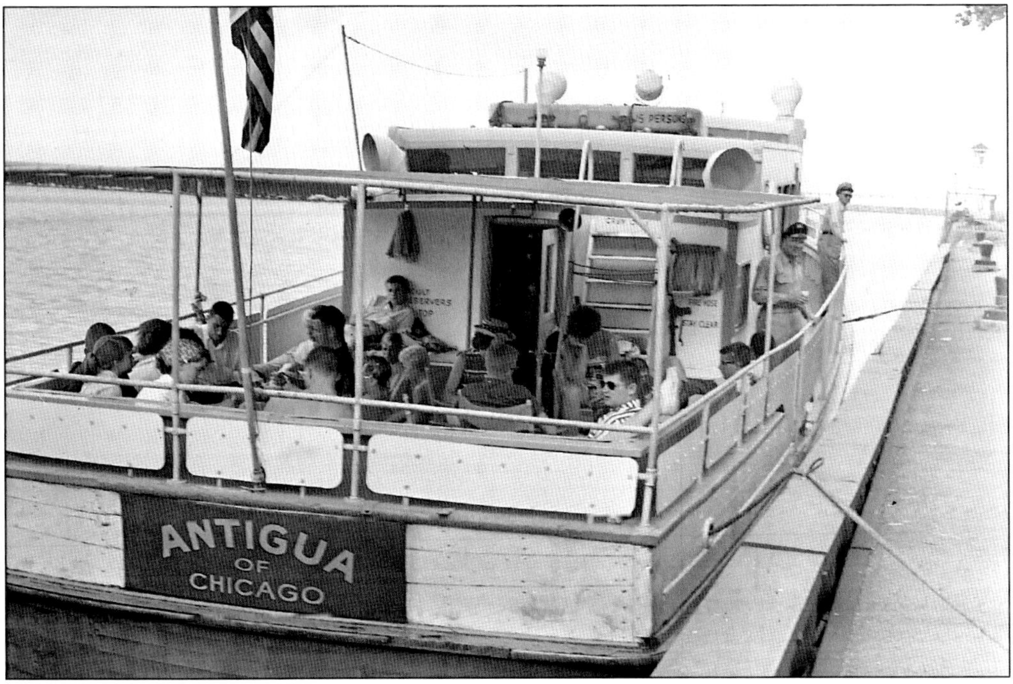

There was more than boating at stake at the basin. Scenic cruises, races, and other events drew tourists and potential revenue to the area. The *Antigua*, pictured here, was a craft used during such tours. (Michigan City News Dispatch.)

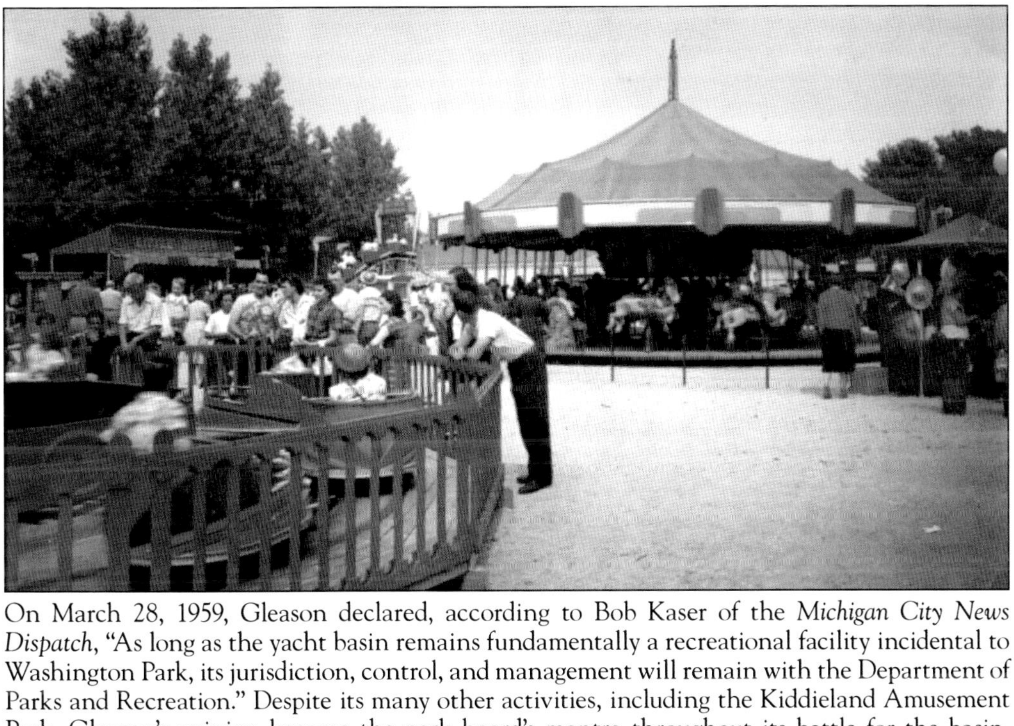

On March 28, 1959, Gleason declared, according to Bob Kaser of the *Michigan City News Dispatch*, "As long as the yacht basin remains fundamentally a recreational facility incidental to Washington Park, its jurisdiction, control, and management will remain with the Department of Parks and Recreation." Despite its many other activities, including the Kiddieland Amusement Park, Gleason's opinion became the park board's mantra throughout its battle for the basin. (Michigan City Park Department.)

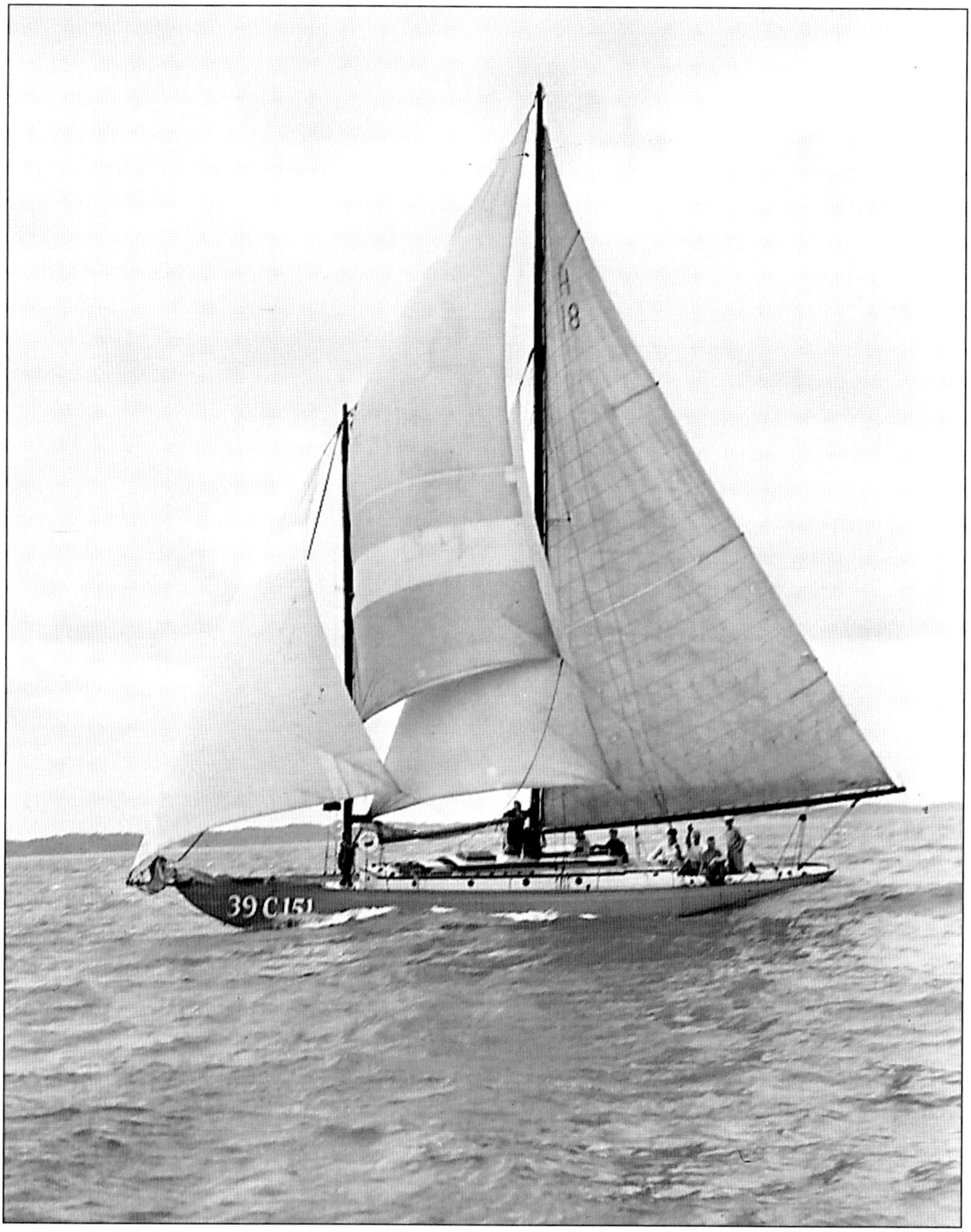

The official opinion did not appease the pleasure-boating community, which included sailboats like the *Fortune* in this 1945 photograph. The issue polarized city and even state officials. Later there was talk of removing the three MCPA board members who were actively fighting the park board. Threats from both sides were ignored as were Mayor Francis Fedder's many appeals for a compromise. (Michigan City News Dispatch.)

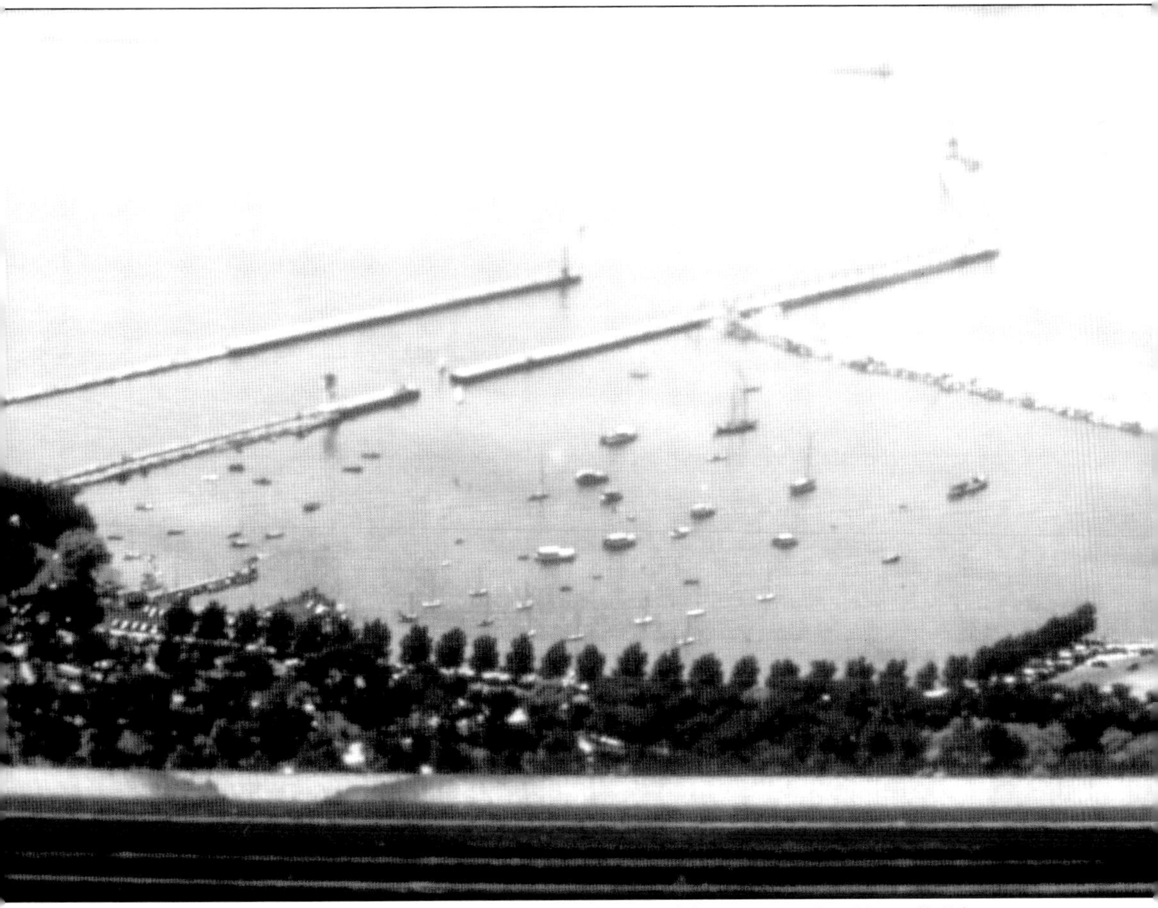

By mid-July 1959, probably frustrated and out of ideas, Fedder suggested a "friendly" lawsuit to give the courts the last say over jurisdiction of the basin, seen in this photograph from about 1950. With Mark Moorman as the first chairman of the board and Hartley Job as the first vice chairman and treasurer, the *Michigan City News Dispatch* reported that the board sent a final letter ordering the park department to "surrender jurisdiction of the basin." Or, prepare for a lawsuit. (Michigan City Public Library.)

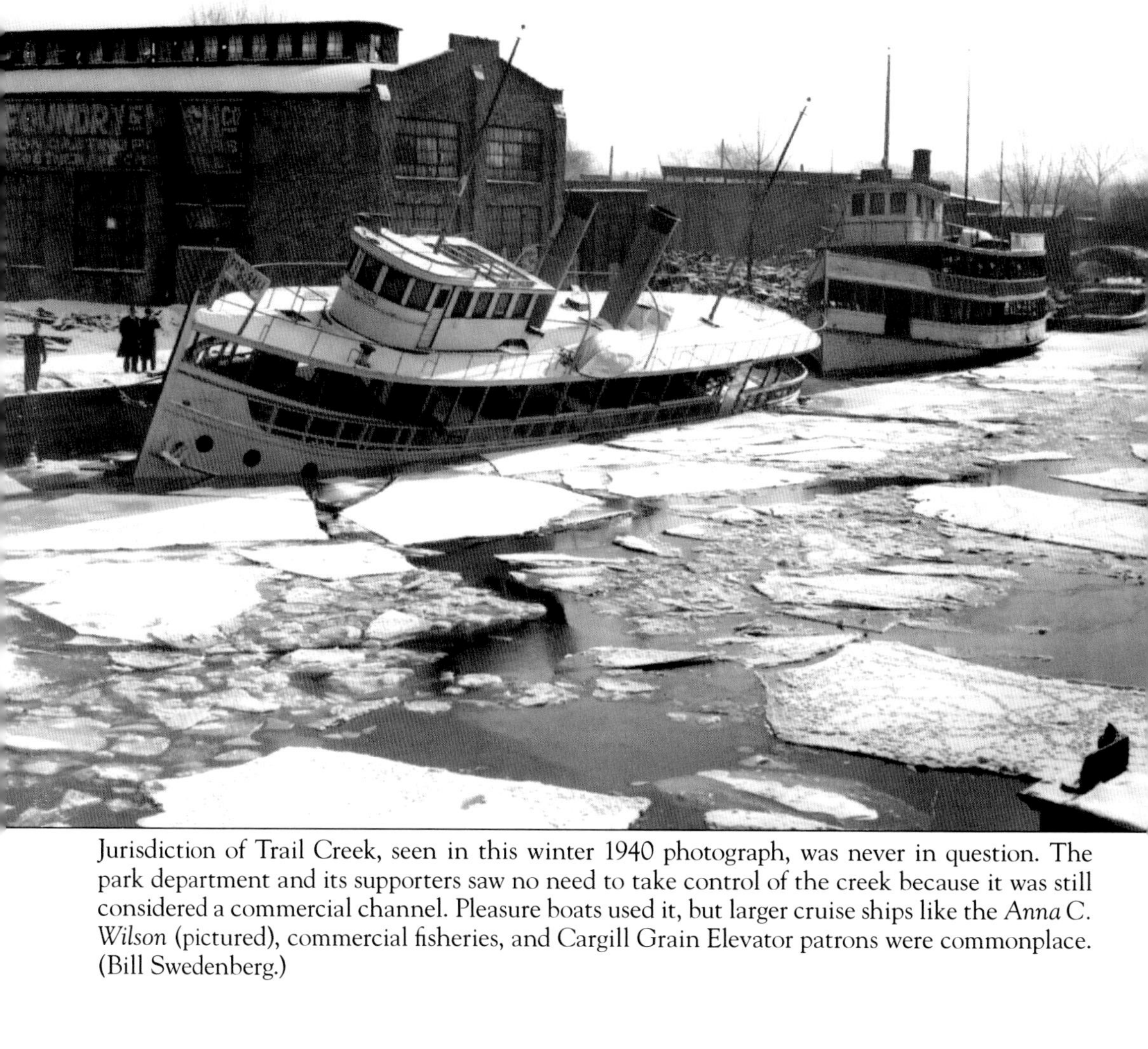

Jurisdiction of Trail Creek, seen in this winter 1940 photograph, was never in question. The park department and its supporters saw no need to take control of the creek because it was still considered a commercial channel. Pleasure boats used it, but larger cruise ships like the *Anna C. Wilson* (pictured), commercial fisheries, and Cargill Grain Elevator patrons were commonplace. (Bill Swedenberg.)

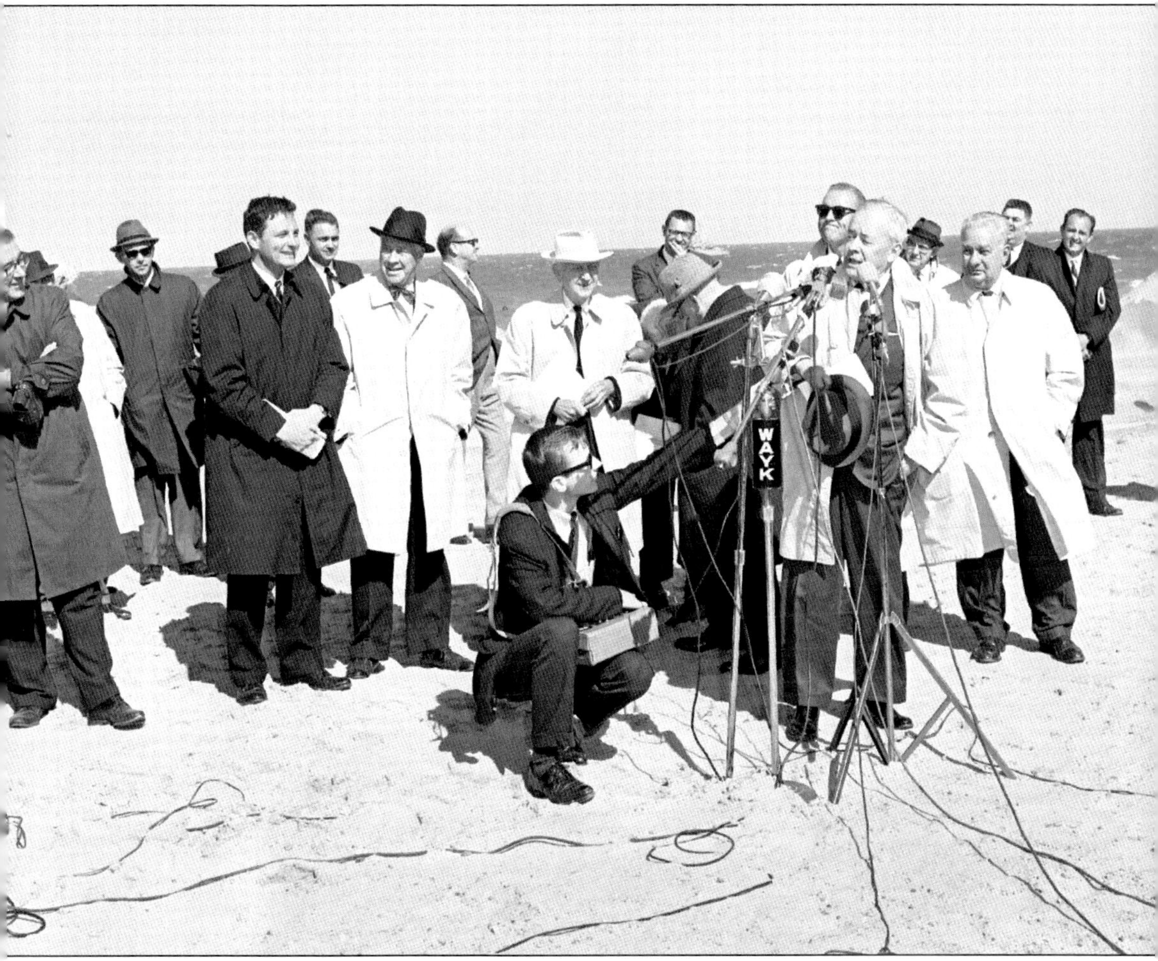

The MCPA board felt that it was the rightful owner of the basin. After all, it was not the commercial shipping industry that pushed Rep. Henry Kintzele to get the bill passed, it was the boating community of Michigan City. The opening of the seaway promised increased commercial shipping, but the boaters simply used the event to get their agenda passed, while everyone in government was on the port-building bandwagon. The press, along with several government officials, including Sen. Birch Bayh (second from left in black trench coat and no hat), is seen here at the opening. (Michigan City News Dispatch.)

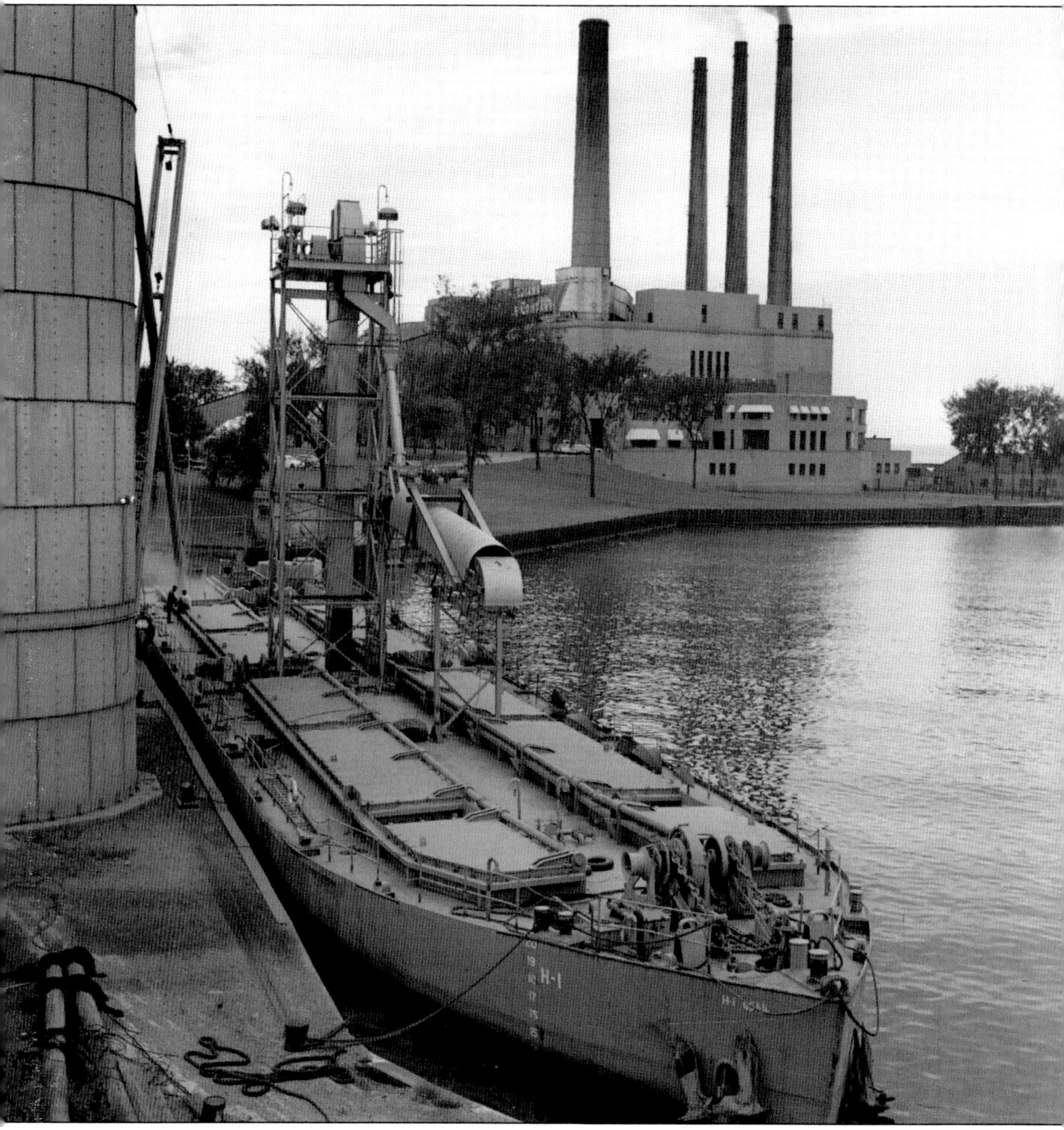

Those same boaters were now loudly voicing their opposition to the park's control of the pleasure-boating industry in Michigan City. Half of the MCPA board members were avid boaters. Made up of pleasure boaters, backed by pleasure boaters, and born of their efforts, the board pledged to fight until the basin belonged to it. (Michigan City News Dispatch.)

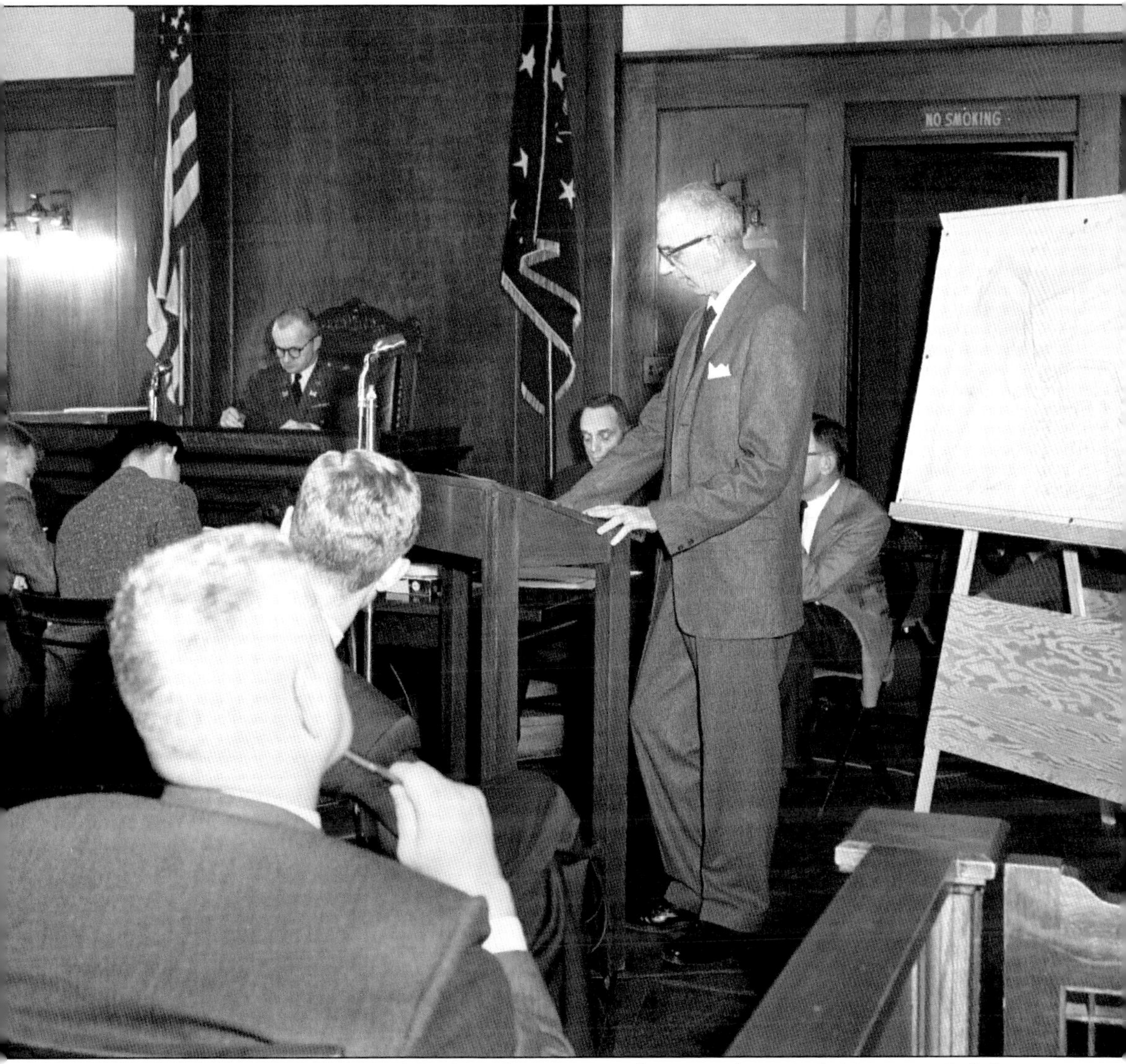

The threat to remove members of the board arose in midsummer, but Mark Moorman led them on undaunted. On September 23, 1959, the board hired attorneys Paul M. Butler and J. Patrick O'Malley to bring the issue before the courts. According to the *Michigan City News Dispatch*, it filed suit in the LaPorte County Circuit Court "seeking a declaratory judgment" in the basin dispute. This 1960 photograph shows attorney Fred Krueger arguing in yet another hearing about the harbor; the focus was dredging. (Michigan City News Dispatch.)

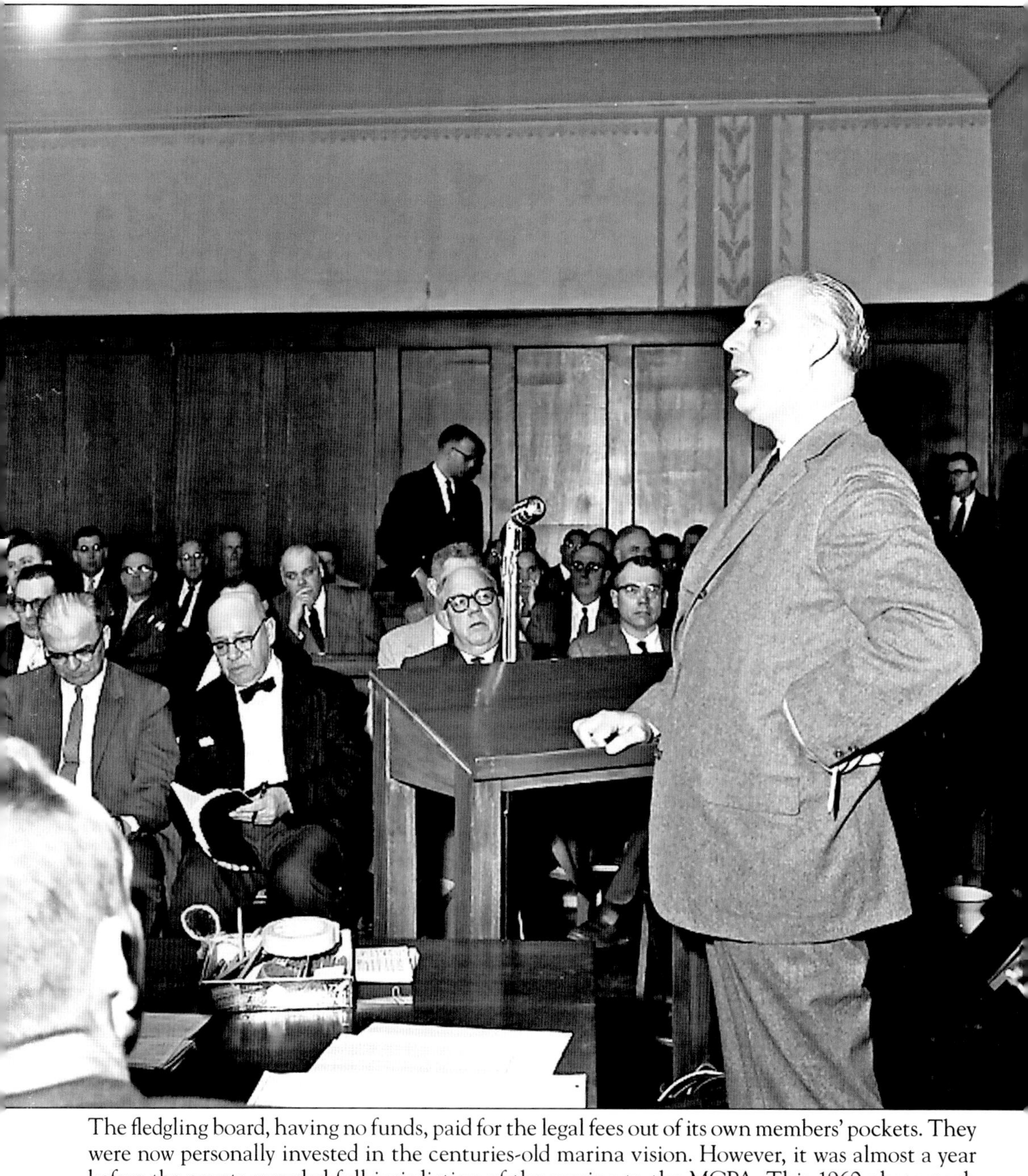

The fledgling board, having no funds, paid for the legal fees out of its own members' pockets. They were now personally invested in the centuries-old marina vision. However, it was almost a year before the courts awarded full jurisdiction of the marina to the MCPA. This 1960 photograph illustrates just one of the hearings on the MCPA's jurisdiction of the basin. In 1960, the MCPA was granted control of the basin. (Michigan City News Dispatch.)

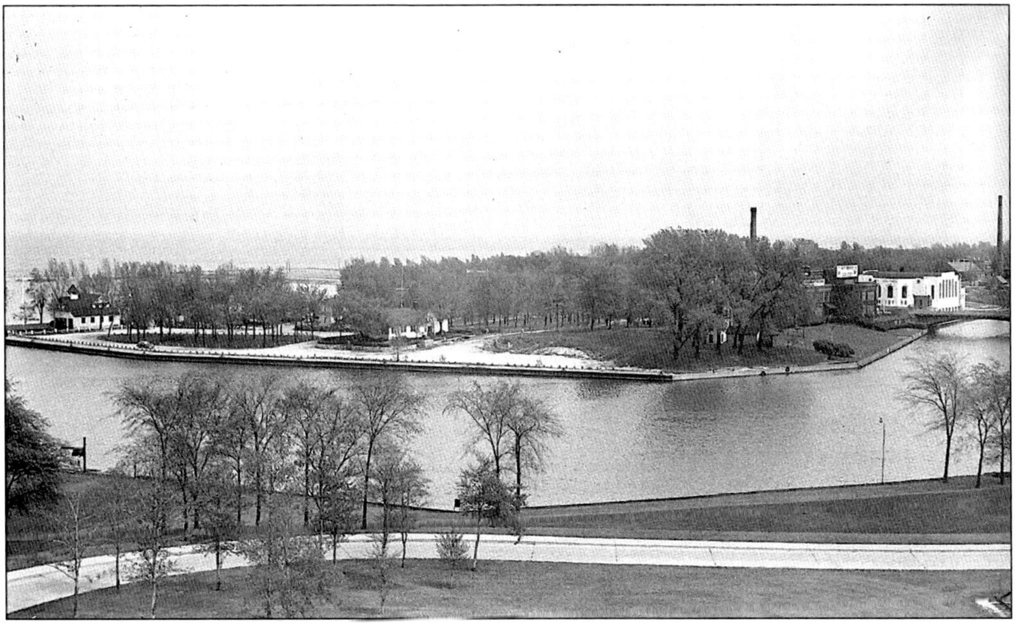

This tranquil view of the Municipal Dock from atop the Cargill Grain Elevator masks a deeper problem. Before anyone could begin work in the harbor or basin, a full dredge of the area was needed. This included the upstream area of Trail Creek. However, there was no money available. Until 1959, business owners along Trail Creek paid for their dredge; that is, those who could afford the major expense did. (Michigan City News Dispatch.)

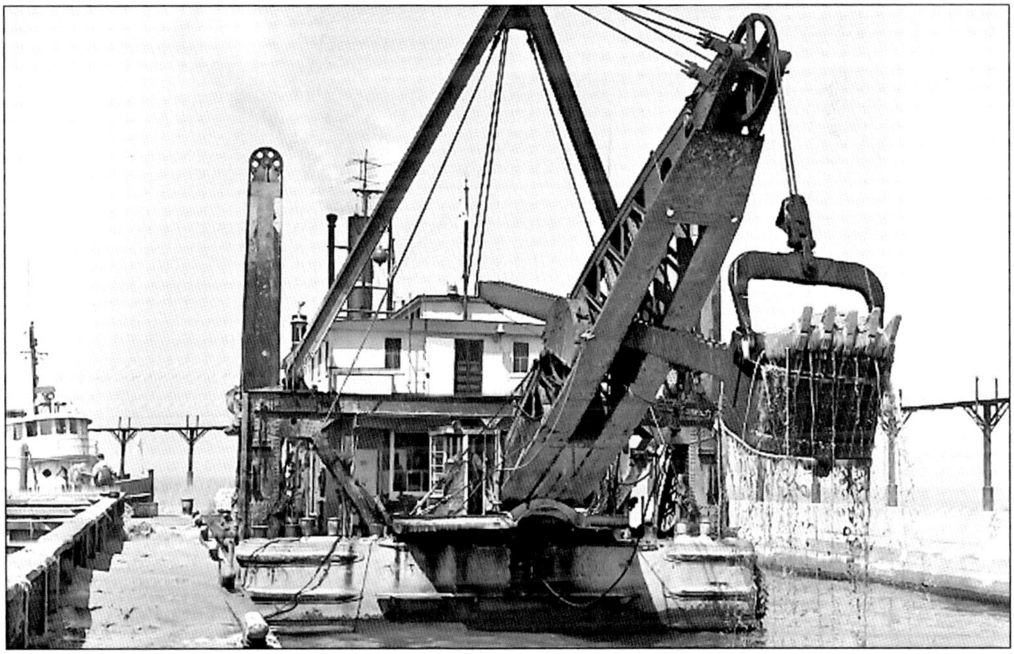

To prevent the problem from worsening, a full dredge was needed, like that being performed in this photograph. In February 1959, before the enabling act was passed, Mark Moorman hatched a plan to the Michigan City Harbor Advisory Commission to get the city a full dredge that would be practically free. (Michigan City News Dispatch.)

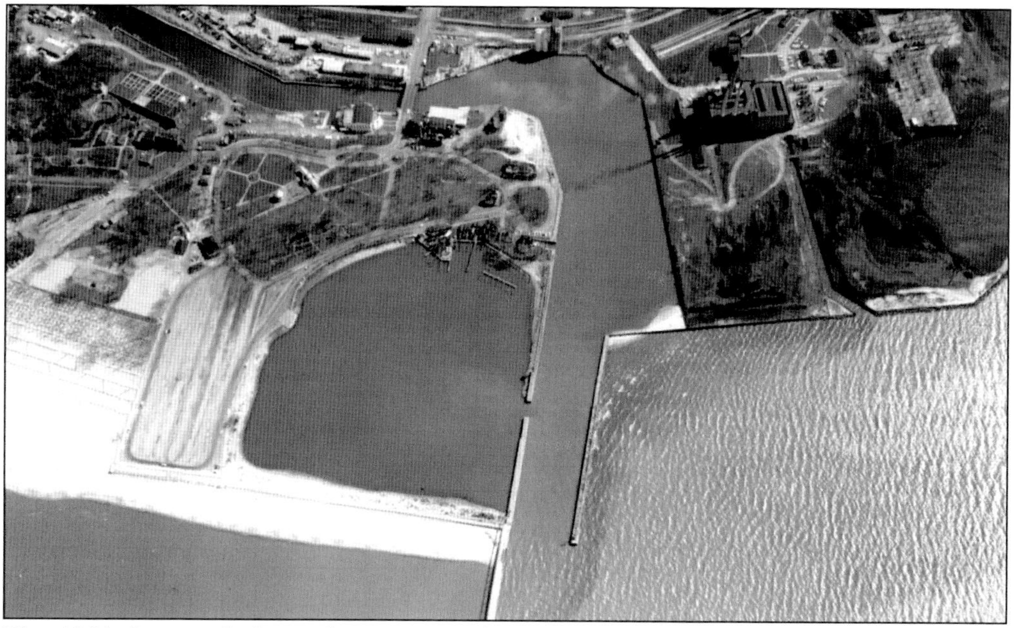

This 1964 photograph shows the marina under construction, the Cargill Grain Elevator, and the salt deposit spot on the Municipal Dock. Mark Moorman's goal was to reactivate the harbor, using the shipments from Morton Salt and the Cargill Grain Elevator. The harbor's commercial status warranted a dredge funded by the U.S. Army Corps of Engineers, if there was enough tonnage passing through the harbor. (Bill Swedenberg.)

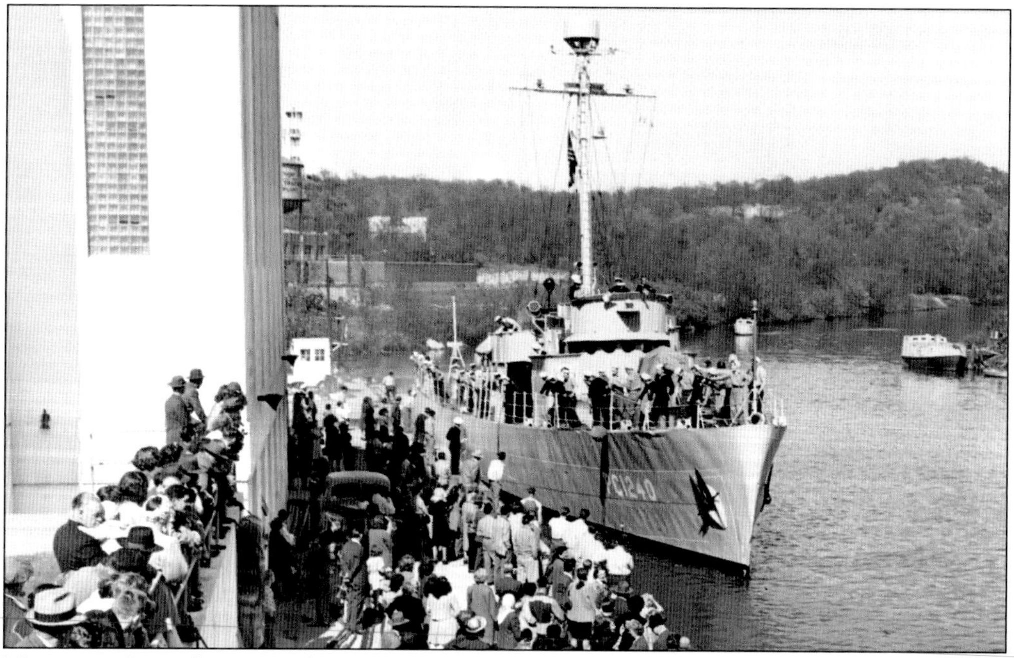

Moorman planned to prove that enough tonnage did come through Michigan City's waters. He cited the amount of business that could potentially come to the commercial fisheries upstream if there was a dredge. Moorman began by initiating a letter-writing campaign to the U.S. Army Corps of Engineers. He also urged Morton Salt to increase its shipments. (Bill Swedenberg.)

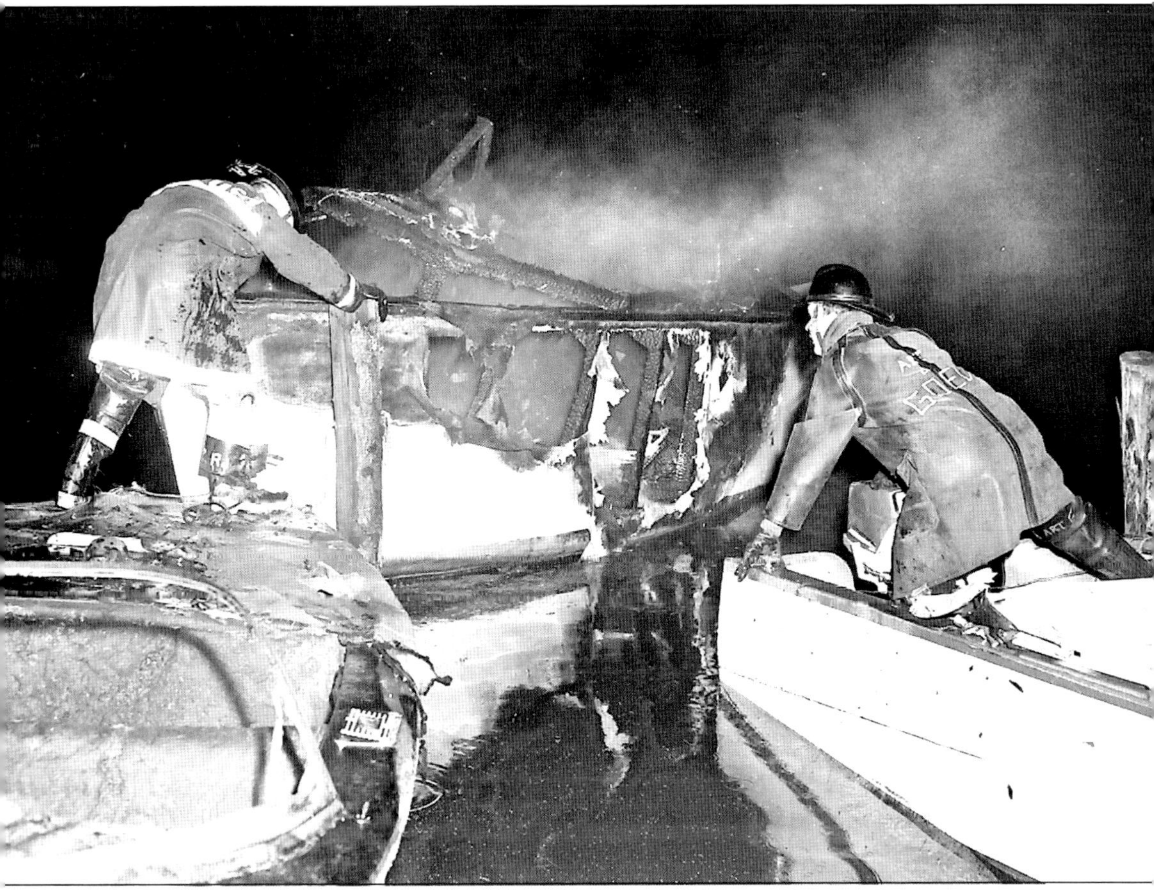

By the end of the year, the U.S. Army Corps of Engineers agreed to a dredge. Coming up with a date was a much harder task. Meanwhile, the board was hard at work preparing the development plans. The basin was included in these plans; the board felt confident that the enabling law would get the park department out of the basin. However, it also prepared for the alternative. (Bill Swedenberg.)

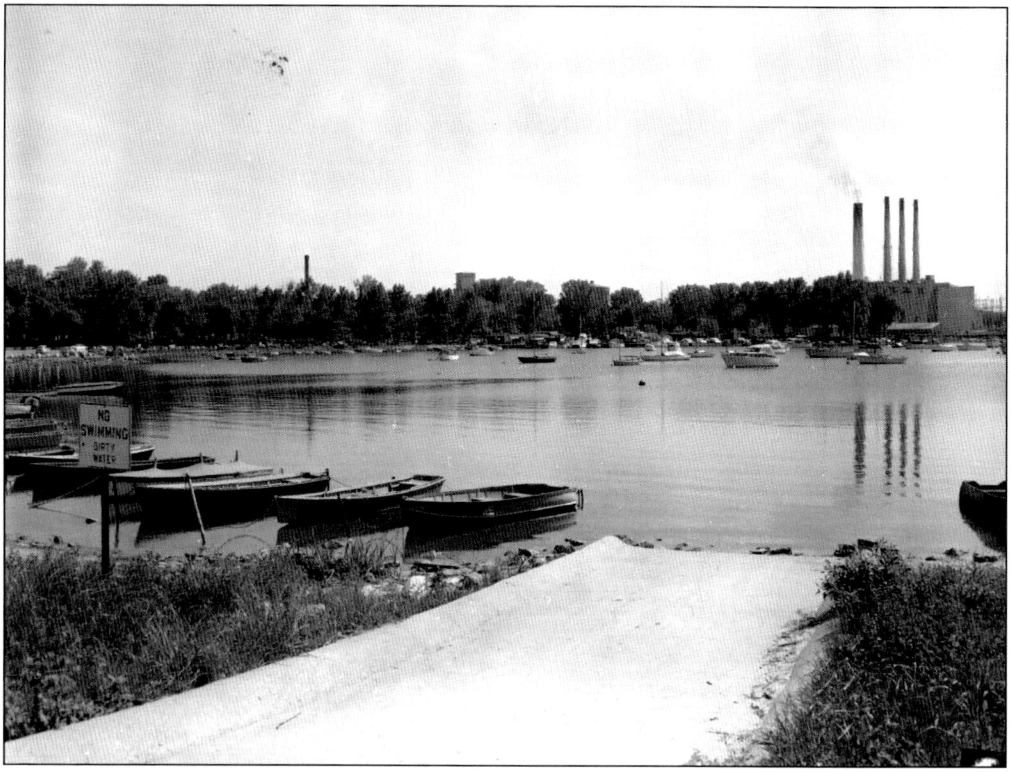

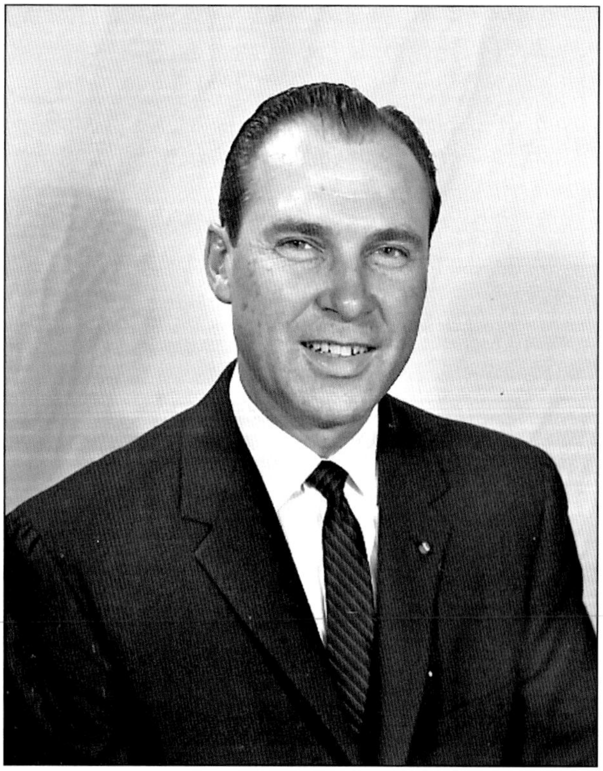

Hartley Job (pictured at left) set to work on the master plan for the entire project. Soon after, John Kelley and Job submitted plans for slips in the basin, and then Job presented the board with the first draft of the master plan. Mark Moorman was impressed; he placed Job in charge of the development planning. To fund the process, the board used a type of municipal bond adapted for a marina. The bonds were said to be the first of their kind. The city would issue them, but slip rentals would pay the bonds. If the marina failed, then the bondholders, not the city, absorbed the risk. To learn about running a thriving marina, Moorman and Job took numerous trips to private marinas along the shores of the Great Lakes, even going to a few Canadian marinas for ideas. (Above, Bill Swedenberg; left, Michigan City News Dispatch.)

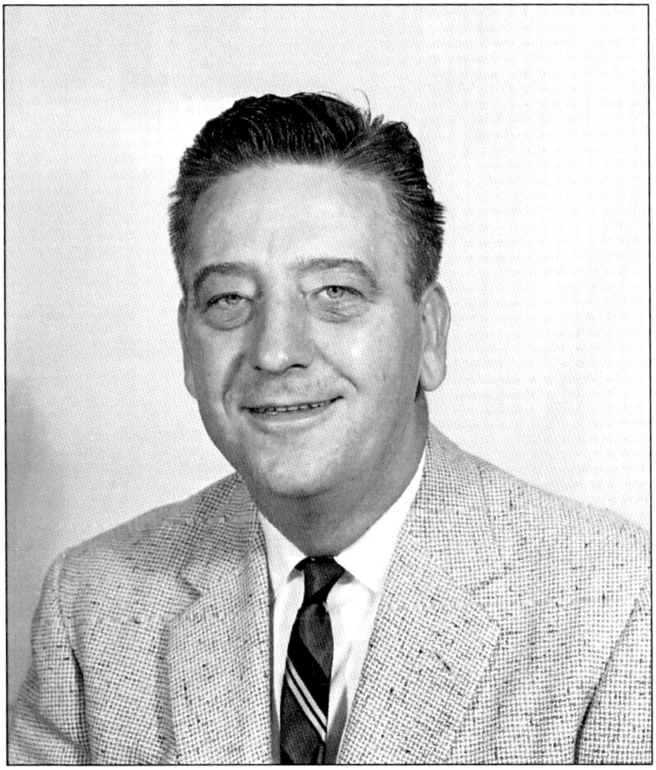

The board grew in 1961, with the addition of two new members. Mayor Francis Fedder passed an ordinance in April that gave the MCPA board seven seats like the rest of the boards in city government. Stanley Przybylinski (right, in 1960) and Louis Cotts (below) were appointed to those new positions. Fred Krueger from the advisory council was hired as the MCPA attorney. (Right, Michigan City News Dispatch.)

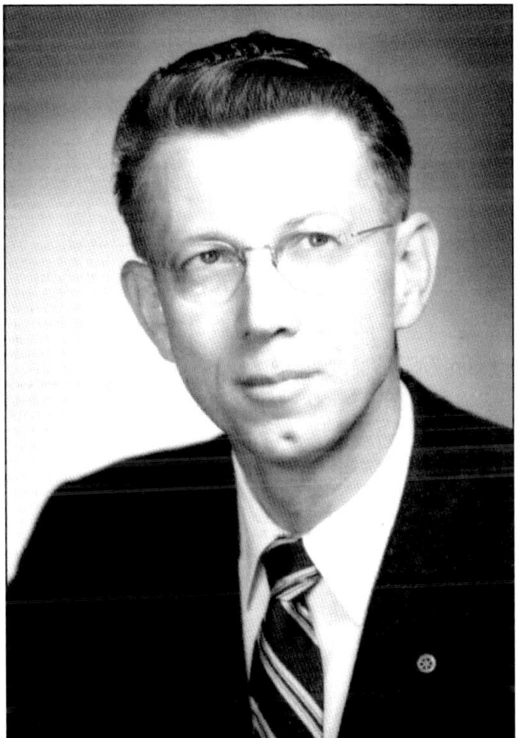

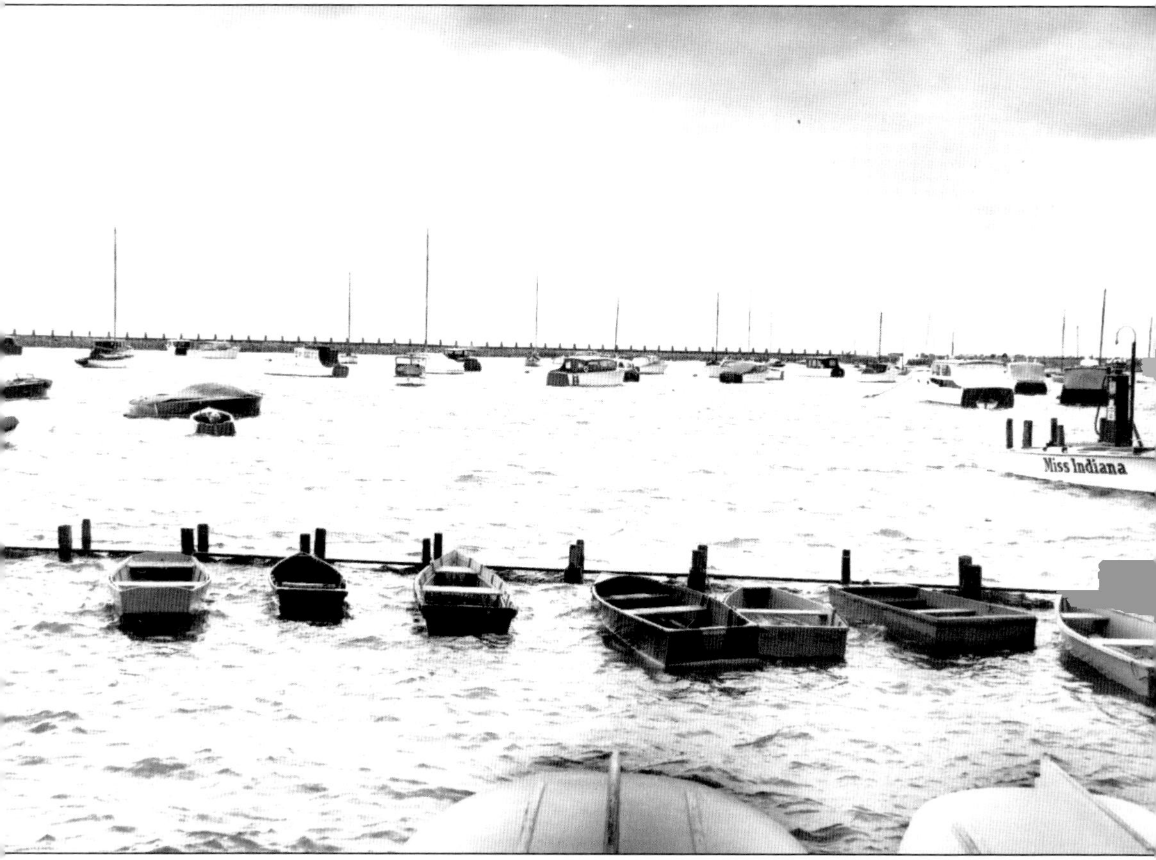

With control over the basin, the board could begin reconstruction. It hired the Ralph K. Burke Company to perform the preliminary tasks, including surveys and feasibility studies. The company also worked to finalize development plans. The board then unveiled the plans at a mandatory public hearing. J. L. Donoghue, president of Ralph K. Burke Company, opened the meeting with a detailed description of the master plan. No objections were lodged specifically. Instead, a debate arose that had been brewing since the first government moneys were received. Participants were divided regarding the need for a commercial port versus a pleasure-boat marina. Marina supporters cited the benefits of boating: tourism could become a large source of revenue. The *Michigan City News Dispatch* reported that G. E. McGrath of the Michigan City Chamber of Commerce referred to the marina as "a first step to the north end's rehabilitation." (Bill Swedenberg.)

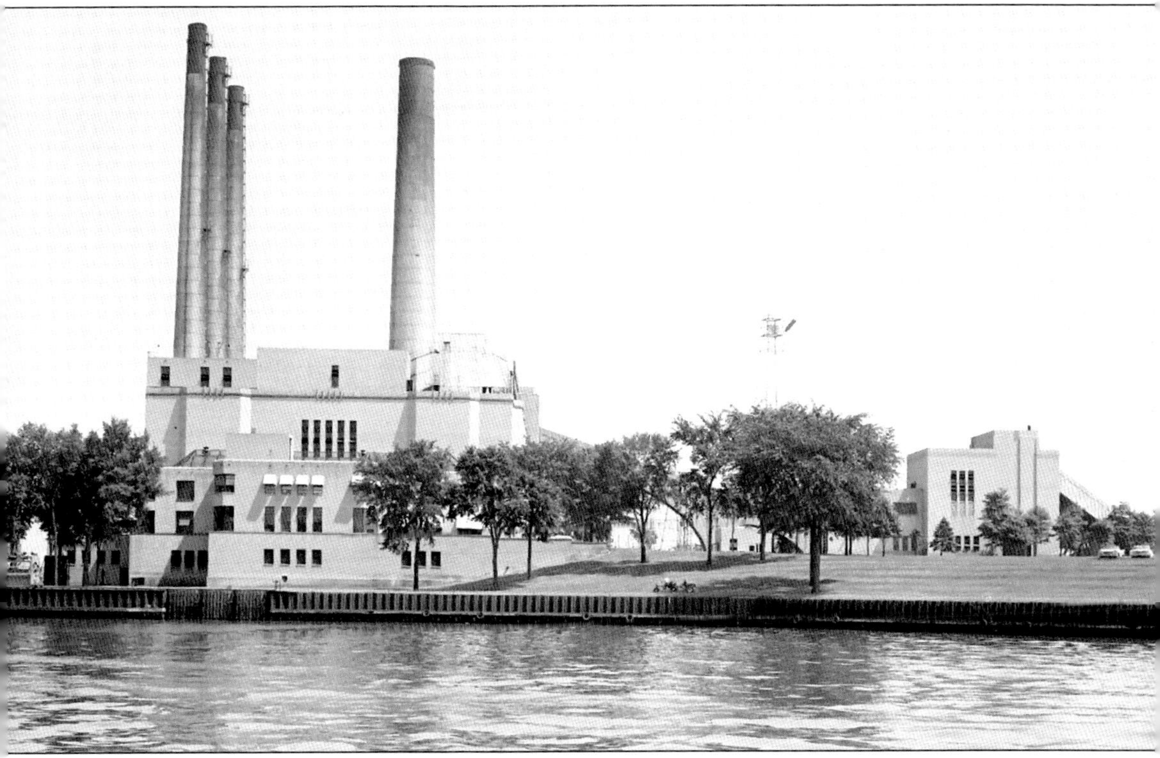

In the beginning, several commercial organizations tried to build a private dock. In 1961, Northern Indiana Public Service Company (NIPSCO) officials went to the state to request permission to purchase 250 feet of submerged land north of their current plant's location in order to build a dock. The board realized that it could not allow the transaction, thinking that NIPSCO was trying to block any future expansion of the proposed marina. NIPSCO's plans failed, but the MCPA never did start a western expansion. (Michigan City News Dispatch.)

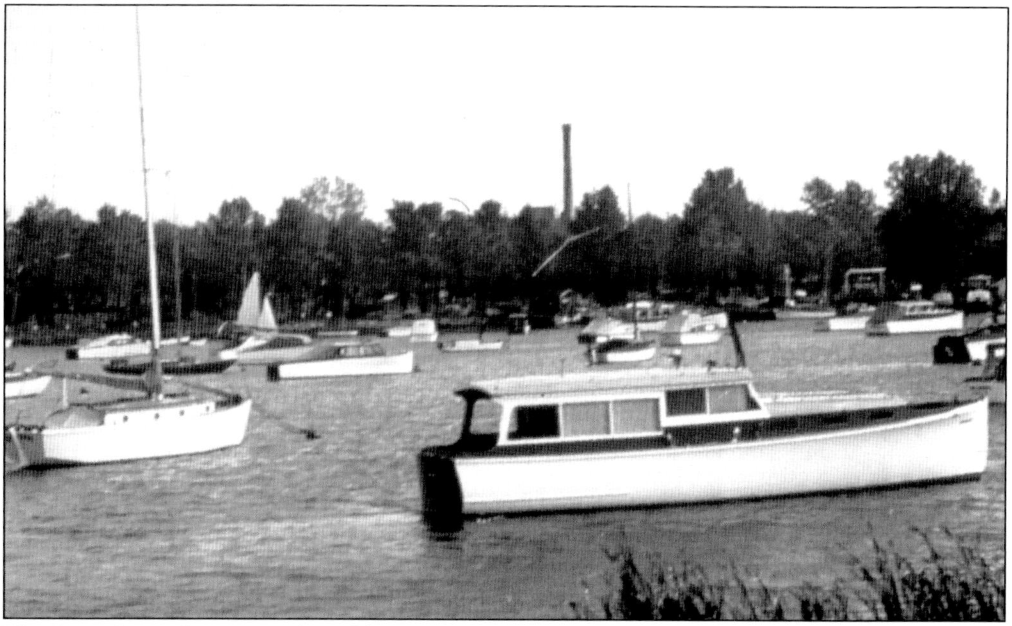

The boat shown here is anchored by cans in a basin surrounded by weeds. Turning this into a proper marina was not cheap, even in the early 1960s. The city council refused to allocate taxes for the new marina and quickly denied a loan until the bonds were issued. Only a few years into their term, the men were tired of paying from their personal funds but still in desperate need of seed money. (Bill Swedenberg.)

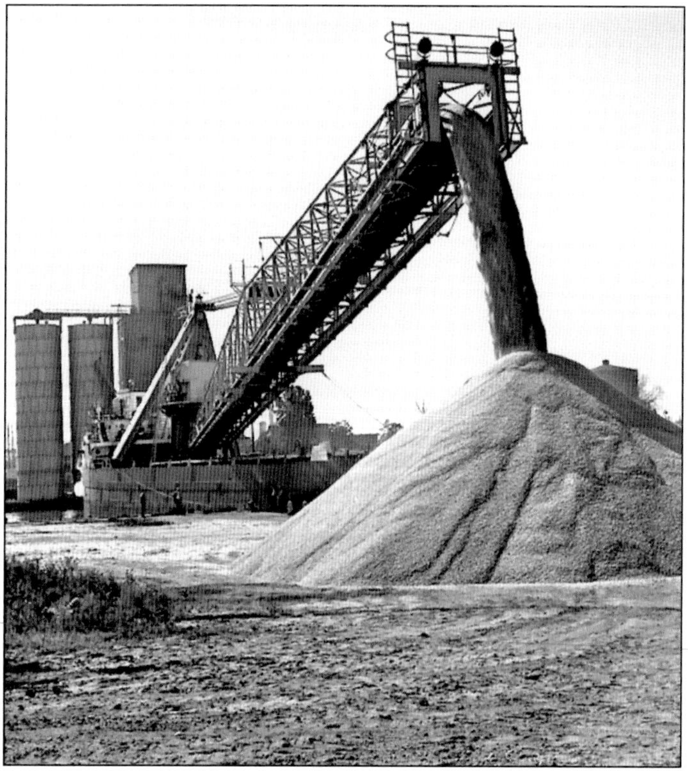

The Morton Salt agreement initially brought in approximately $5,000 a year, which was not enough to get the construction started. In September 1962, the Michigan City Chamber of Commerce helped obtain a $50,000 loan from the Housing and Home Finance Company of Michigan City. According to the *Minutes of the Michigan City Port Authority I*, the bank required a written contract guaranteeing the salt shipments long enough to pay back the loan if the bond issue failed. (Michigan City News Dispatch.)

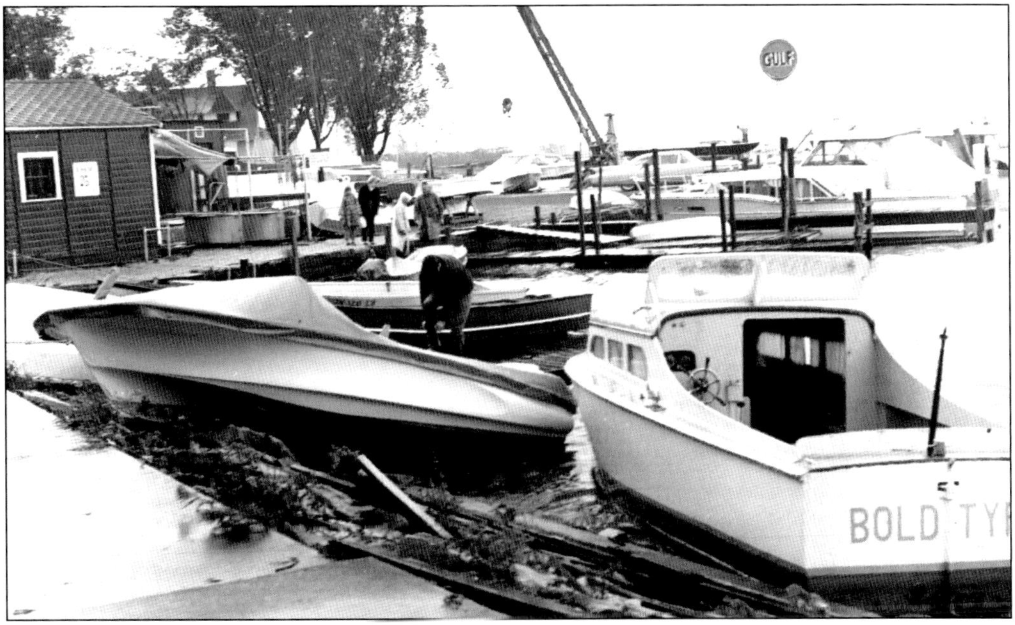

By 1963, Marcellus Meyer replaced the overworked Fred Krueger as MCPA attorney. The bond issue was not finished. Once again, the board found itself in dire need of funds. Slips in the basin (seen here after a 1961 storm) were filling with silt, making it difficult to dock a boat. It even had to turn down the city engineer/harbormaster, who came to a board meeting asking to have his slip dredged. (Bill Swedenberg)

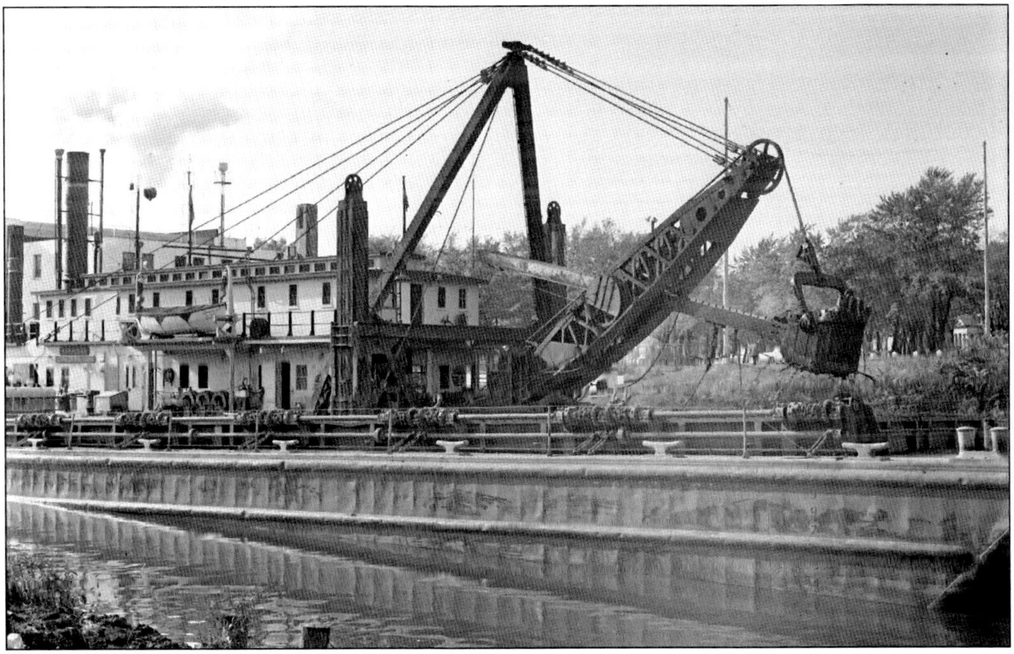
The MCPA was overextended. It was awaiting funds to construct the marina while also scraping pennies to keep Trail Creek and the Municipal Dock maintained. Those two areas were not going to be covered by the bond money because they belonged to the city not the MCPA. The MCPA was just the caretaker. (Bill Swedenberg)

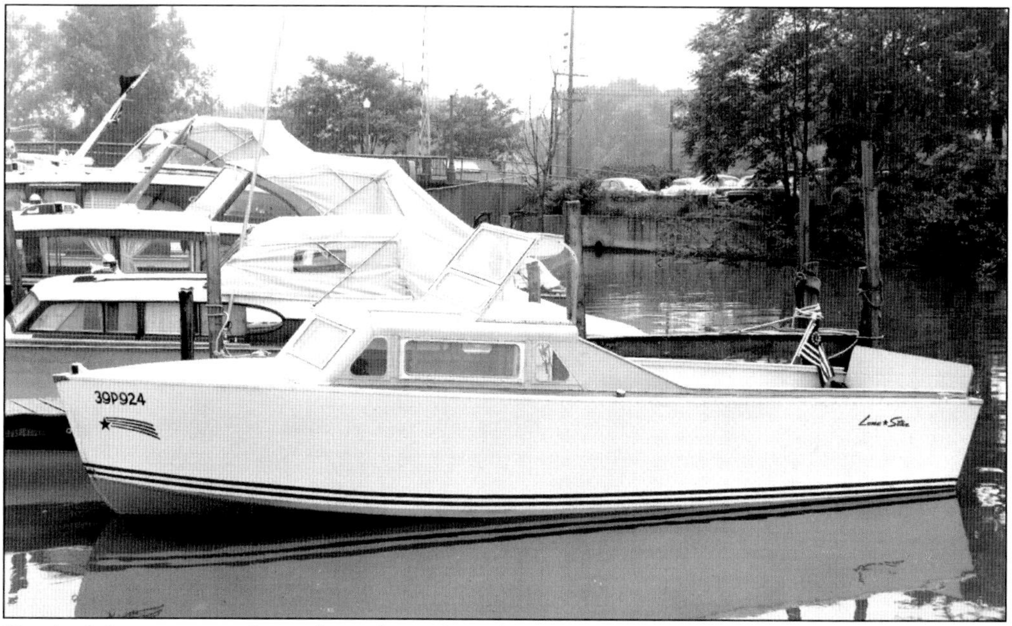

Hartley Job came up with an idea to keep the public areas maintained. Job reasoned that because they were city property, the Municipal Dock and channel needed to benefit from city funds for maintenance. His idea was to make the fund cumulative, derived from taxes on boats bought and sold in the area. The money would pay for the maintenance of the channel, with dredging as one of those maintenance tasks. (Michigan City News Dispatch.)

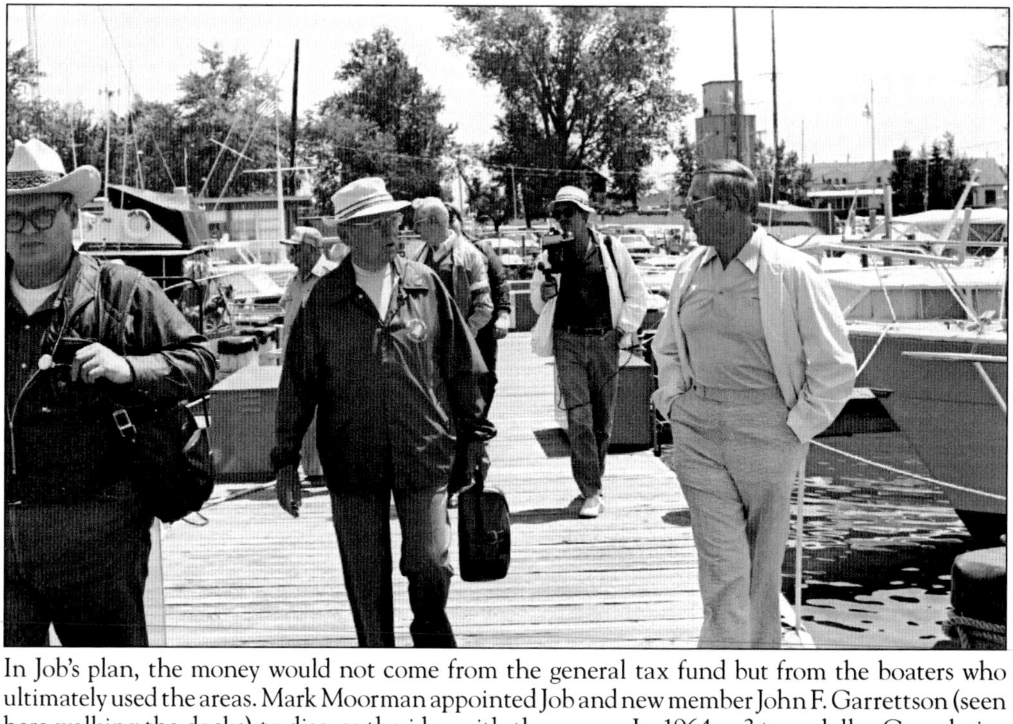

In Job's plan, the money would not come from the general tax fund but from the boaters who ultimately used the areas. Mark Moorman appointed Job and new member John F. Garrettson (seen here walking the docks) to discuss the idea with the mayor. In 1964, a 3¢ per dollar Cumulative Channel Maintenance (CCM) fund levy was approved. (Michigan City News Dispatch.)

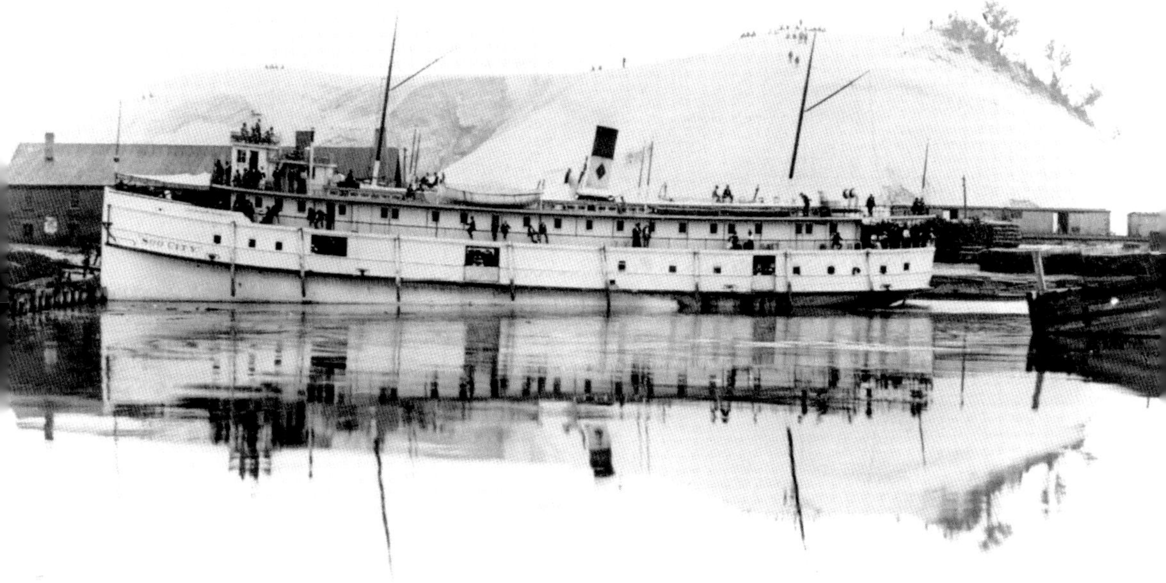

Although the CCM fund levy seemed like a small victory, the fund was the first step since the 1800s to devote tax money to regular maintenance of Trail Creek. This 19th-century image captures the channel at a time when money for maintenance was uncertain. At the time, ships like the one seen here at the base of the Hoosier Slide dune in the place where the NIPSCO factory now stands entered the harbor at their own risk. (Bill Swedenberg.)

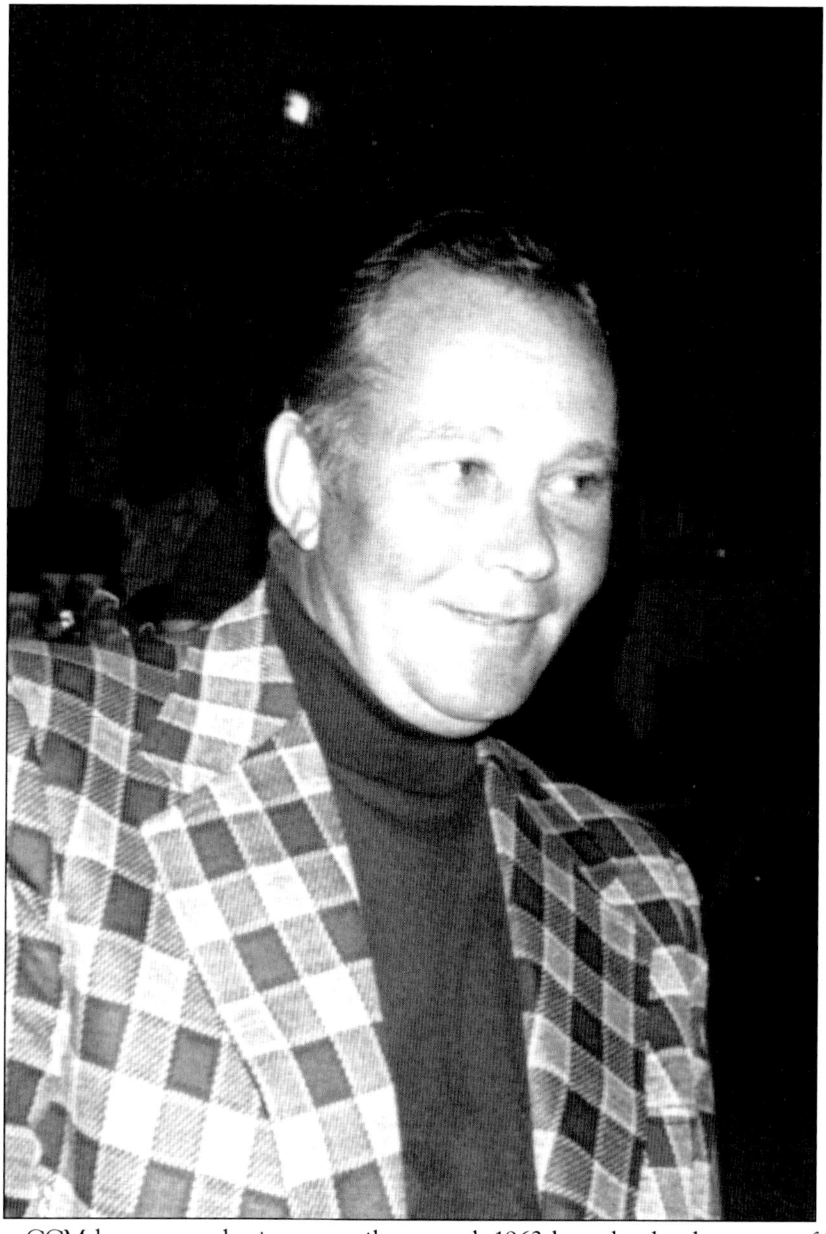

While the CCM levy was gathering council approval, 1963 brought the departure of Maurice Brooks (pictured) and John Kelley and the appointment of three new members, Merle Swendsen, Bernard (Bernie) Solberg, and Matt Goerg. Also added in 1964 was the office of the harbormaster, which was moved under the jurisdiction of the MCPA from that of the city engineer's office. Hartley Job and Kelley's harbormaster ordinance was drafted and passed by the city in 1963. A year later, Ben Lisiecki became the first MCPA harbormaster. More staff came in 1964. John Carow became the first MCPA maintenance worker, and Adele Faroh became the first secretary. The new three-person staff now freed the board to attend to other issues that were cropping up in the marina construction. However, it soon found the intricacies of marina development too much to handle and hired Herb Peterson as MCPA engineer. His job was to inspect work that was finished and advise the board on the work to be done.

The year 1963 closed with Mark Moorman announcing that he was stepping down from his post on the board, leaving the harbor in the hands of Job, Louis Cotts, Stanley Przybylinski, and the newcomers. Cotts was elected to take Moorman's vacant seat, Job kept his dual position of vice chairman and secretary, and John F. Garrettson became treasurer. (Michigan City News Dispatch.)

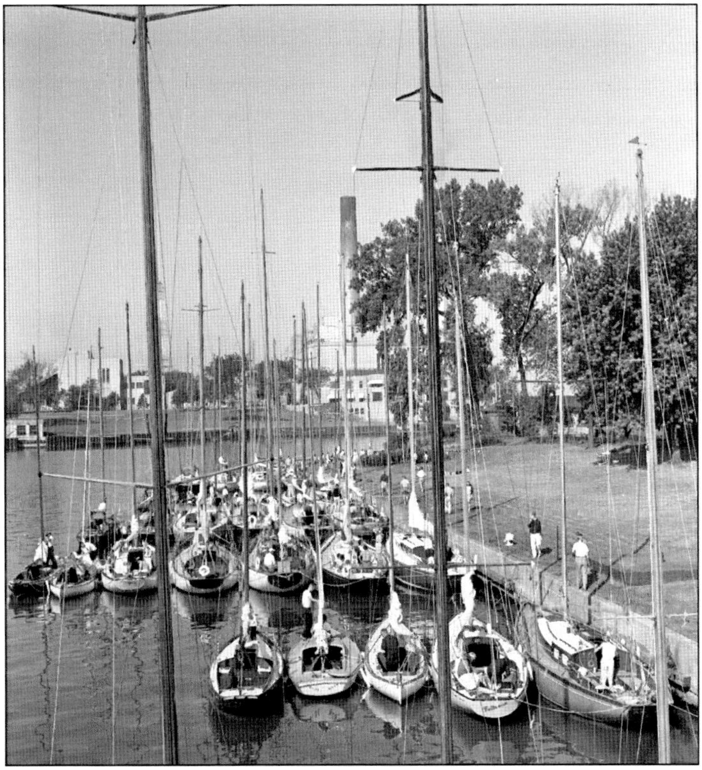

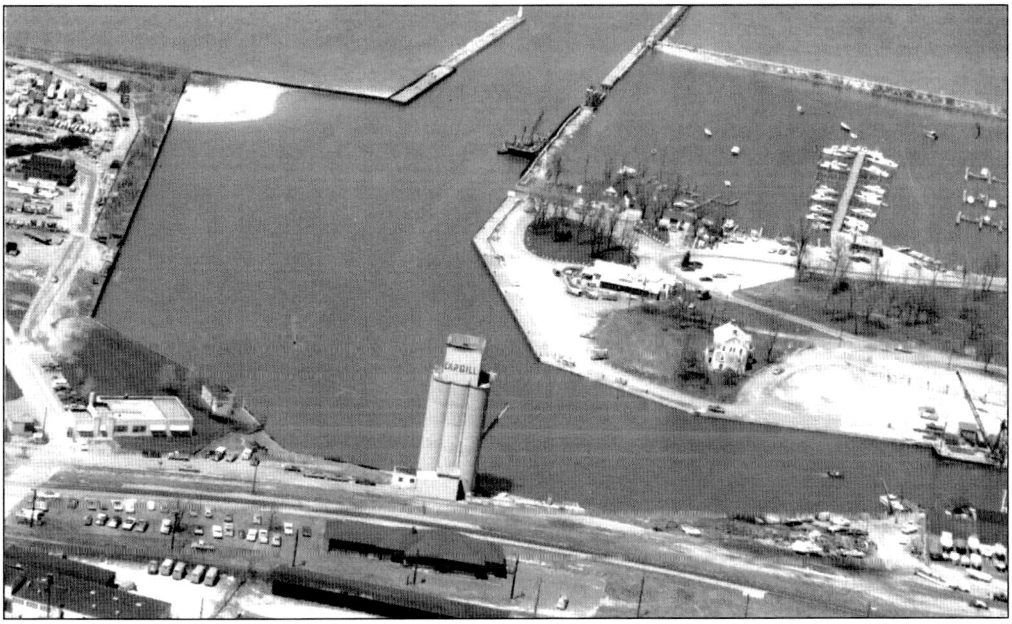

The board realized early in 1964 that in order to complete its plans, outside help was going to be needed. This meant burying the hatchet with its neighbor and rival, the park department. Still smarting from the basin suit five years earlier, dealings between the two boards was civil at best. Cotts made it his mission as chairman to warm relations with the park board. (Bill Swedenberg.)

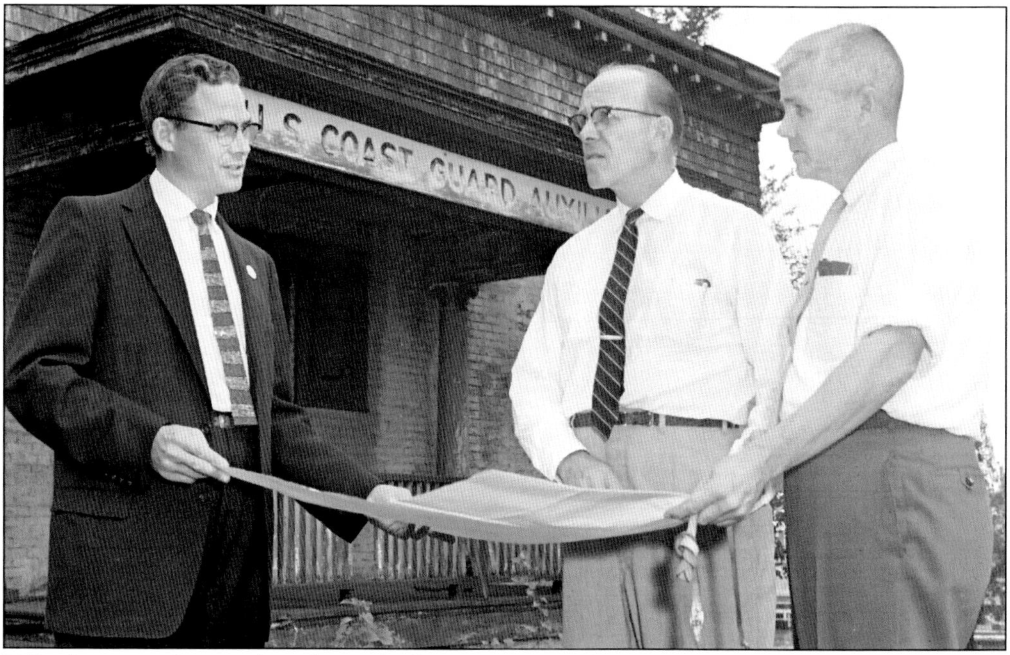

Talks between the two boards resulted in a new air of cooperation. That cooperation led to the agreement that gave the Old Lighthouse Museum, which sits on a piece of land that runs through both the park and MCPA properties, to the historical society. The park board even decided to rent the first floor of its Heisman House building to the MCPA. This measure was one of many that helped save the lighthouse from annihilation. In 2008, it celebrated its 150th year on Michigan City's lakefront. Above, park superintendent James W. Cook (far left) is speaking with George H. Thompson (center) and Peter DeGelleke of the U.S. National Park Service. (Above, Michigan City News Dispatch; below, Bill Swedenberg.)

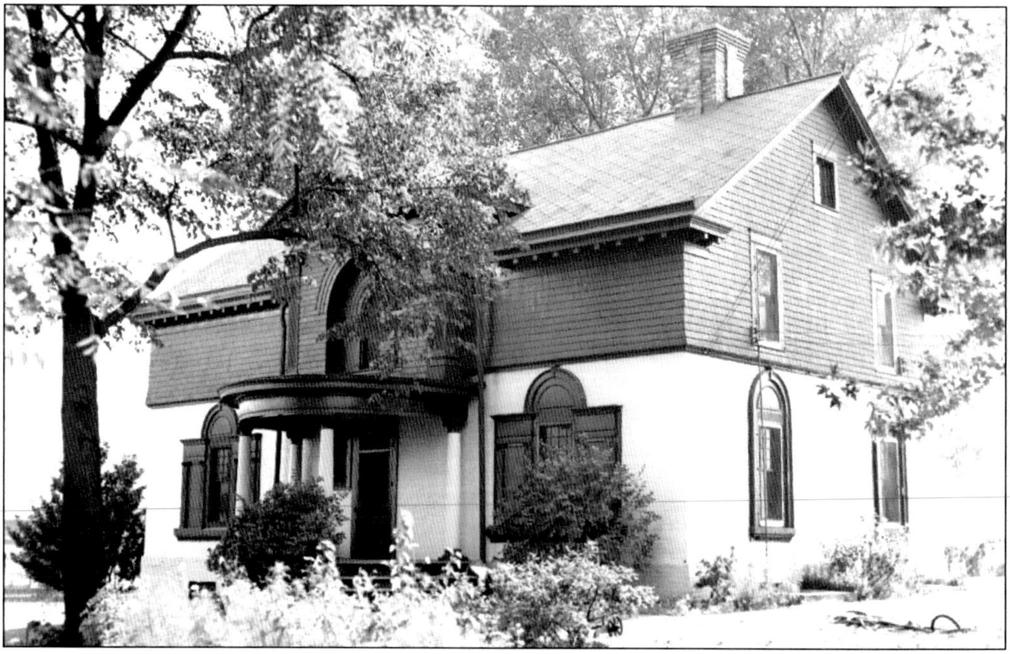

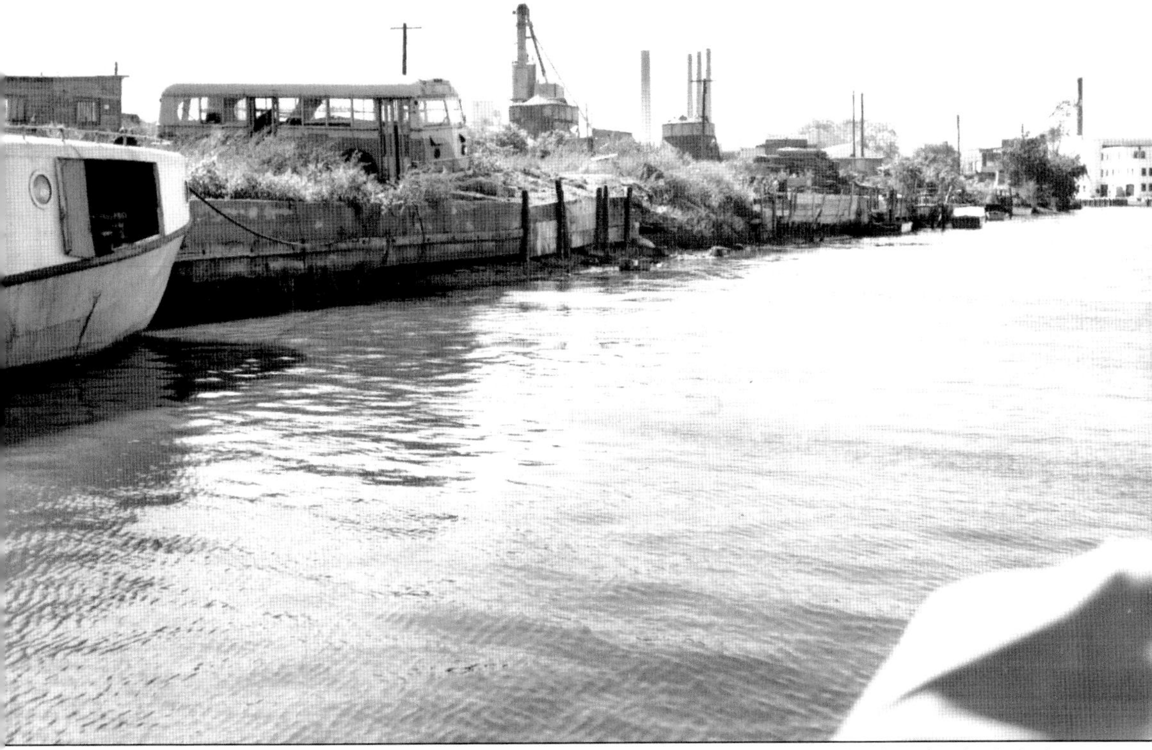

Getting the upstream portion of the channel dredged was also a problem solved with a little help from the MCPA's neighbors. The U.S. Army Corps of Engineers announced that it would dredge the entire channel if the MCPA could come up with a portion of the costs. The board had all but $4,200. The pending bond issue could only pay for the marina. Louis Cotts saw no other way to get the funds but to go to the city for it, a task that would most likely get them nowhere. Matt Goerg, being a marina owner himself, knew just how badly the dredge was needed upstream. He knew that the business owners upstream would jump at the chance to help in any way. Goerg met with each one and came back to the board with pledges totaling the amount needed to pay its share of the bill. The channel is pictured here at the site of the future Tonn and Blank facility. (Bill Swedenberg.)

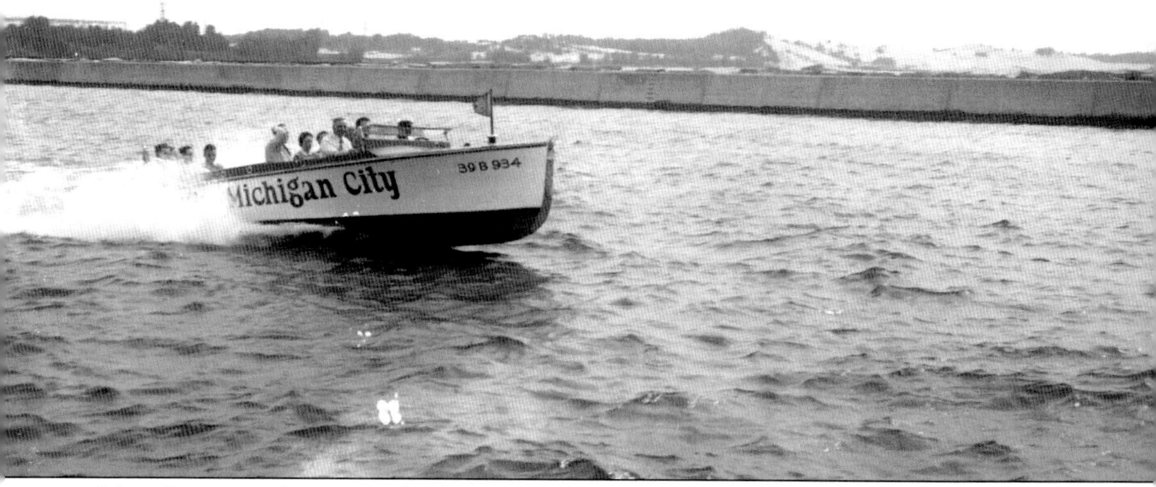

Matt Goerg was known for his boat tours on *Miss Michigan City*, shown here. His donation gathering was the last of the MCPA's creative funding ideas. Later that year, the board succeeded in getting Harley Job's CCM tax levy put into the city budget. The board would then have money to maintain the channel—if the levy was renewed every year. The funds for marina construction were also obtained in 1964. Boater Frank Collins was working closely with the board to get the master plan and bond ordinance passed. He also worked closely with bond attorneys and the MCPA attorney, Marcellus Meyer, to get the bonds ready for sale. He warned the board that the bonds would be a difficult sell because they were municipal bonds backed by marina revenues. This concept was too new for most investors. After sitting on the market for months, the bonds were bought by an unidentified investment firm. They then had $425,000 to begin phase one of the master plan. (Bill Swedenberg.)

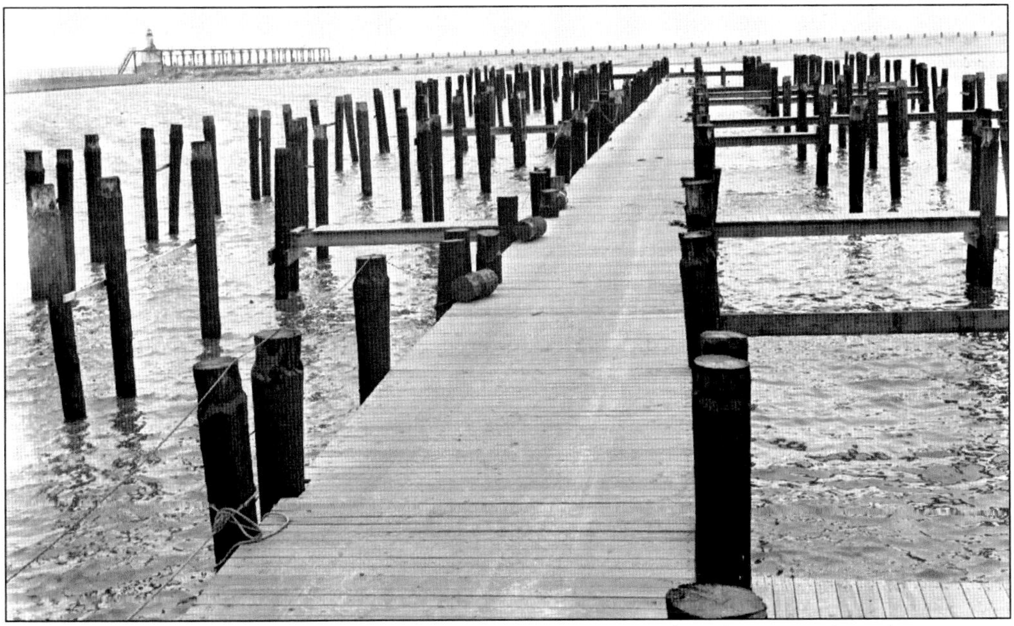

Immediately, D. C. Cameron Construction of Chicago was hired to complete the in-water portion of the project (above), building the docks shown here. General Construction Company of Michigan City was hired to handle the land construction portion of phase one. Boater Herman Jenkins even chipped in by donating crushed gravel for constructing a parking lot. (Michigan City News Dispatch.)

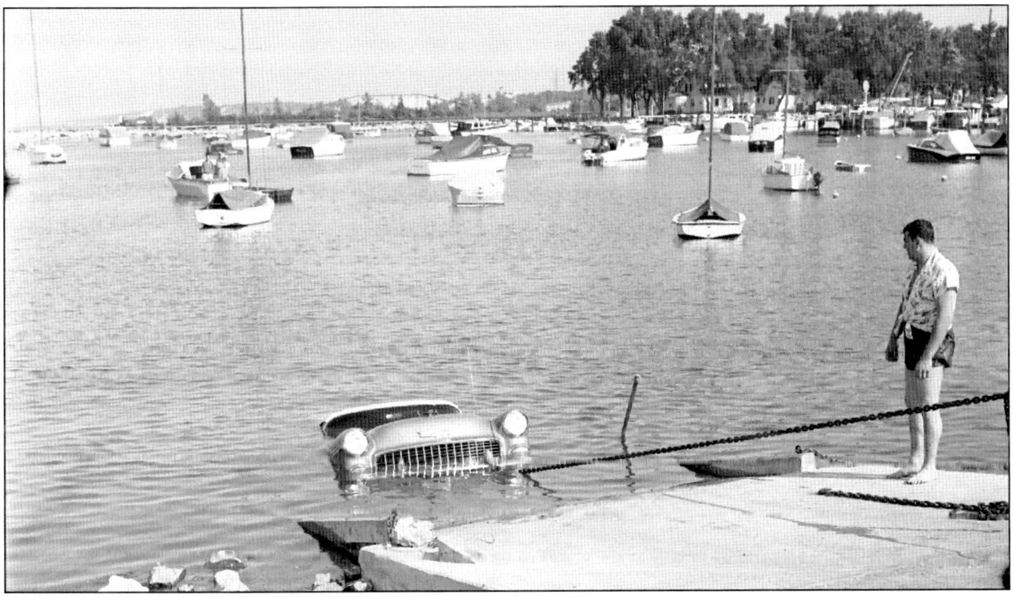

In 1965, the Washington Park Marina was completed. The Wilson Oil Company built gas docks. There were new docks, a comfort station, a parking lot, sidewalks, and a new launch ramp. Cars frequently went into the lake on the old ramp (in this 1958 image). Michigan City now had the marina that Isaac Elston, Pop Heisman, E. G. "Babe" Browne, and Harry Frey had dreamed of. It was dedicated on July 23, 1965, as the Washington Park Marina. (Michigan City News Dispatch.)

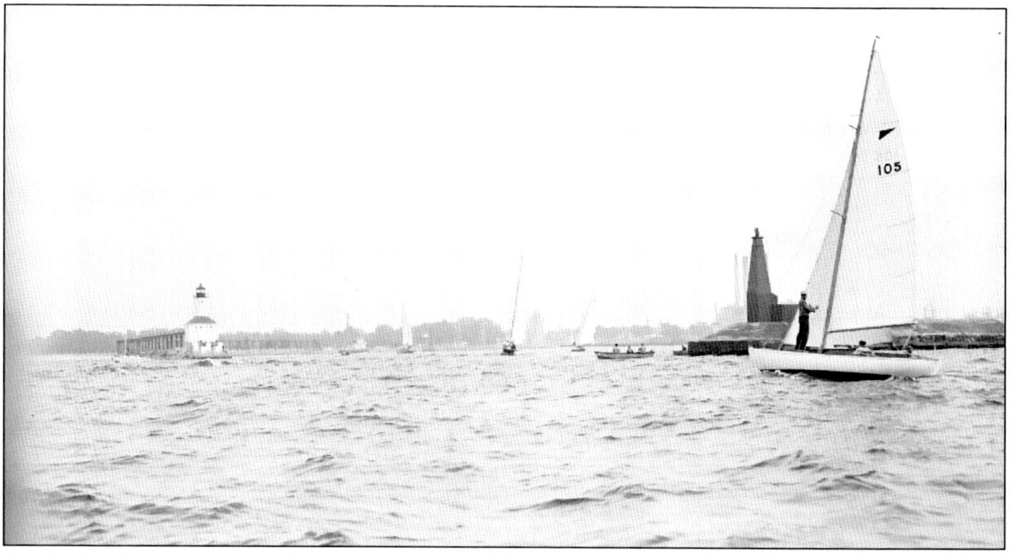

As the final additions were being made around the marina, the board was busy trying to build a community relationship with its boaters. A dock committee was set up to be a liaison between the board and boaters. It consisted of boaters, one from each dock, as well as representatives of outboard boaters and sailboaters (pictured above in a 1959 yacht race). They were Jack Little; Frank Collins, who handled the bond issue; Larry Wendt; Irv Frigon; George Mayfield; Dick Kimball; and Herman Jenkins. These men kept the relationship between the board and boaters running smoothly. In fact, things were going so well at the marina that the board threw a dock party (below) to show its appreciation for the boaters. Held at the end of boating season, the party became an annual event for the next 11 years. In this picture are, from left to right, Jim Jordan of the U.S. Power Boat Squadron, opposite Bernard (Bernie) Solberg, Hartley Job, and Norman Cipares from the board. (Michigan City News Dispatch.)

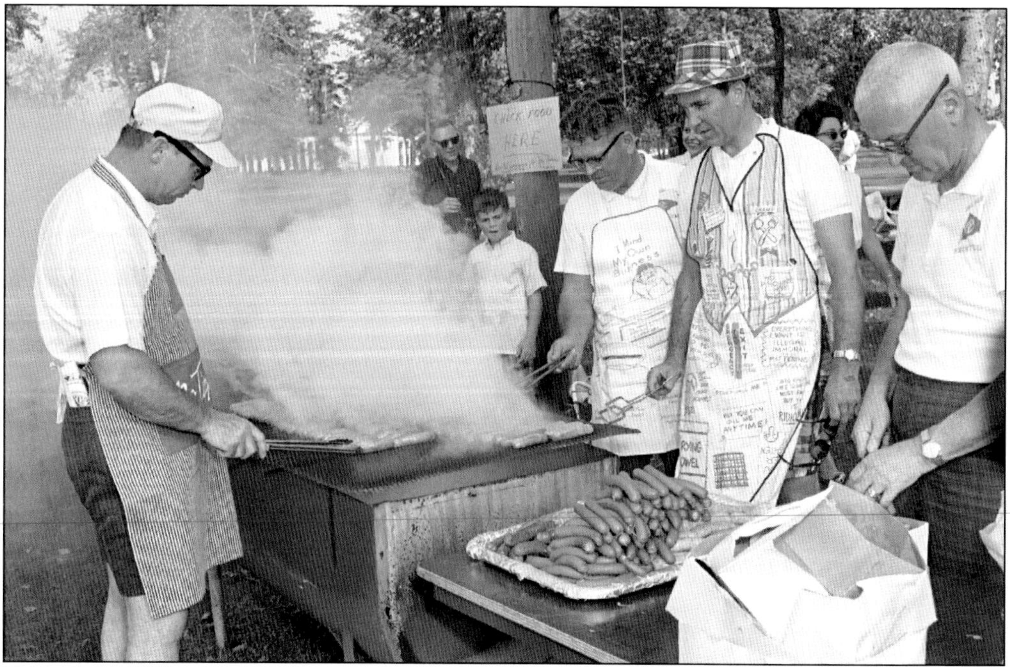

Three

GONE FISHING

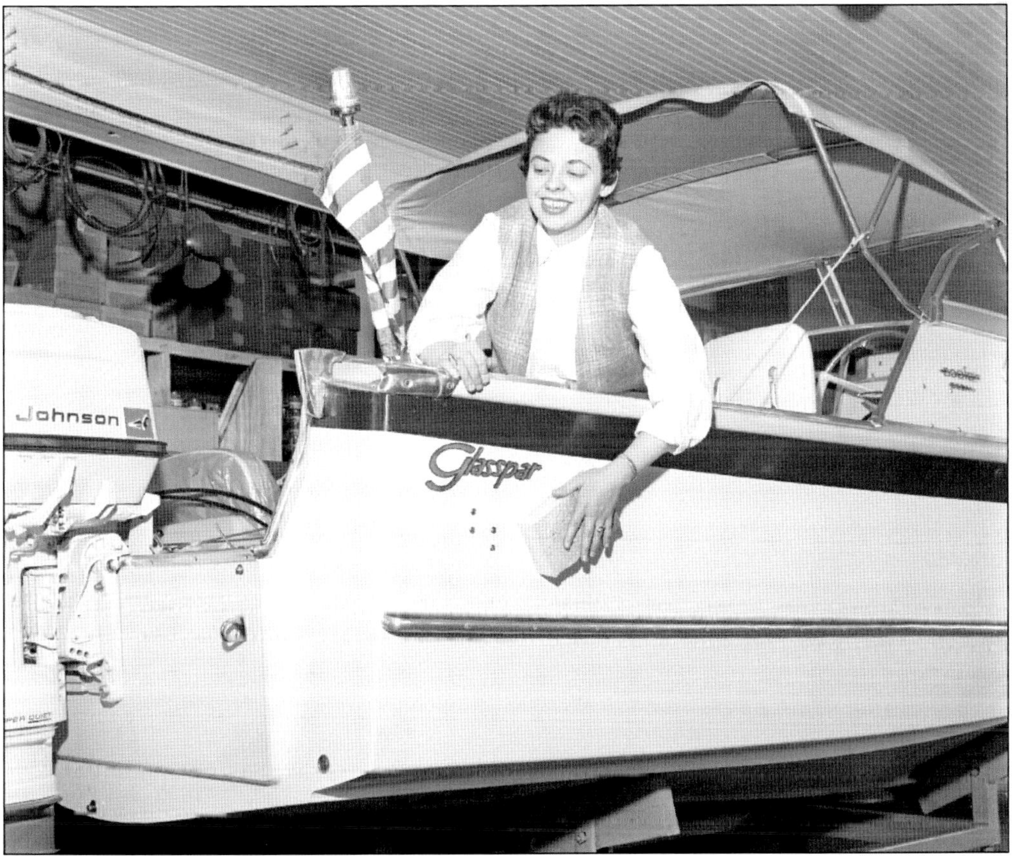

A woman identified as Mrs. Ellison washes a boat. The idea of building a commercial port in the harbor had fallen by the wayside, as pleasure boating took center stage. Morton Salt and Cargill Grain Elevator shipments served as a means for the city to get a federally funded dredge for the harbor. The boating populations exploded, bringing in huge revenues and increasing tourism. As stated in the MCPA meeting minutes, Hartley Job made a sign touting Washington Park Marina as "the first marina built without tax dollars." (Michigan City News Dispatch.)

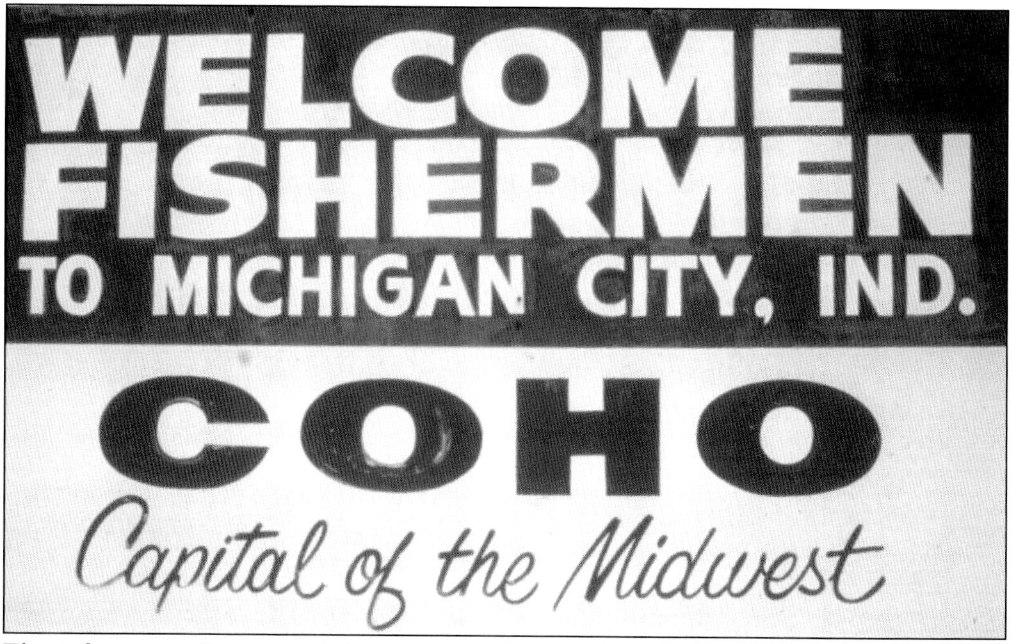

The influx naturally attracted the attention of event planners around the Great Lakes and beyond. By 1970, the MCPA had become host to a full slate of events such as the Hoosier Coho Seminar (later to become the Coho Derby and then the Coho Classic), the Columbia Yacht Races (pictured below in a 1958 photograph), and the U.S. Power Squadron rendezvous for the Chicago, St. Joseph, and Michigan City chapters. The boating season events drew in tourists and their money. Hartley Job made a point to remind city officials and residents of the revenues boating created when the CCM fund request was submitted every year. He also jogged their memories every time a citizen campaign arose against improvements at the Municipal Dock and up Trail Creek. To keep the boating industry in Michigan City going, Job believed the harbor must be maintained. (Above, Michigan City Public Library; below, Michigan City News Dispatch.)

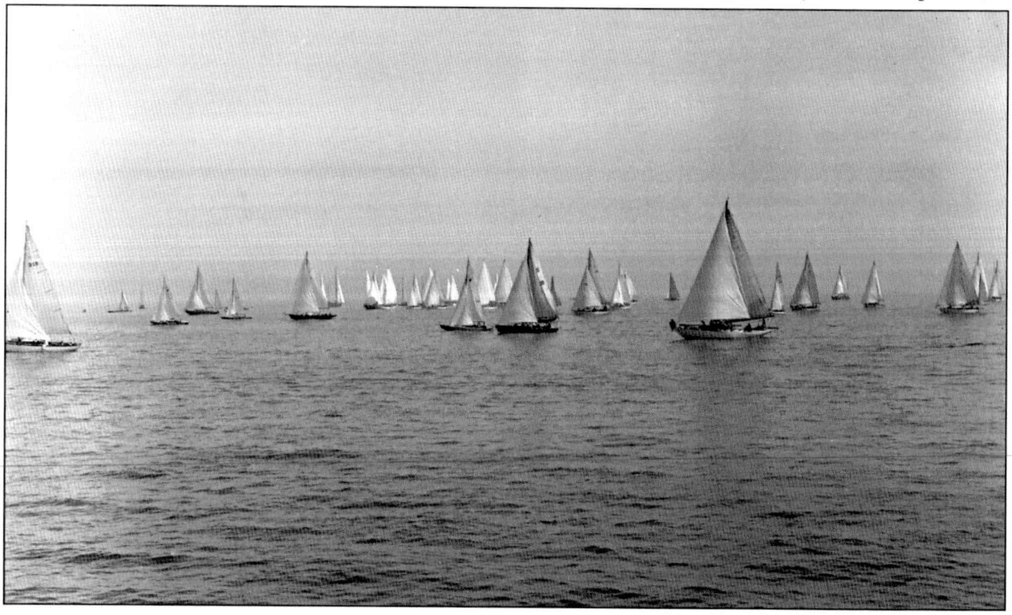

Another event took place in the late 1960s to boost the marina's popularity. In the summer of 1967, Michigan City awakened to a stench on its beautiful beaches. The cause of the "die-out" of alewives is still debatable today. The event drew an even bigger problem in the lake—lamprey. They attacked the marine life to an unusual extent, leaving little for sport or commercial fishermen. Not so for Felix Wroblewski, the angler in this photograph. (Michigan City News Dispatch.)

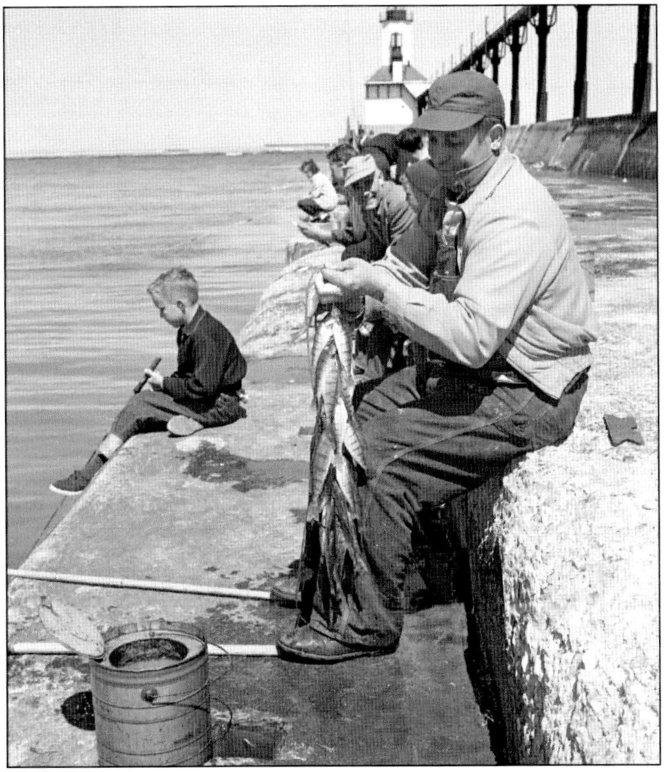

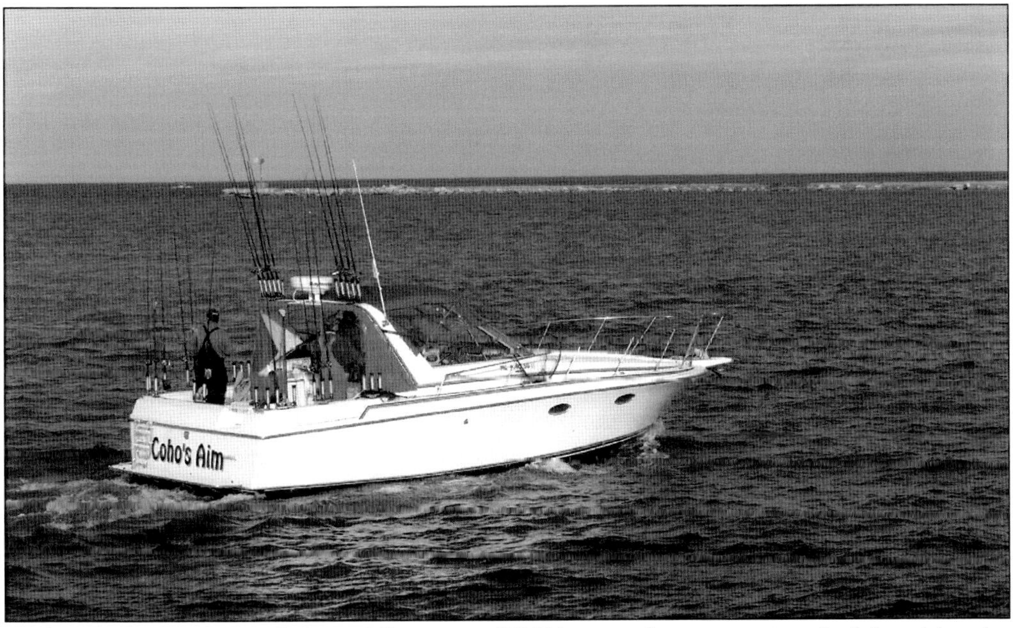

Michigan's Department of Natural Resources (DNR) stepped in, saturating the lake with coho salmon, a predator to the lamprey. The coho eliminated the parasitic fish and became a boon for Lake Michigan anglers. By 1970, there was "the revival of sport fishing." Men descended on the harbor with a net and a pole in a tradition that still survives today. The *Coho's Aim* is pictured here in the 2008 pro-am fishing tournament. (John Haynes.)

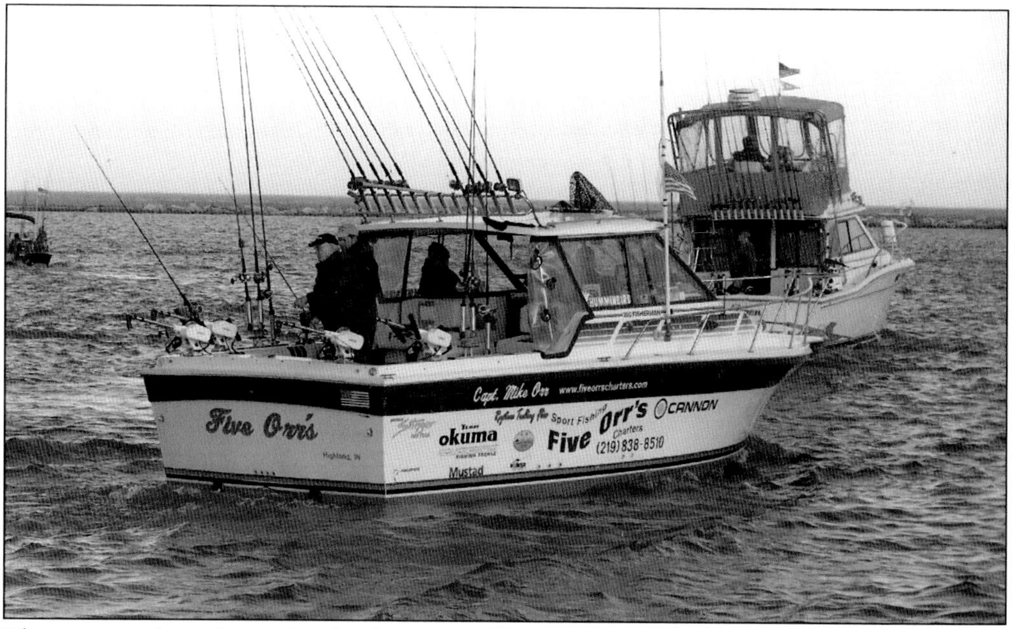

The revenue brought in by the booming fishing industry was undeniable. Charter boat businesses sprang up in the marina. Paul Wilhelm was actually the first charter boat captain to request permission to load and unload his clients from his slip. As the number of charters, like Capt. Mike Orr's *Five Orr's*, grew, the board began to allow all captains to load passengers from their slips. (John Haynes.)

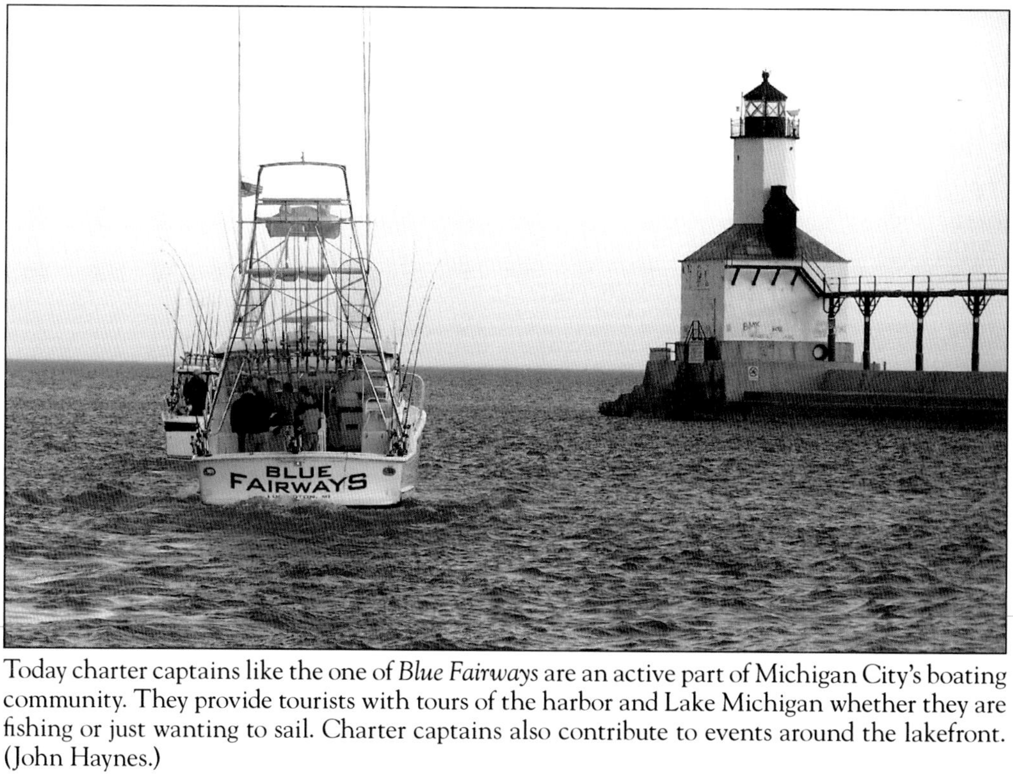

Today charter captains like the one of *Blue Fairways* are an active part of Michigan City's boating community. They provide tourists with tours of the harbor and Lake Michigan whether they are fishing or just wanting to sail. Charter captains also contribute to events around the lakefront. (John Haynes.)

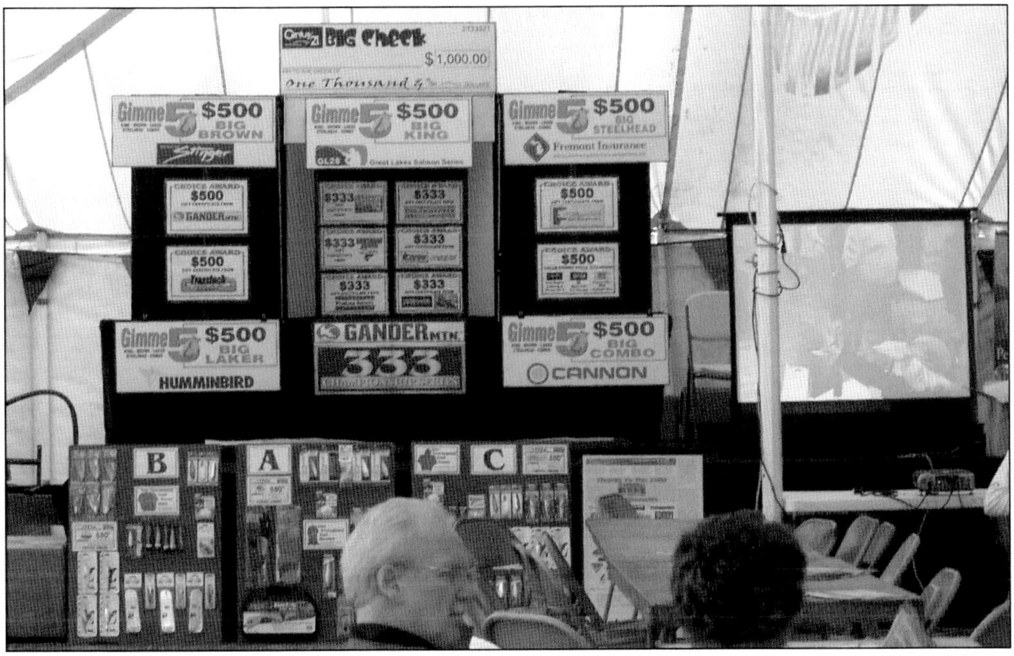

The annual Hoosier Coho Classic began in 1964 and contributed immensely to the sportfishing industry in Michigan City. In 2008, the event gained renown, as it became an official part of both the Michigan City Summer Festival events lineup and the first event of the Great Lakes Salmon Series (GL2S) fishing circuit, televised on ESPN. (John Haynes.)

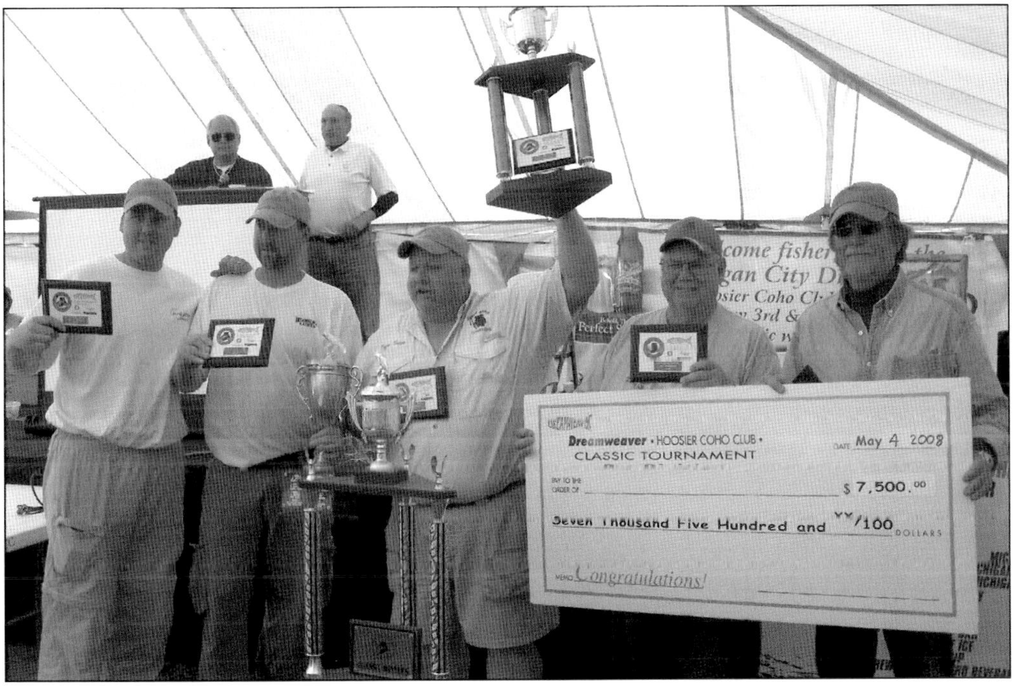

In 2008, the first year of joint competition in the professional division of the GL2S Dreamweaver Coho Classic, the winners were Capt. Carl Stopczynski (center) and his team from the *Fuzzy Bear*. He is pictured here with the first-place trophy and the big check for $7,500. (John Haynes.)

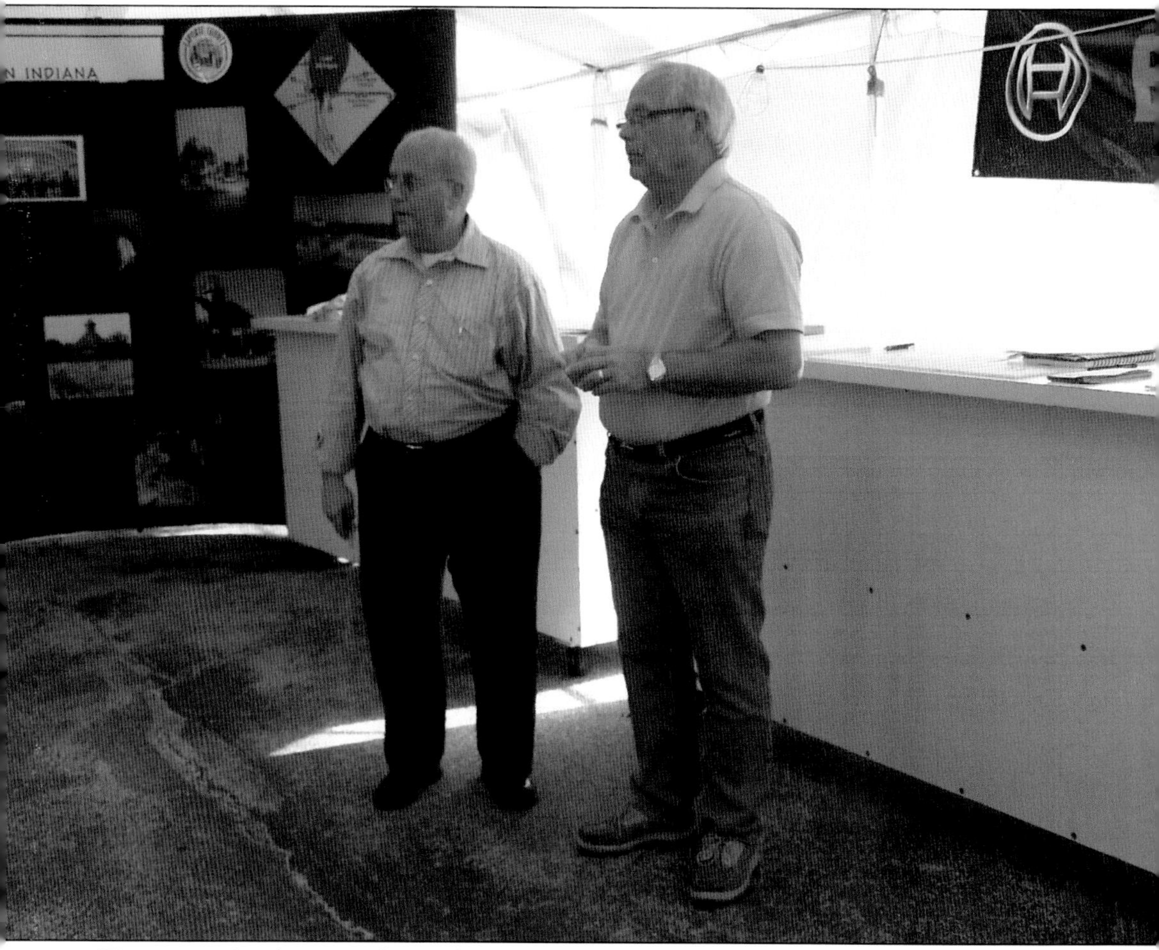

The partnership between the Michigan City Summer Festival, represented by Joe Doyle (left), and the Hoosier Coho Club, represented by Bob Kelsey, is one that many fishermen hope will last well into the future. (John Haynes.)

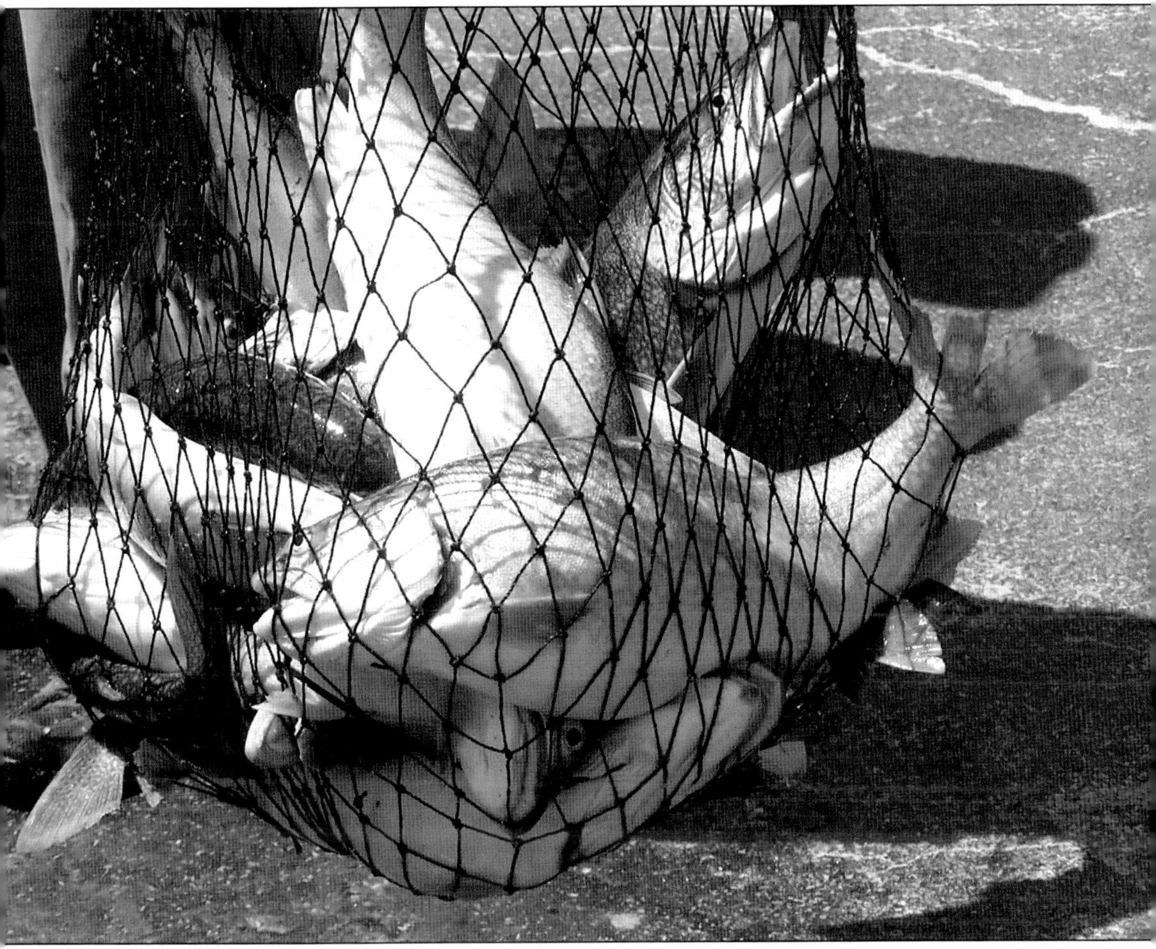

Sportfishing is now a permanent part of the MCPA's history. As sportfishing gains popularity, so will the fishing waters around Michigan City's harbor. This is especially true now that the town's fishing tournament is televised worldwide. (John Haynes.)

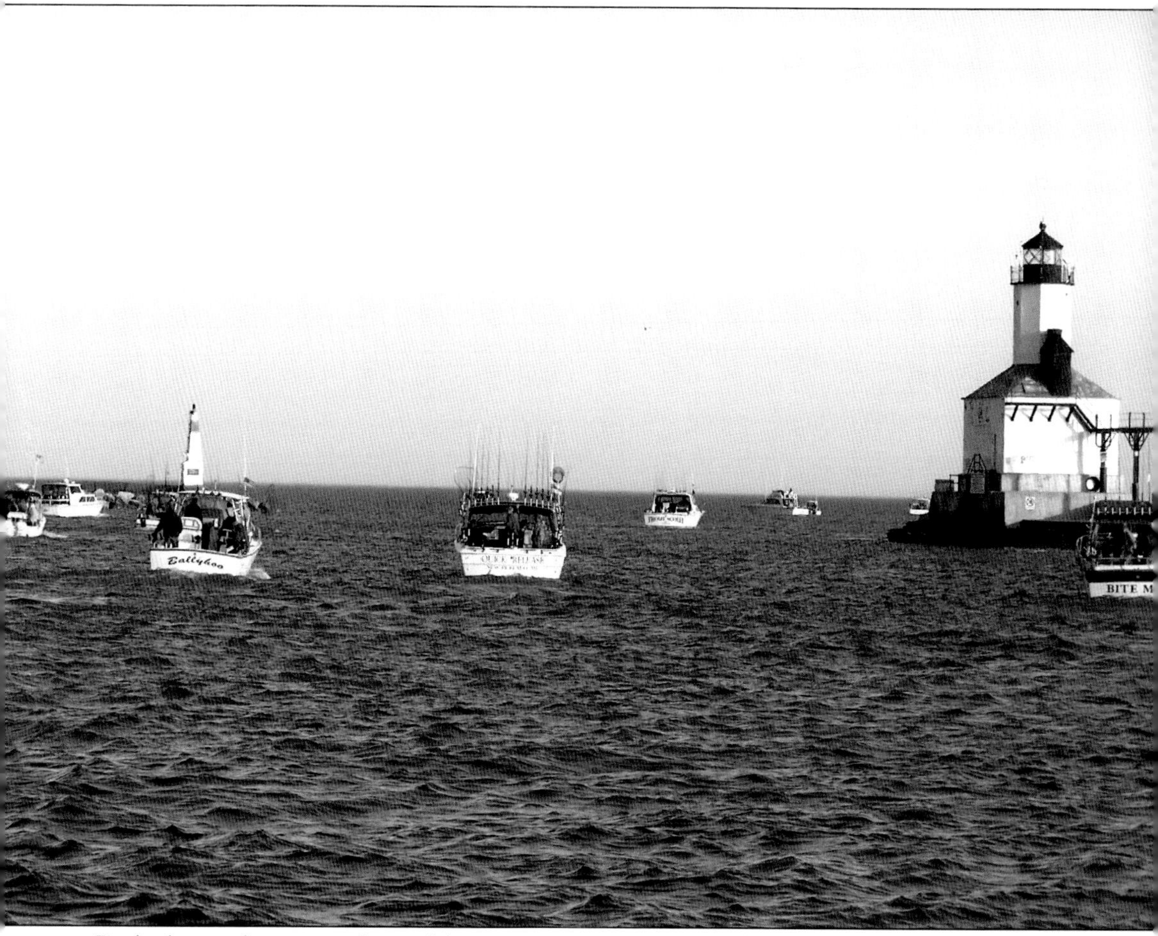

Both pleasure boating and sportfishing are important parts of the MCPA's event roster every year. The Hoosier Coho Club is only one of the many groups that have sprung up around Michigan City's sportfishing industry. Now they are integral parts of the town, bringing more tourists and national recognition to the area. (John Haynes.)

Four

Growing Pains

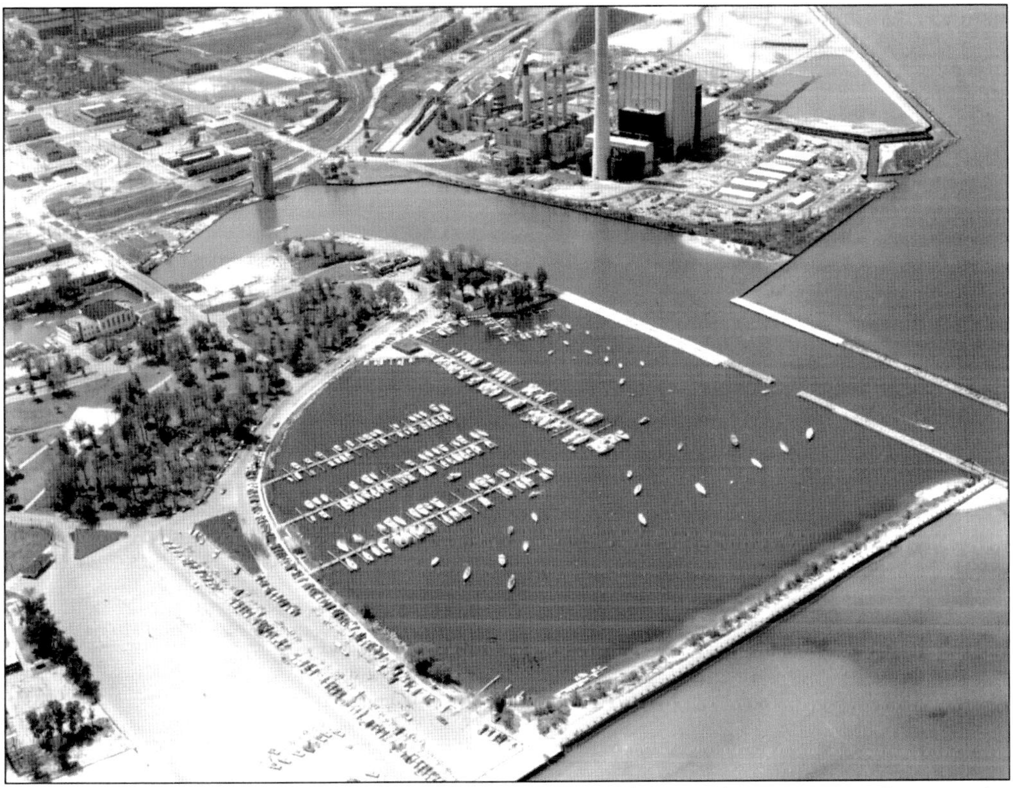

Burgeoning use brought many benefits to the MCPA. Along with paying crowds came the criminals who preyed on them. In 1969, a night watchman was hired. Howington, known by last name only, worked alone; when the crime rate rose, he was joined by others. The facilities, pictured around 1970, deteriorated at a more rapid rate with increased use. In April 1972, the board resolved to begin development of phase two. The focus of the project was a new marina on Trail Creek. (Bill Swedenberg.)

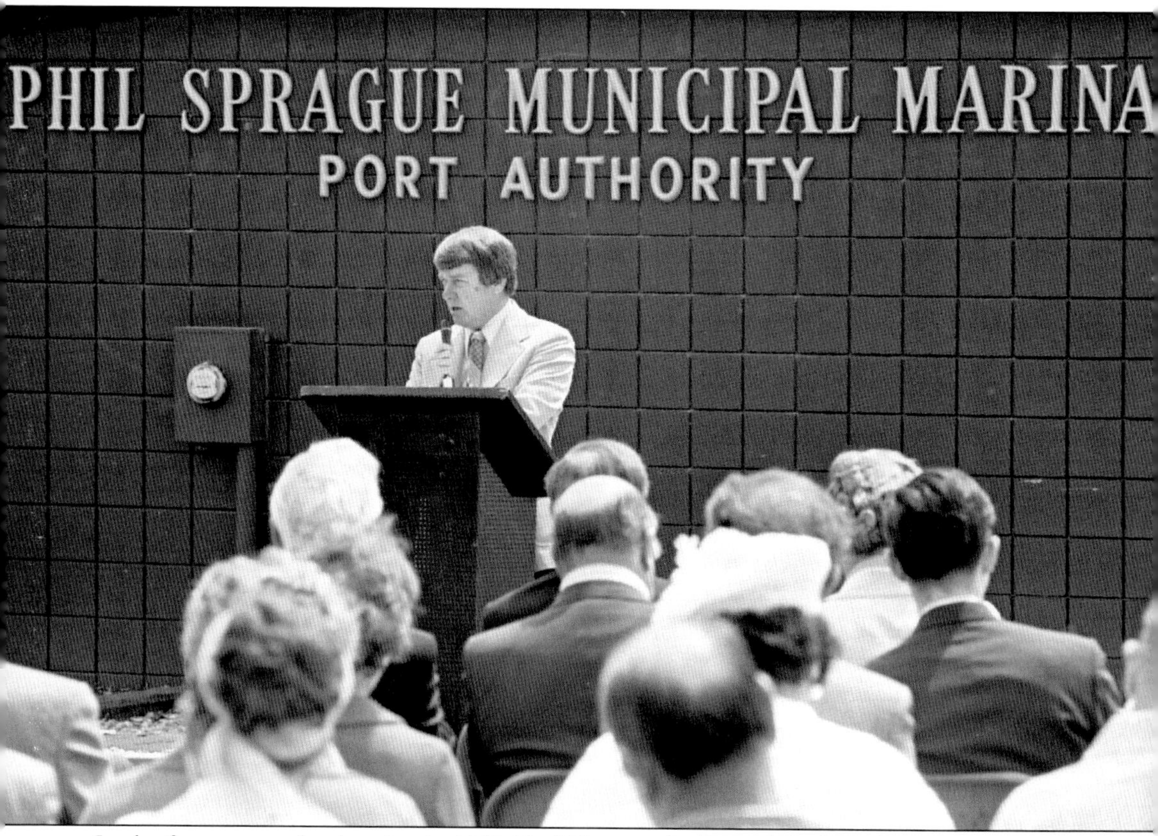

In the first master plan hearing in 1960, Paul Krueger challenged the board's plans to eventually acquire property owned by the Hayes Corporation. Phase two required the land in question along with other properties surrounding it. The board initiated phase two and set out to acquire the land. To its surprise, there was no debate over getting the Hayes Corporation property. Phillip A. Sprague decided to donate the land for use in pleasure boating. This gesture was done in honor of his father, Phillip T. Sprague. A year later, the marina was dedicated as the Phil Sprague Municipal Marina. The younger Sprague told the crowd at the dedication that although his father was not a boater, the man loved the harbor and wanted to see it developed. (Michigan City News Dispatch.)

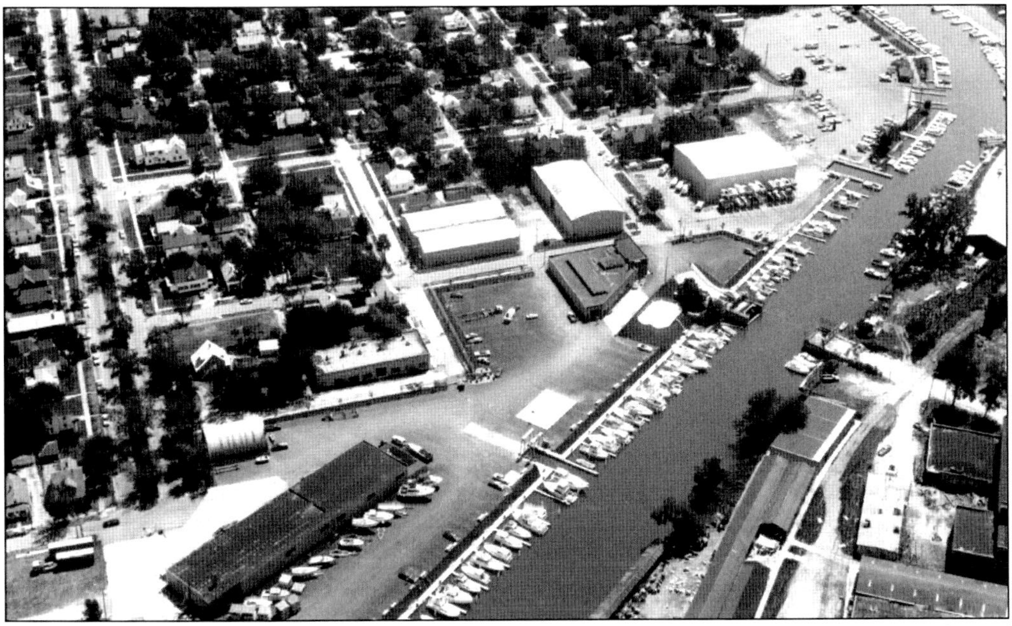

The new marina (second white-roofed building from the top) offered many amenities free of charge for city residents. The launching ramps and parking were free. For nonresident boaters, the marina offered low slip rates, low launch fees, and dry storage for the winter. Lawrence Nowak was recorded in April 1974 as the first Michigan City resident to register to use the launch ramps at the Sprague Municipal Marina. (Michigan City News Dispatch.)

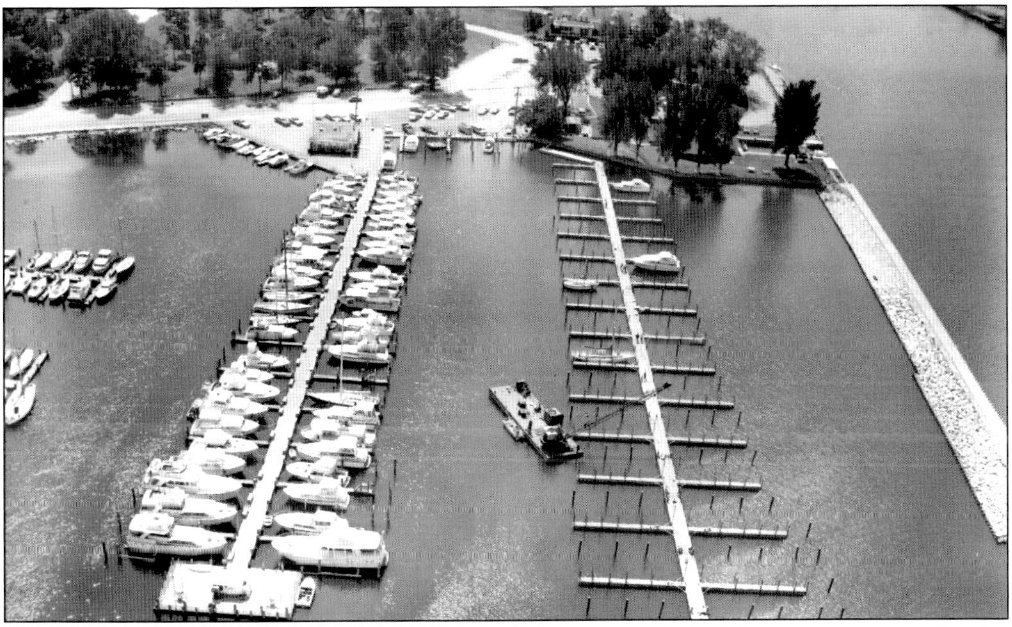

The rest of phase two included upgrades to Washington Park Marina (pictured). By the mid-1970s, however, the nation was in the midst of a crippling recession. Gas shortages and massive unemployment numbers preoccupied the people. Although the revenues at both marinas increased steadily during that period, public sentiment toward boating declined drastically. As a result, the MCPA experienced great difficulty selling the bonds. (Bill Swedenberg.)

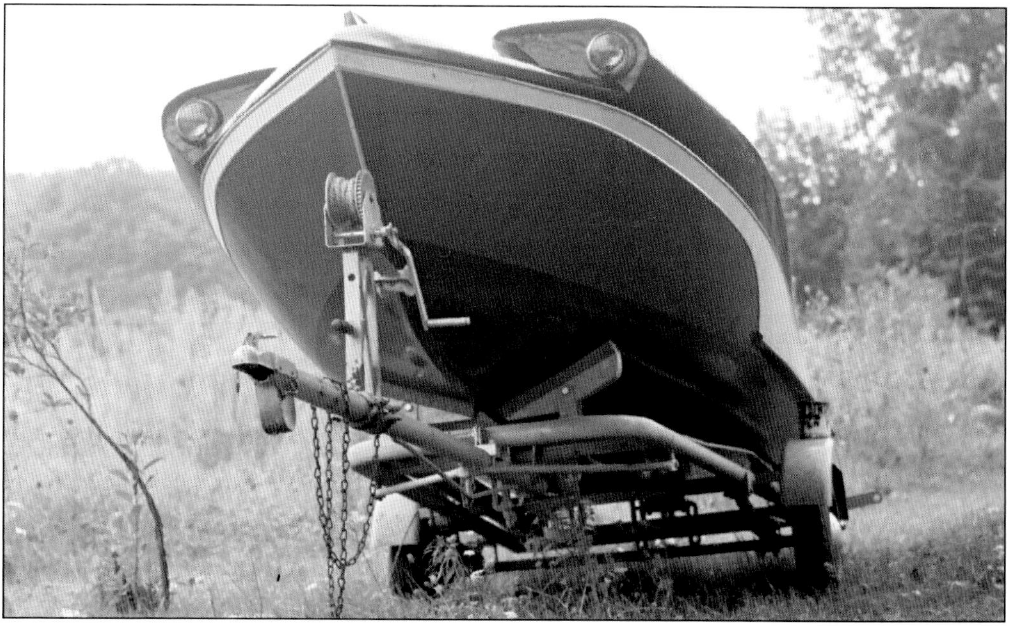

The new marina bonds languished on the markets for months, surpassing that of the first marina bonds. Deadlines for bids were set and exceeded with no takers. Then four years after the resolution to begin phase two passed and two years after the Sprague Municipal Marina opened, the board received a single bid. Moseley, Hallgarten, and Estabrook wanted the bonds, sending a good-faith check of $12,000 to represent its sincerity. (Michigan City News Dispatch.)

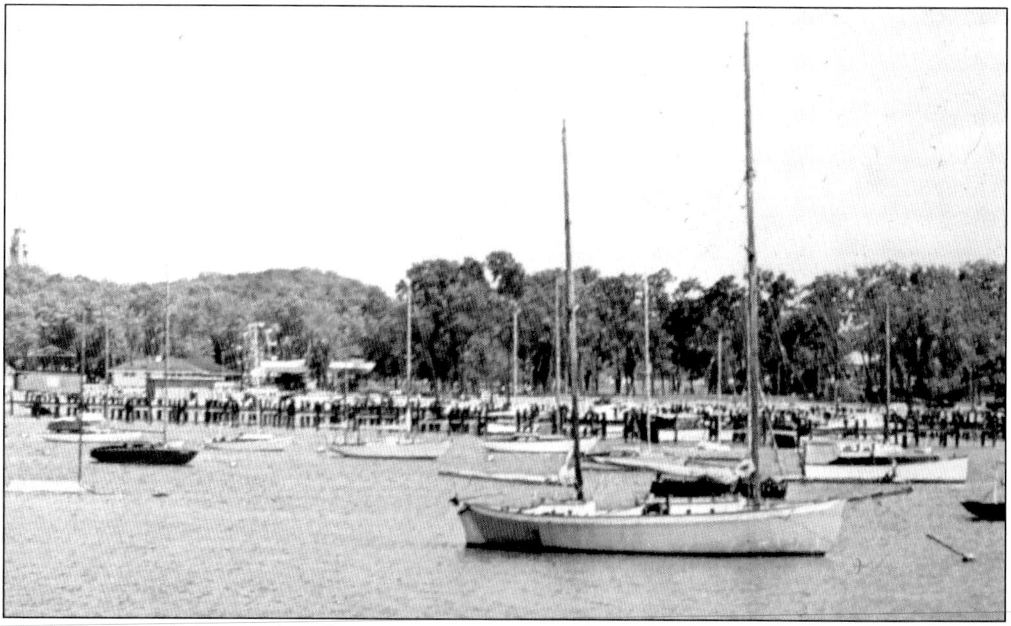

The board was glad to see that there was interest in the bonds, but there was a bit of a controversy about the deadline. Concerns were voiced that included the board's reputation among city residents of making its own rules. After much debate, the board later accepted the offer. Phase two continued after $1.2 million was raised. Harry Miller was hired as the inspection engineer. (Michigan City Public Library.)

The disappointing bond sale was at the beginning of January 1976. By the middle of the boating season, the economic woes of the country reached the MCPA. July was usually a peak revenue month. That year, however, then harbormaster James Maule (pictured) announced the MCPA's first revenue losses. (Michigan City News Dispatch.)

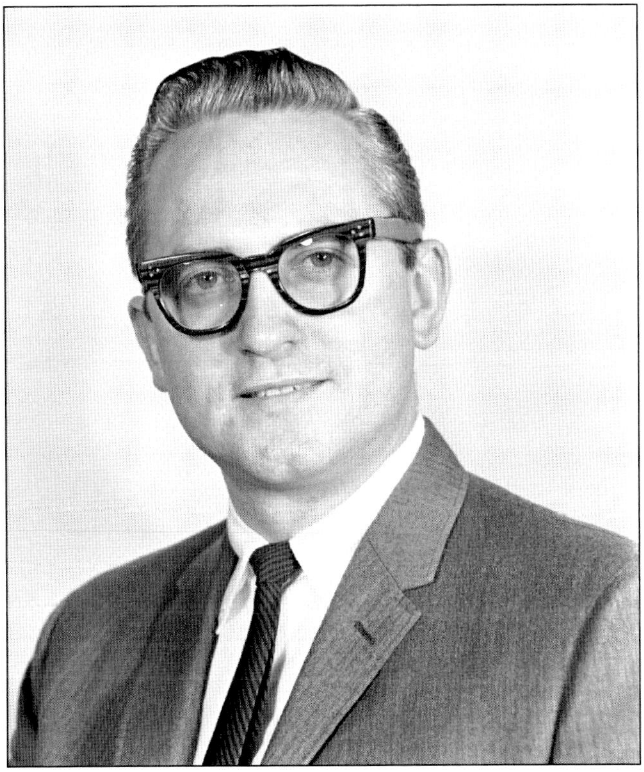

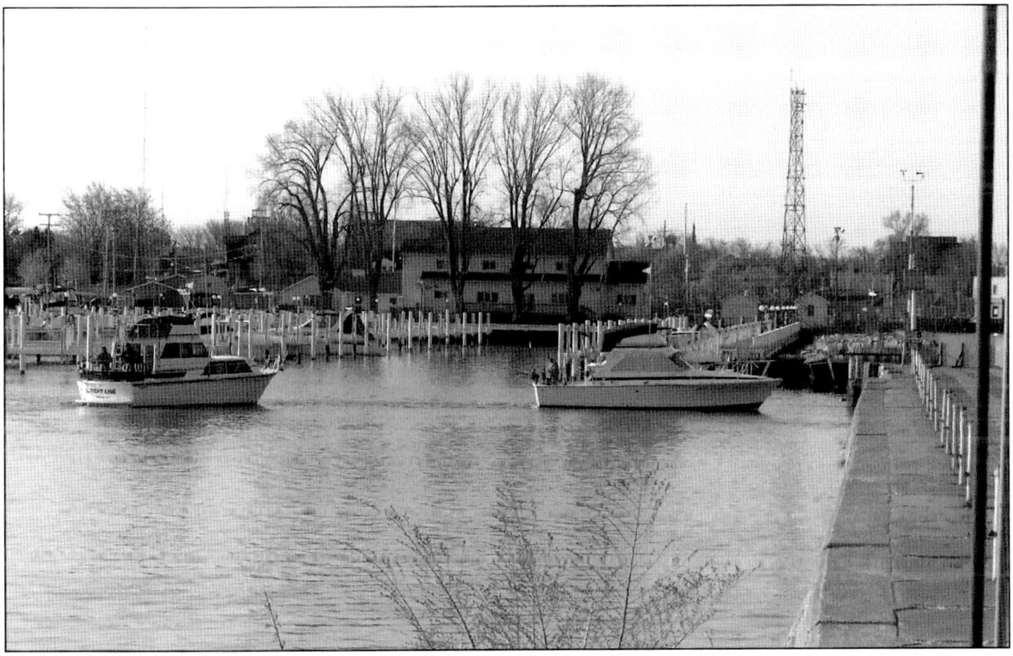

To prepare for what was going to be a season of losses, the board began to cut costs and raise revenues. The slip rates and fees were all increased, and the dock parties were terminated. The board had to adhere to a budget that put it in the red before the year even began. It could only hope to make a soft landing by the end of the year. (John Haynes.)

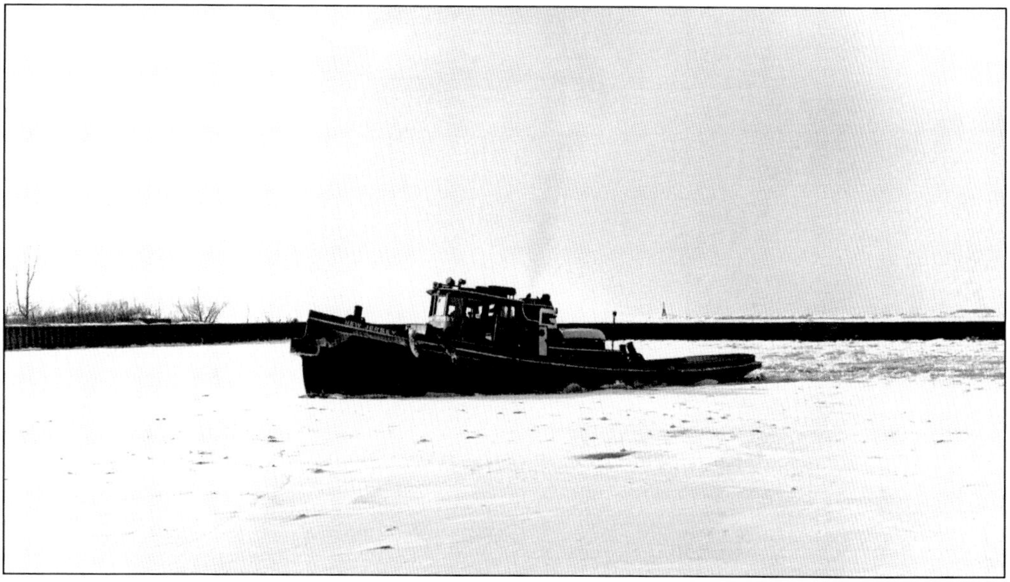

The recession tightened its grip, this time striking the CCM fund. Like the tug in this picture, the board fought icy sentiments toward pleasure boating in an effort to get funds allocated for the Sprague Municipal Marina and Trail Creek. In 1976, that process became like a gauntlet for the board. The city council continuously refused to pay for maintaining the public facilities at the harbor. (Michigan City News Dispatch.)

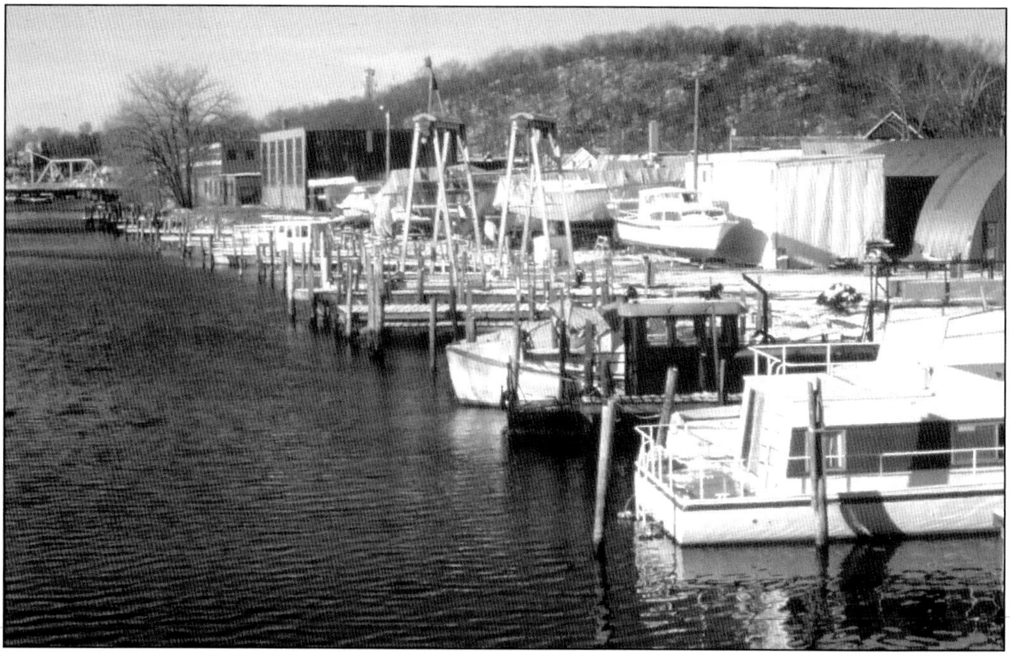

The city residents increasingly aired their resentment, which the board received graciously. Then the council voted to give the MCPA only a fraction of the levy originally requested. This went on until 1978, when the city council refused to appropriate a levy for the CCM fund. The Sprague Municipal Marina was the biggest casualty in this showdown. (Bill Swedenberg.)

Five

Bringing Home the Boat Show

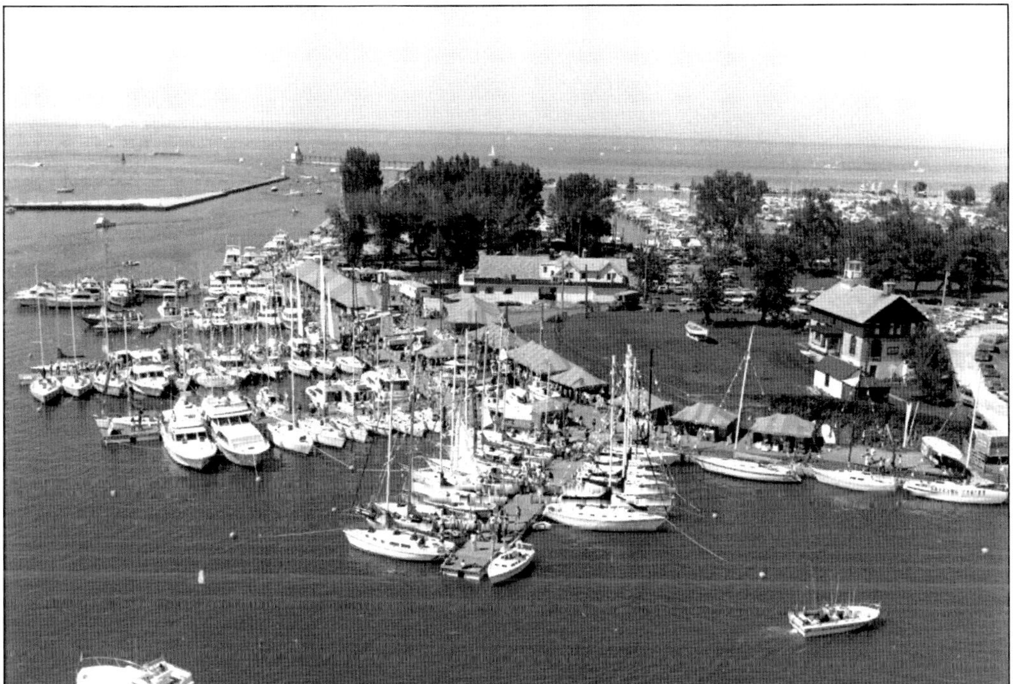

The end of the CCM fund meant an end of maintenance to the channel and the Sprague Municipal Marina. Boaters rallied behind the board with ideas. In a September 1977 meeting, minutes describe an idea presented by charter captains Ron Halus and Mike Stewart: an in-water boat show, complete with boat dealers and food and accessories vendors. The board embraced the idea and began planning. By 1978, it was apparent the plan was not feasible. Undaunted, the board partnered with the chamber of commerce to plan a show for 1979. However, their efforts faltered—until 1980. (Bill Swedenberg.)

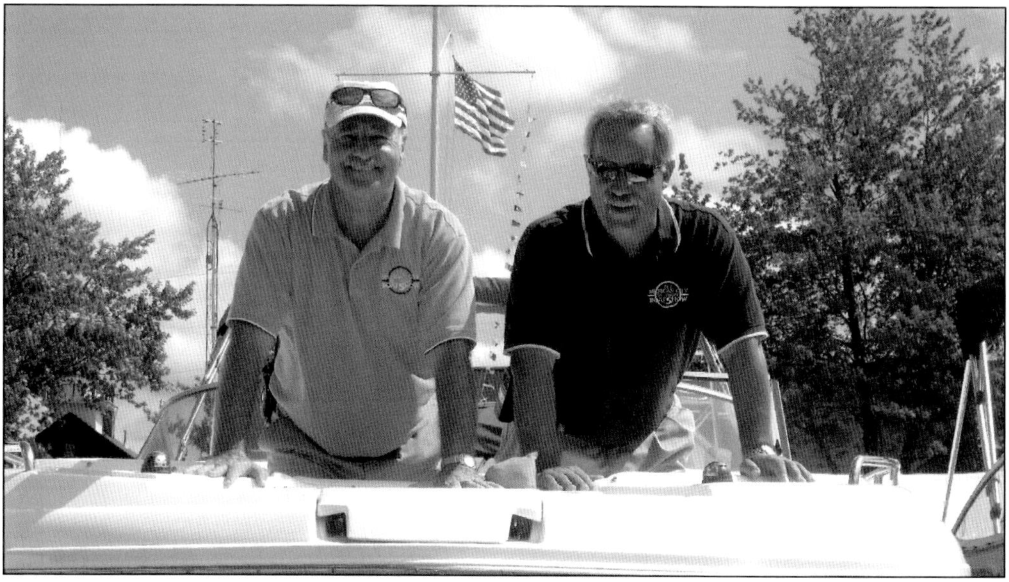

Norm Schultz (left) of the Lake Erie Marine Trades Association (LEMTA) is pictured with Ken Alvey, current LEMTA president. LEMTA and Schultz were the masterminds of the biggest boat show at the time in Sandusky, Ohio. It was in Ohio in 1978 that Hartley Job, Ron Halus, philanthropist Bud Ruby, and others cornered Schultz about hosting a show in Michigan City.

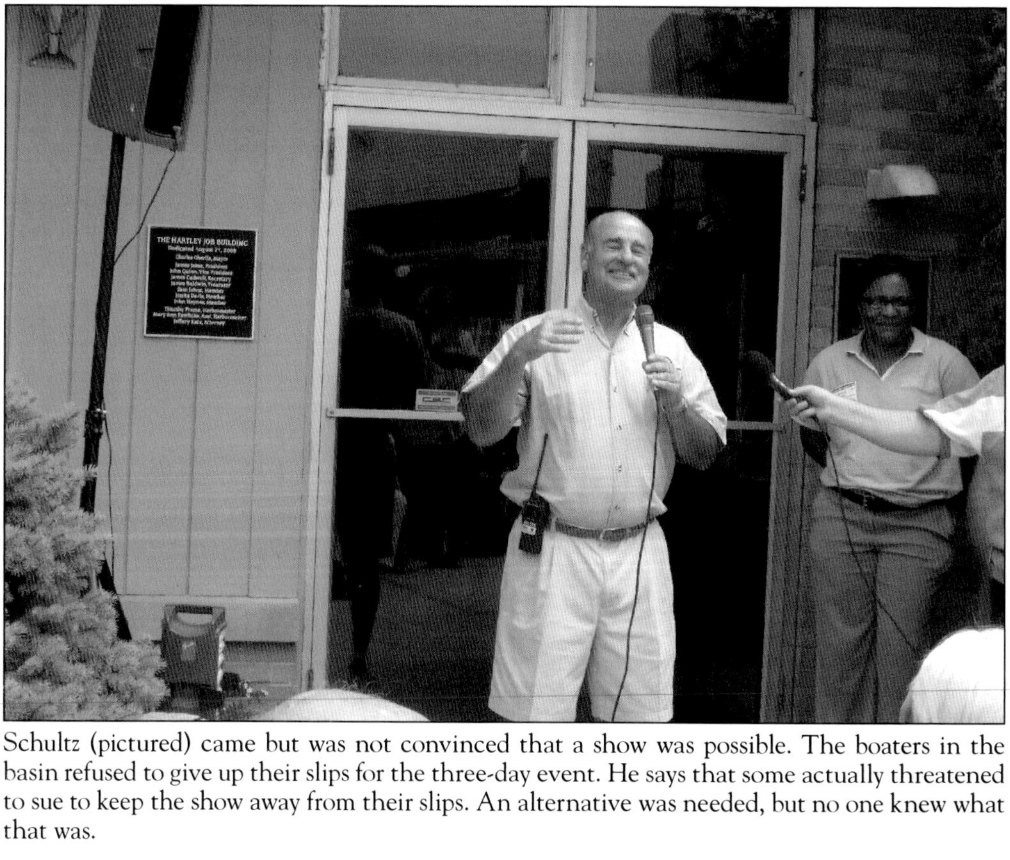

Schultz (pictured) came but was not convinced that a show was possible. The boaters in the basin refused to give up their slips for the three-day event. He says that some actually threatened to sue to keep the show away from their slips. An alternative was needed, but no one knew what that was.

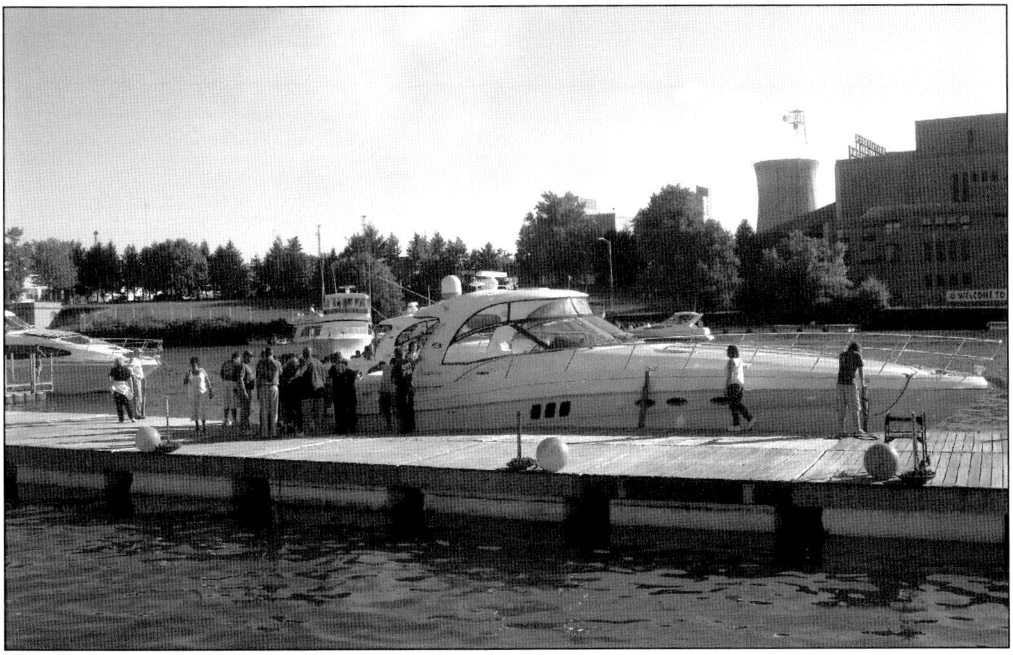

Schultz saw Michigan City as a great location with great facilities for a show. However, he needed somewhere to dock the vendor boats like the one in this picture. There was no room at the Municipal Dock, and the basin was out of the question. He flew back to Ohio, and the board tried to come up with other ideas.

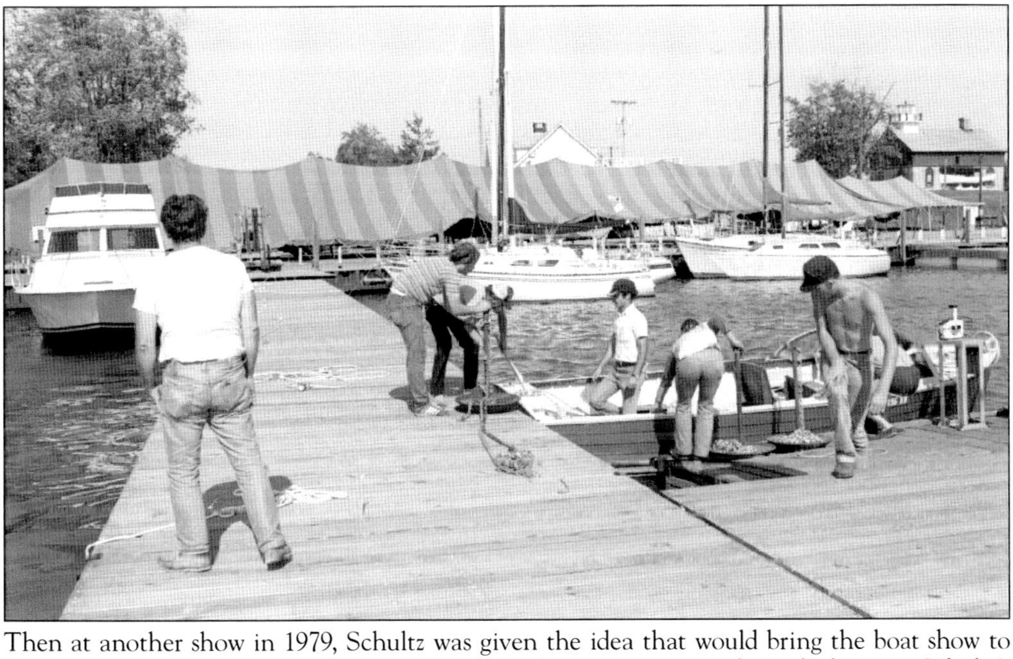

Then at another show in 1979, Schultz was given the idea that would bring the boat show to Michigan City. City residents were still hounding him. However, without dock space, Schultz's hands were tied. The new concept of a floating dock (being assembled here) arose—LEMTA was actually using one in another show—and suddenly Michigan City had a show scheduled for August 1980.

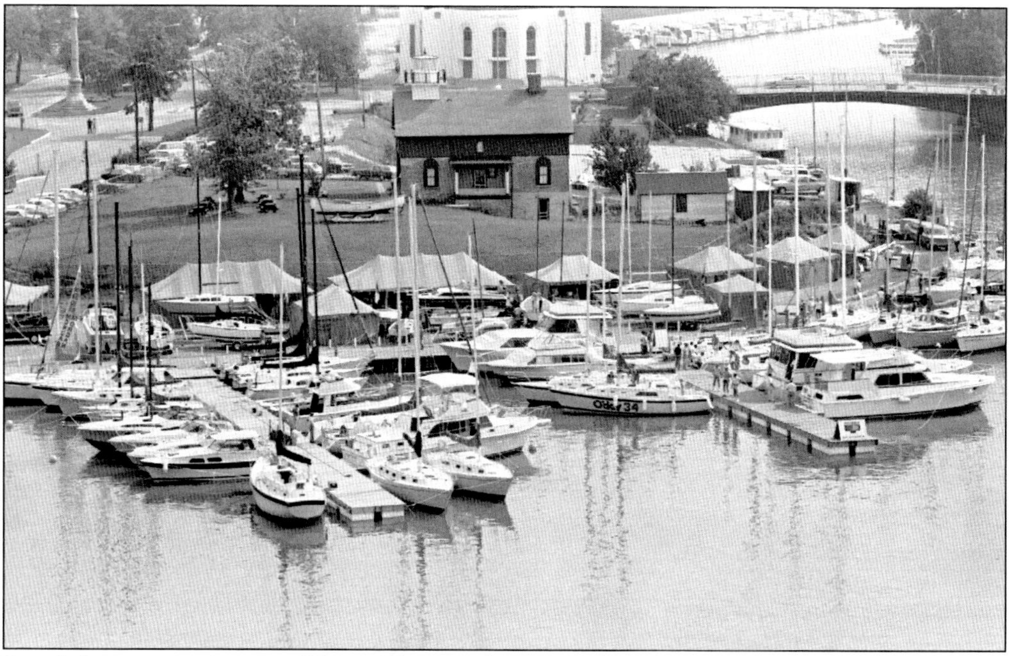

Board chairman at the time, Warren Sherwood appointed a boat show committee to work closely with Norm Schultz. Floating docks were stretched out from the Municipal Dock (shown here). The dock was tented to make booths for vendors of food, clothing, jewelry, and even boat loans. (Michigan City News Dispatch.)

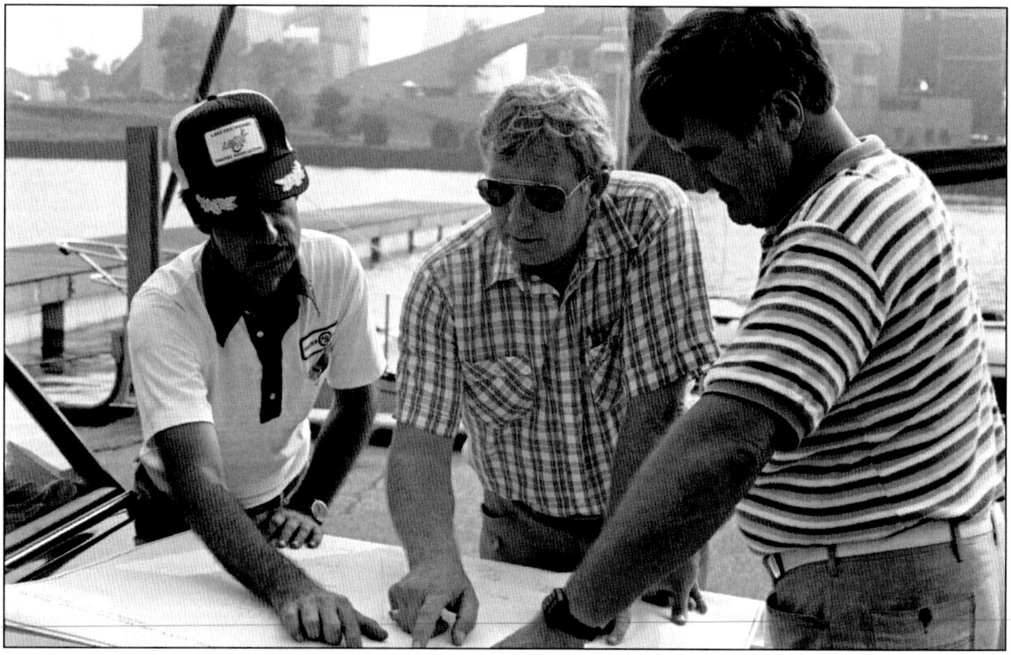

By the end of January 1980, a five-year contract was signed, committing Schultz (far left) and LEMTA to Michigan City's show. The revenue share from the boat show was a godsend to the MCPA. Although it was not much in the beginning, the money helped repair and maintain the Sprague Municipal Marina until the CCM was reinstated. (Michigan City News Dispatch.)

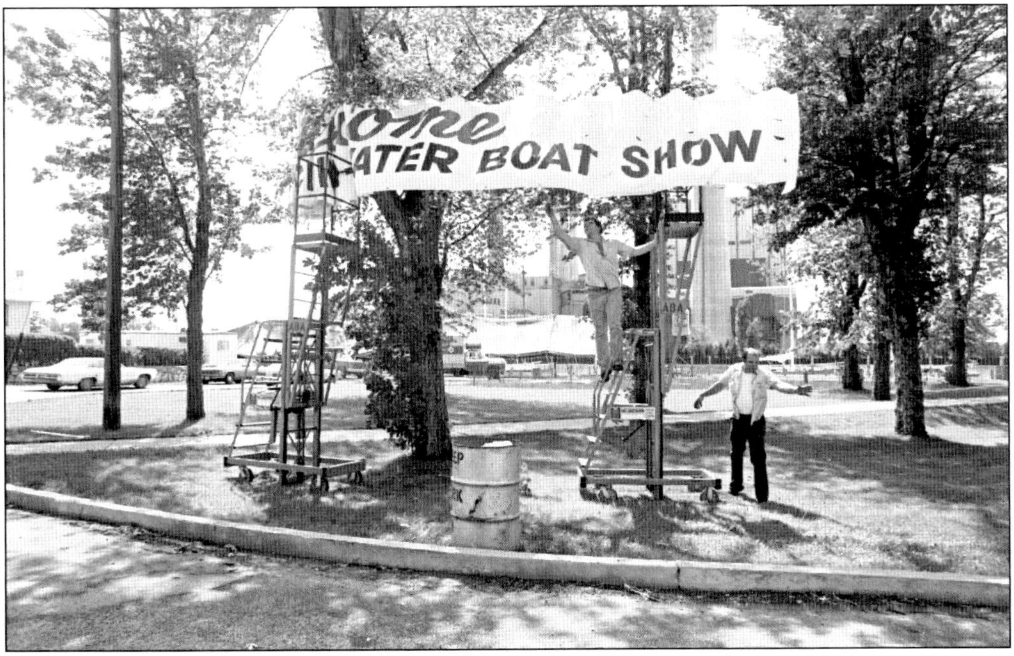

The first show was a glowing success. The amount of traffic brought into Michigan City was unexpected but welcomed. The visitors benefited not only the marina but also businesses all over town. The Michigan City In-Water Boat Show quickly became a fixture in the city's summer activities roster. (Michigan City News Dispatch.)

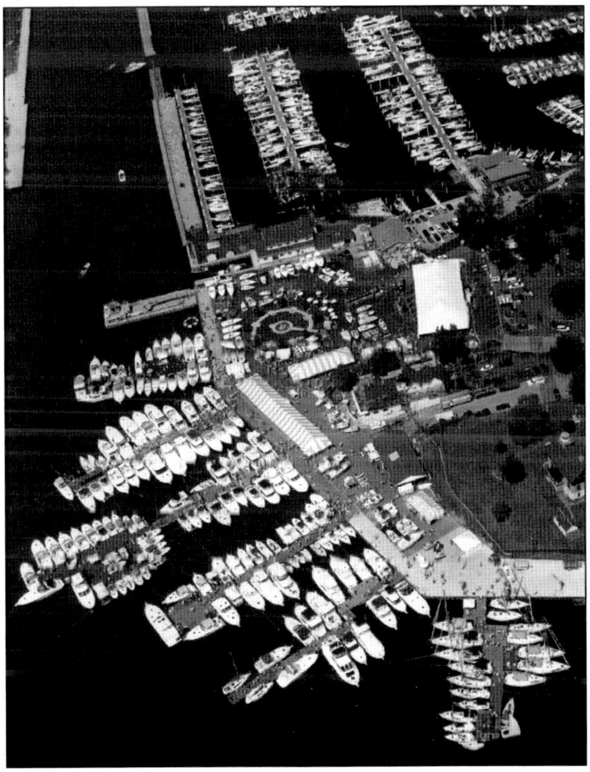

This 2006 aerial photograph shows how much the boat show has grown since the first year. The 2009 boating season marks 30 years of partnership between the boat show, Schultz, LEMTA, and the MCPA. Schultz is adamant that Michigan City's show has beaten all expectations. "In the beginning, they said we couldn't do it, we wouldn't last. Look at [the Michigan City In-Water Boat Show] now."

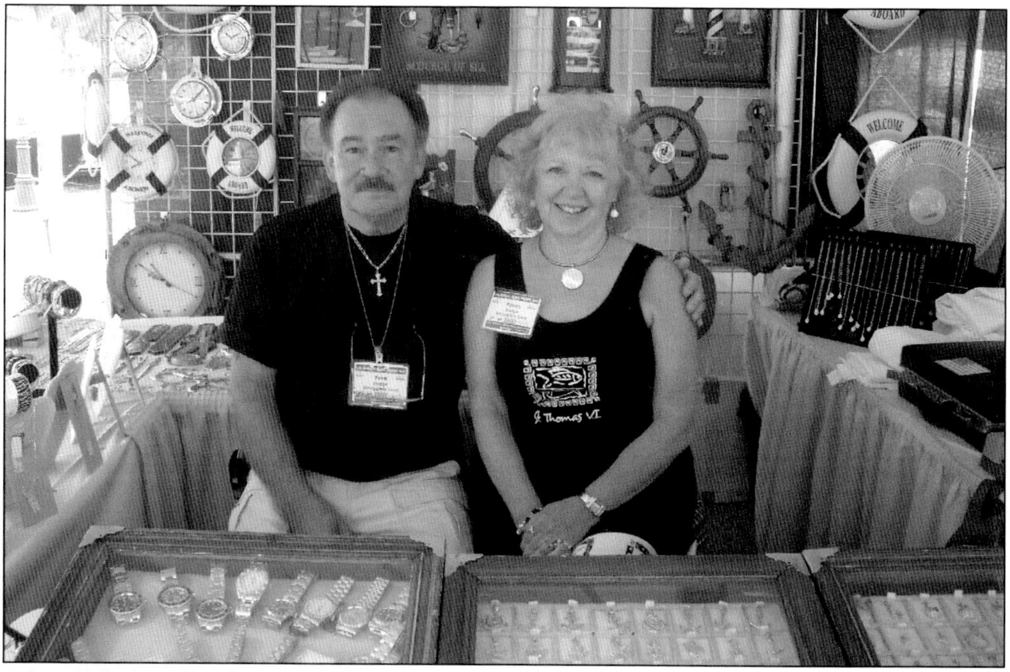

A handful of vendors from 1980 have become a fixture in the Michigan City In-Water Boat Show. Jewelry vendors Fred and Sandy Dodge of Smuggler's Cove and Hans Buchbach of Avalanche Jewelry have been selling their wares since that first show. Over the years, many vendors have joined Buchbach and the Dodges at the Michigan City show. Today one can find everything from deck shoes to superabsorbent chamois. There is even a vendor selling hammock chairs and nylon sacks that one can carry the weight of a kindergartner in.

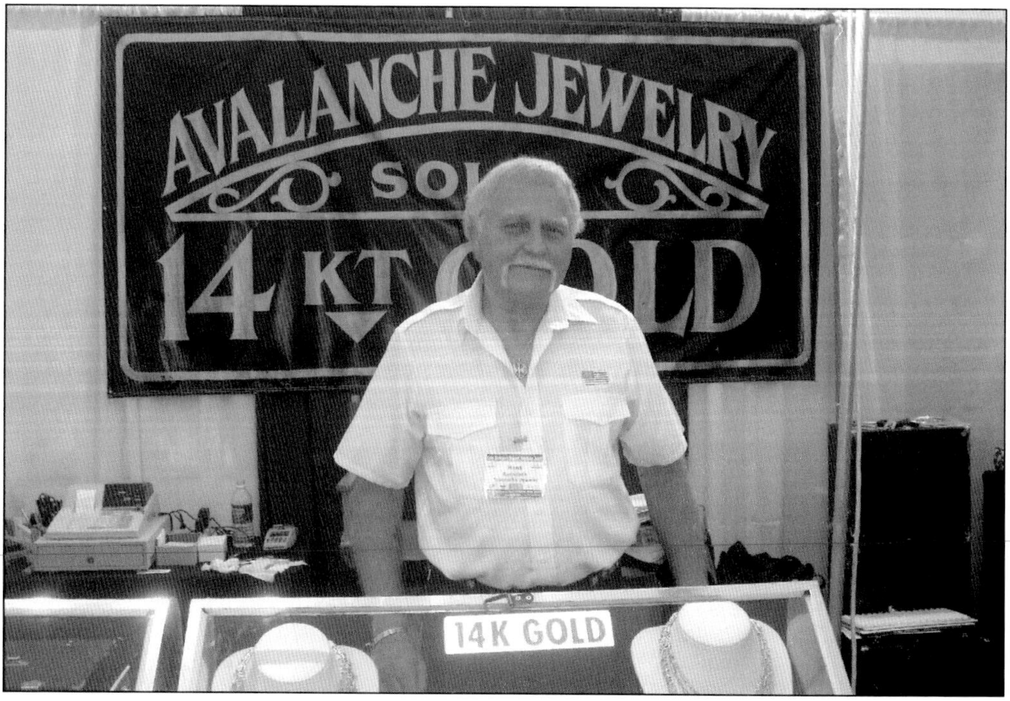

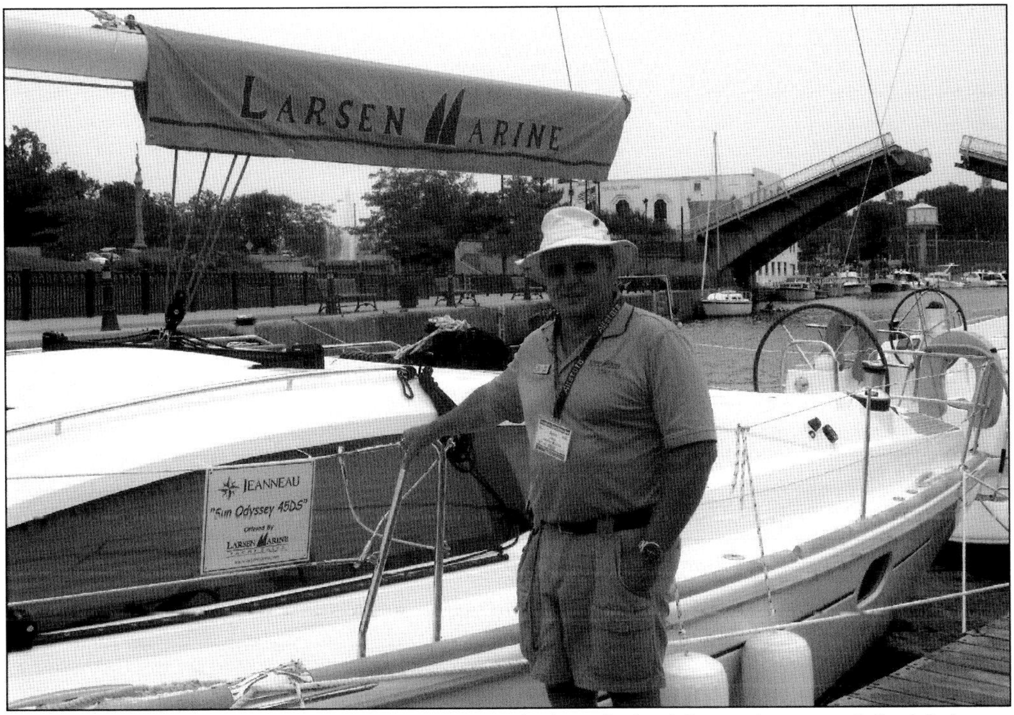

Sailboat vendors Larsen Marine (above) and Sail Place (below) have also graced the Michigan City harbor with the latest in the sailboating world. Recognizing the growing revenues achieved at the show, banks and other boating lenders have joined these vendors over the years. After finding a sailboat, showgoers could then finance it on the spot. This move surely benefitted the sales for vendors like Larsen Marine and Sail Place. Some vendors also offer boating rides and other gimmicks to draw the crowds to their boats.

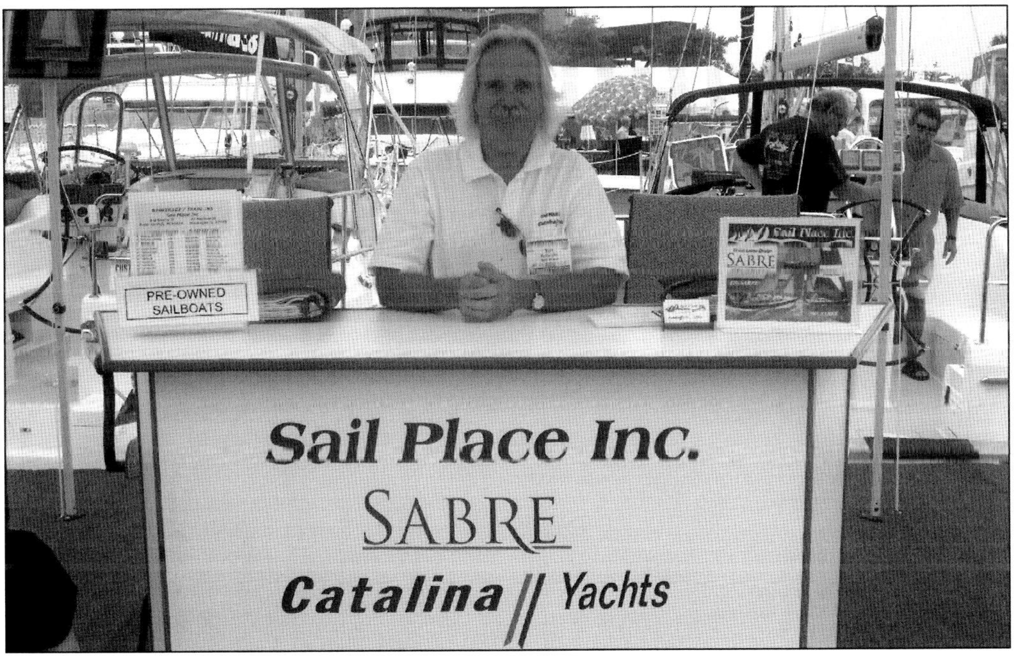

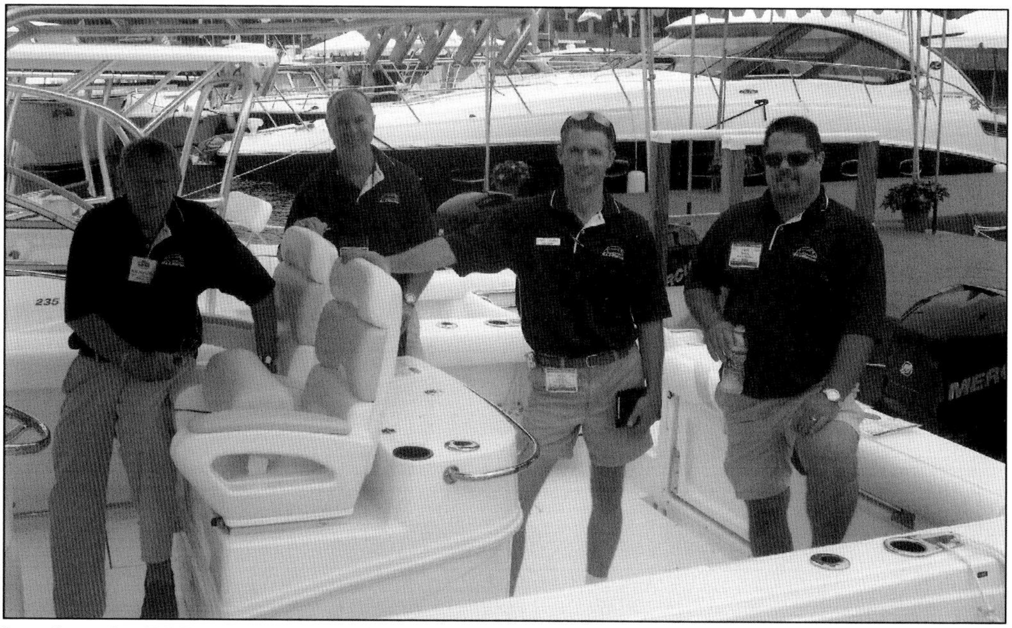

Local vendor B&E Marine is owned and operated by Ronnie Bensz and family. Bensz was among the group who convinced Norm Schultz to consider Michigan City as a place for an in-water boat show. B&E Marine also has another link to MCPA history in Chris Cipares (third from the left), grandson of 24-year board member Norman Cipares, who was chairman of the board for five of those years.

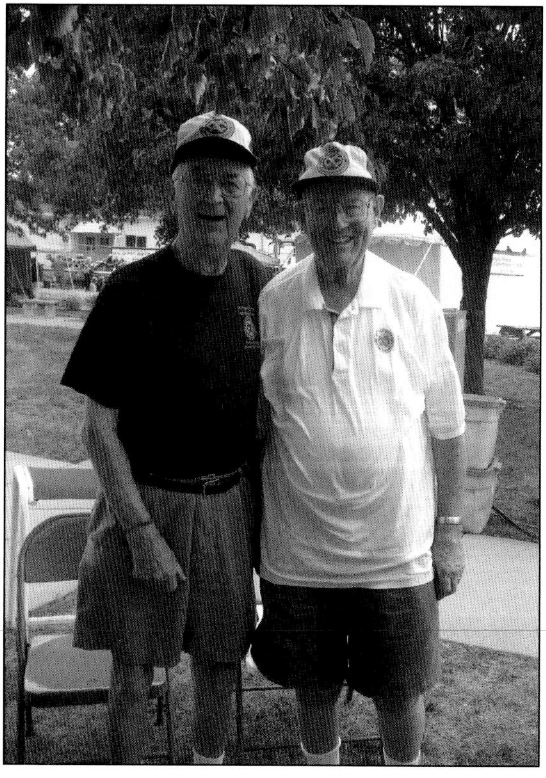

The Exchange Club has been providing the boat show visitors with food since 1980. Members Thomas Lernihan and Edward Vail have returned each year along with a revolving roster of new Exchange Club members. Their array of burgers, roasted corn, and much more make the Exchange Club's booth popular with the crowd.

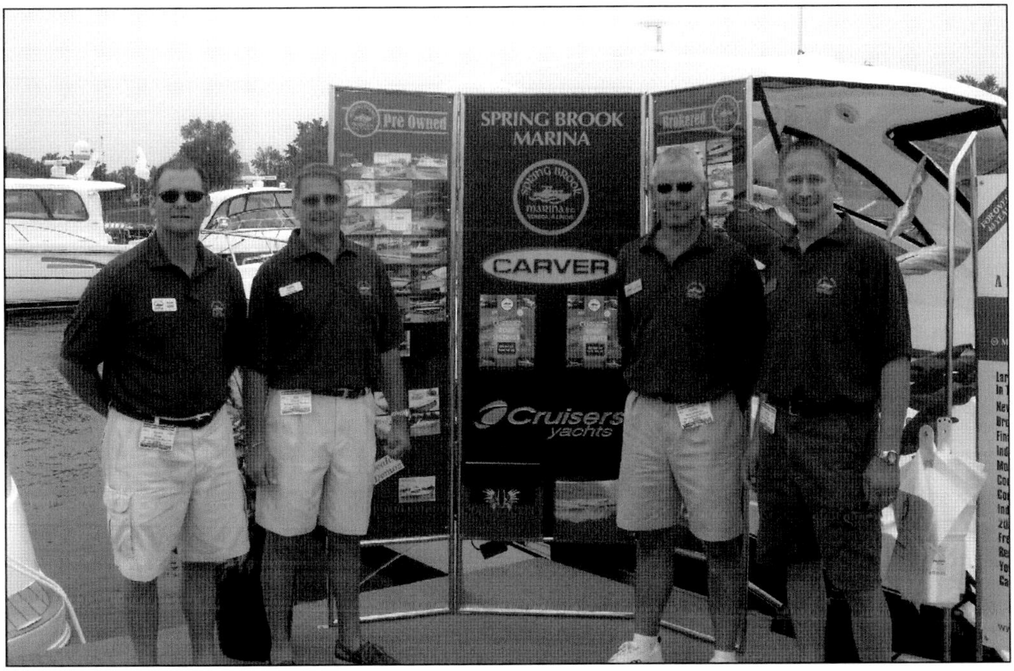

Spring Brook Marina (above) and Tiara Yachts (below) are among the several vendors who offer boat show visitors a tour of some of the latest vessels for the year. According to Norm Schultz, the Michigan City In-Water Boat Show is the first in the boat-show circuit, which includes shows in Florida and Ohio. Many buyers and even vendors come to Michigan City to get an early view of what the next season has to offer. They can also get a feel for the economic atmosphere toward boat buying through Michigan City's show. This show sets the tone for others across the country.

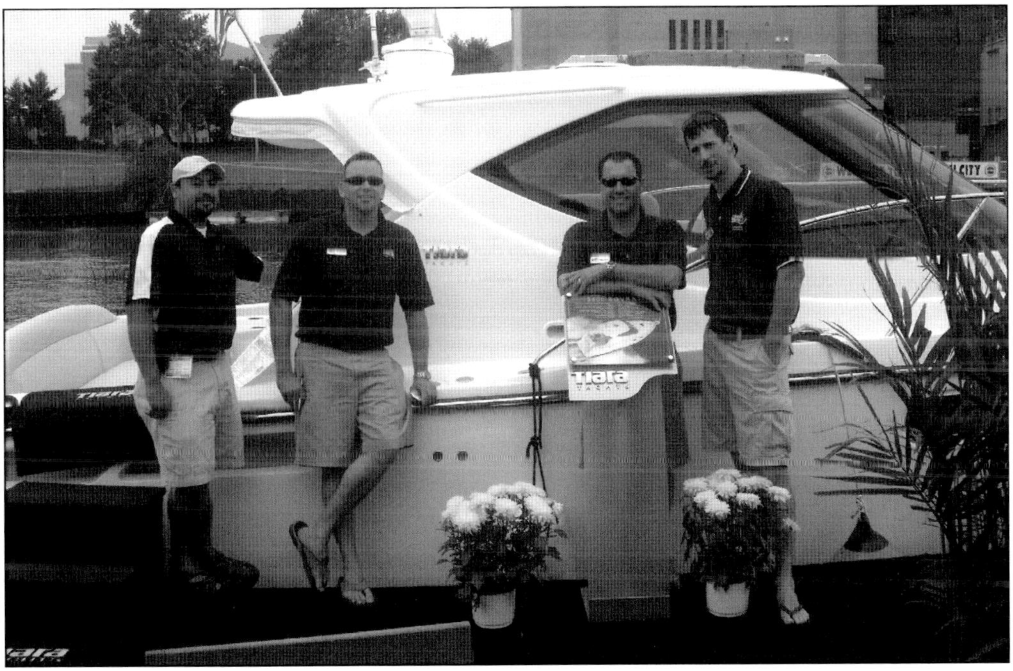

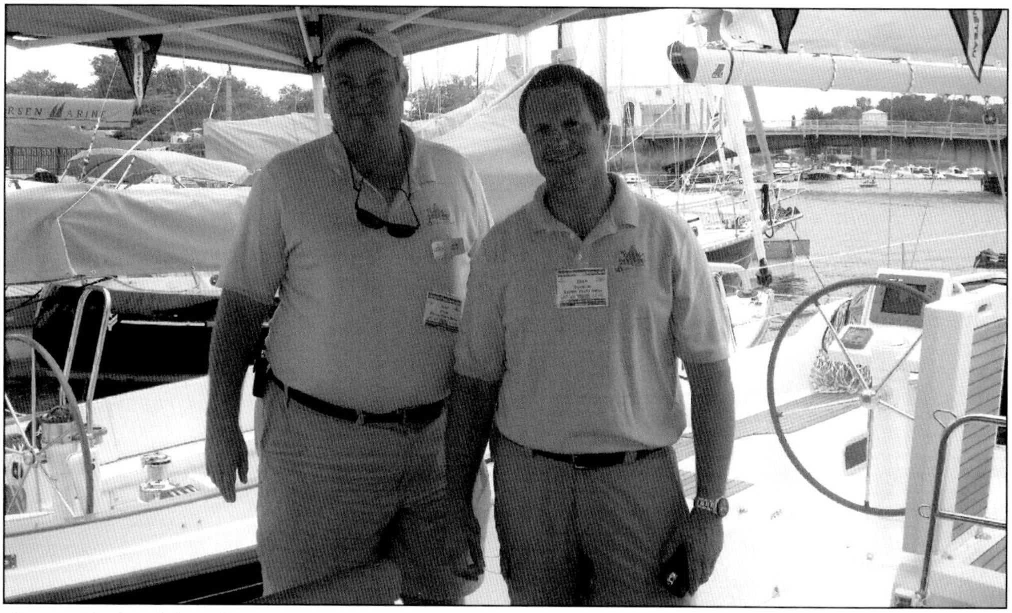

Karma Yachts (above) came to the boat show in 1980 as Darfin Marina. Although its name has changed over the years, it has continued to bring its vessels to display in Michigan City. North Shore Marina (below) is a large vendor that has enjoyed a spot at the Michigan City boat show since the beginning, bringing several varieties of yachts for sale and display. New boats were not the only ones available. Showgoers could find both new and used vessels vying for attention at the docks. Lenders who had set up shop across the pavement from the sailboat vendors' dock to snag customers soon joined yacht vendors.

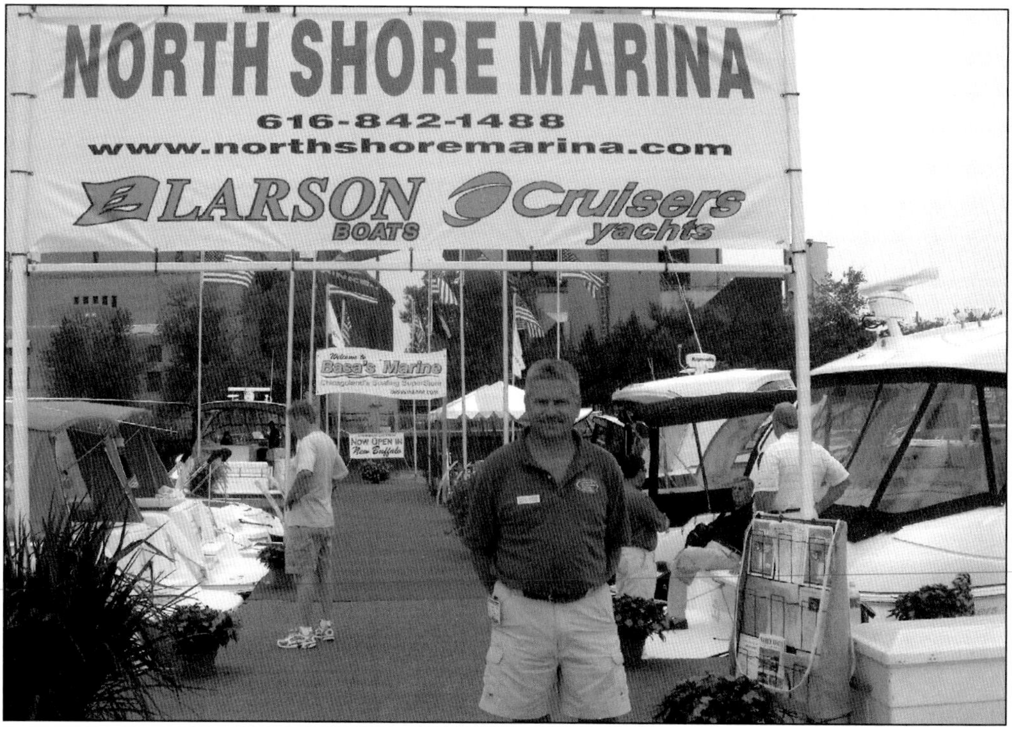

Six

Concerned Citizens

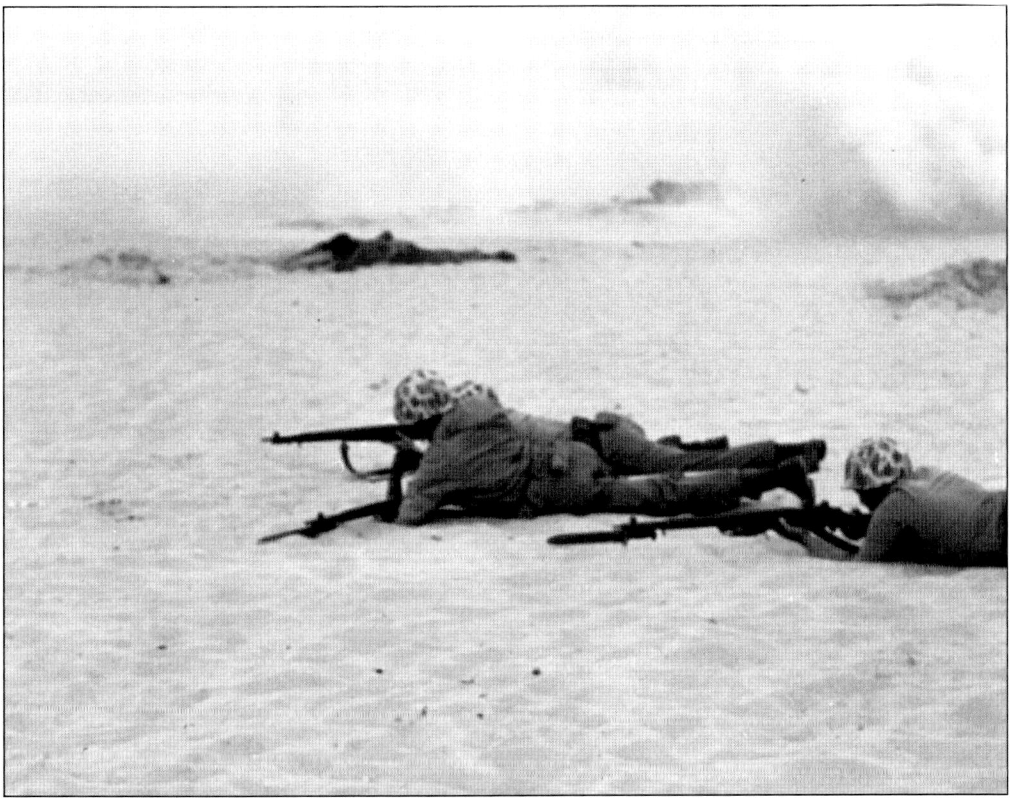

This image from a mock invasion staged on Michigan City's beach in 1958 symbolizes the MCPA's struggle with the public during the 1980s. Growing public resentment toward the MCPA overshadowed the boat show's success. Fueled by the harsh economy, much of the bad blood stemmed from reaction to a parking plan offered by the park department and MCPA. The plan angered residents and local politicians, and "Raze the Maze" became the slogan du jour. Another sore subject was the channel maintenance fund. (Michigan City News Dispatch.)

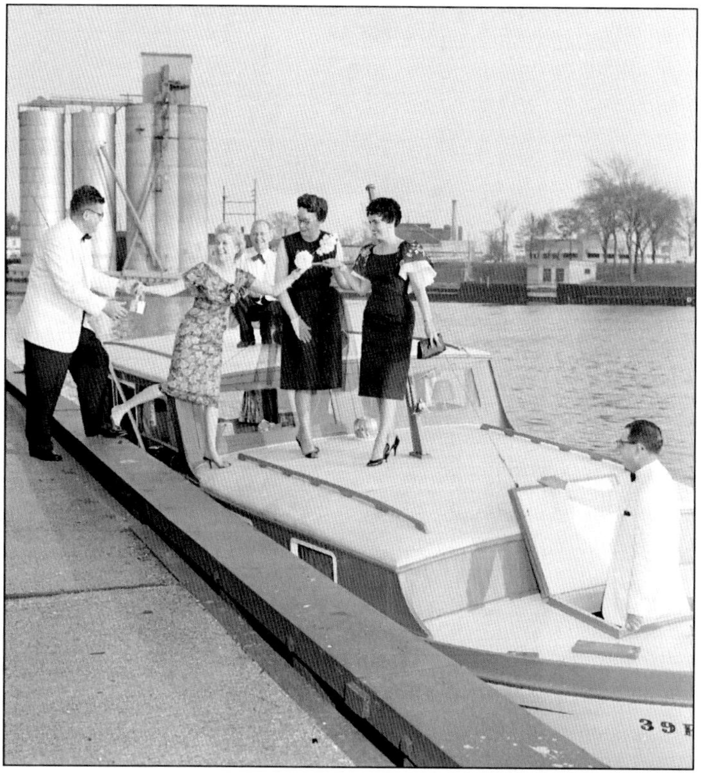

This 1940s snapshot of MCYC members embarking on a boat ride illustrates the city's view of boaters as a privileged lot. This was yet another sore spot with city residents. According to the *Michigan City News Dispatch*, one Michigan City resident summed up the public's view by saying that board "members have expressed their desire for the taxpayers to pay for their pleasure boats and yachts." (Michigan City News Dispatch.)

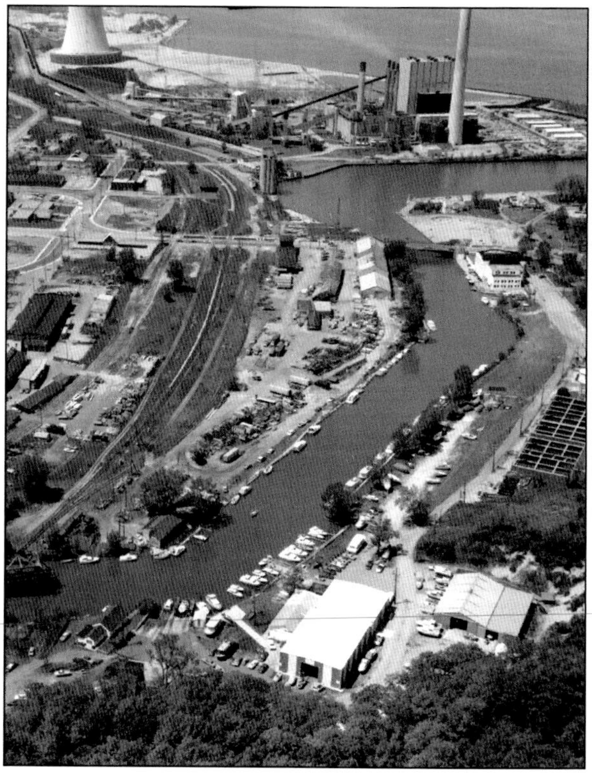

In 1980, the CCM fund had been cut from the city's budget entirely. The city council believed that since the MCPA had money in an account and generated revenues through its many activities, there was no need for the tax funds. Meanwhile, the channel filled with silt, and the Sprague Municipal Marina fell into disrepair. (Bill Swedenberg.)

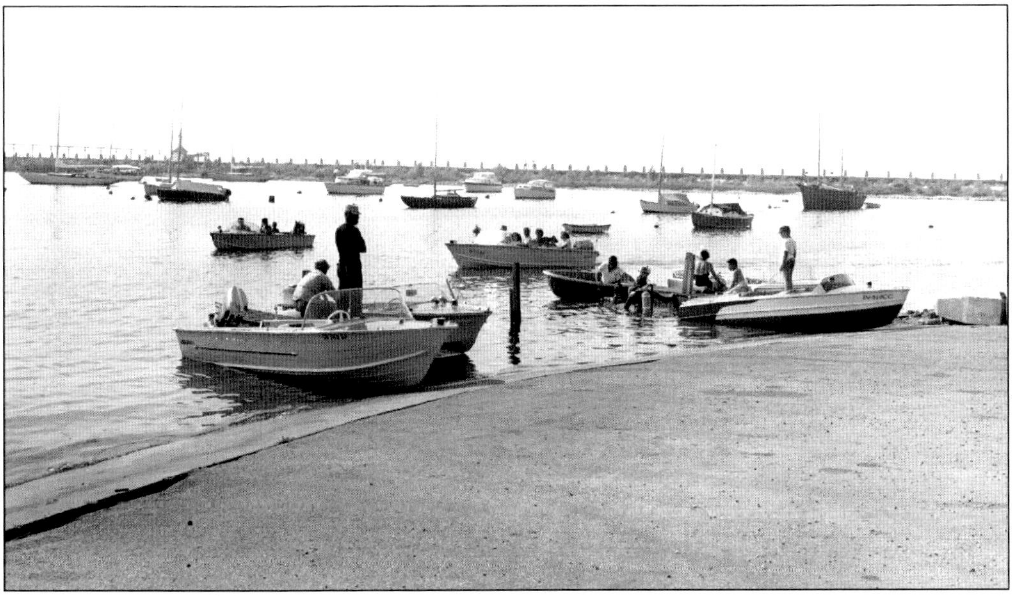

Michigan City needed to understand that the bond prohibited the use of yacht basin proceeds on city-owned property like the Municipal Dock, the Sprague Municipal Marina, and Trail Creek. The MCPA is actually charted by the state as an agency with powers to buy, sell, and maintain its own property. Furthermore, the CCM tax money was for maintaining Michigan City's property not the MCPA's. MCPA property was paid for by boaters like the ones in the yacht basin in this 1950s photograph. (Bill Swedenberg.)

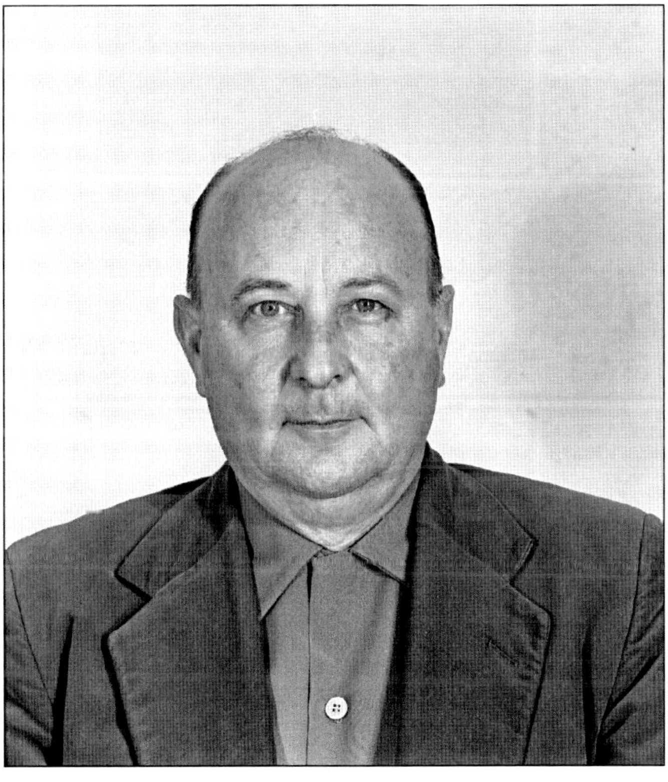

Hartley Job and Al Spiers (pictured) decided, along with the rest of the board, that the problem was ignorance. Job commissioned a boating impact study prepared by Indiana University. Job believed that once the city saw that they too were benefiting from boating, the council and residents would gladly contribute to the CCM fund. Spiers, however, thought the focus of the public's education should be more specific. (Michigan City News Dispatch.)

Through media interviews and city council meetings, Al Spiers tried to explain the framework of the MCPA's finances, using facts from Hartley Job's study. "There may have been a time in the past when boating was big boat oriented," he said at a public MCPA meeting. "But those days are past—boating is now for the middle class citizens. Seventy-five percent of the boaters are middle class citizens." This photograph of the 1961 Columbia Yacht Race shows many city residents enjoying just one of the pleasure-boating events that Spiers spoke of. This and other activities, including the coho and other fishing tournaments, drew not only tourists but also local spectators and participants. He reminded everyone that once the CCM fund dried up so would Trail Creek, and the Sprague Municipal Marina would be forced to shut down. The self-sufficient Washington Park Marina would survive. (Michigan City News Dispatch.)

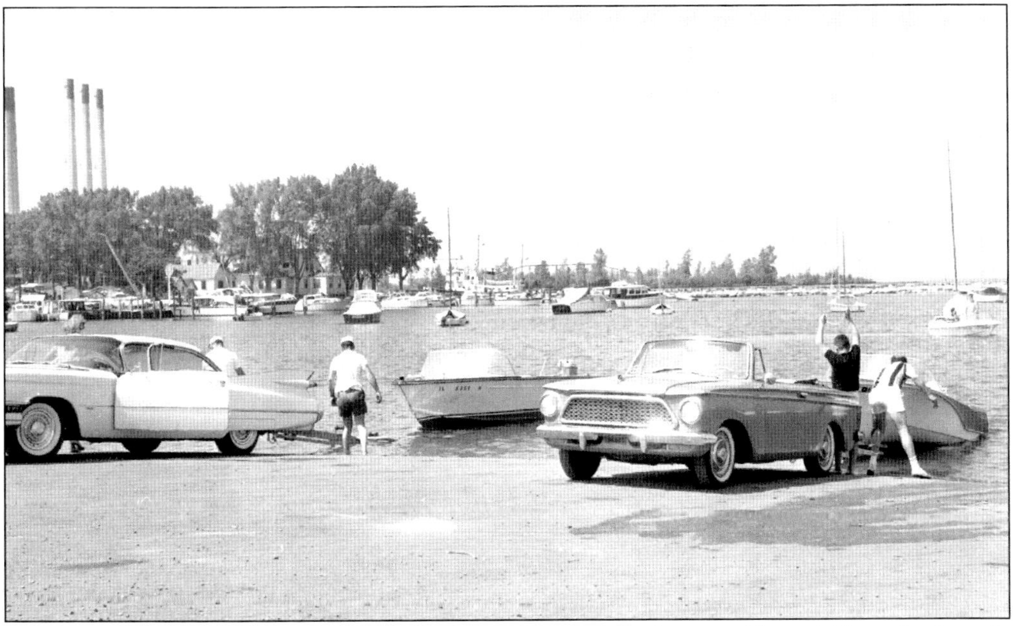

In 1982, Mayor Clifford Arnold decided to lend a hand to the frustrated board. He spoke directly to the board members at an April 5 meeting and had a proposition: a skeptic's tour. According to the *Minutes of the Michigan City Port Authority II*, it would be "40 minute tours along the channel with narration pointing out improvements being made." This 1950s photograph measures improvements enacted after the MCPA took over. (Bill Swedenberg.)

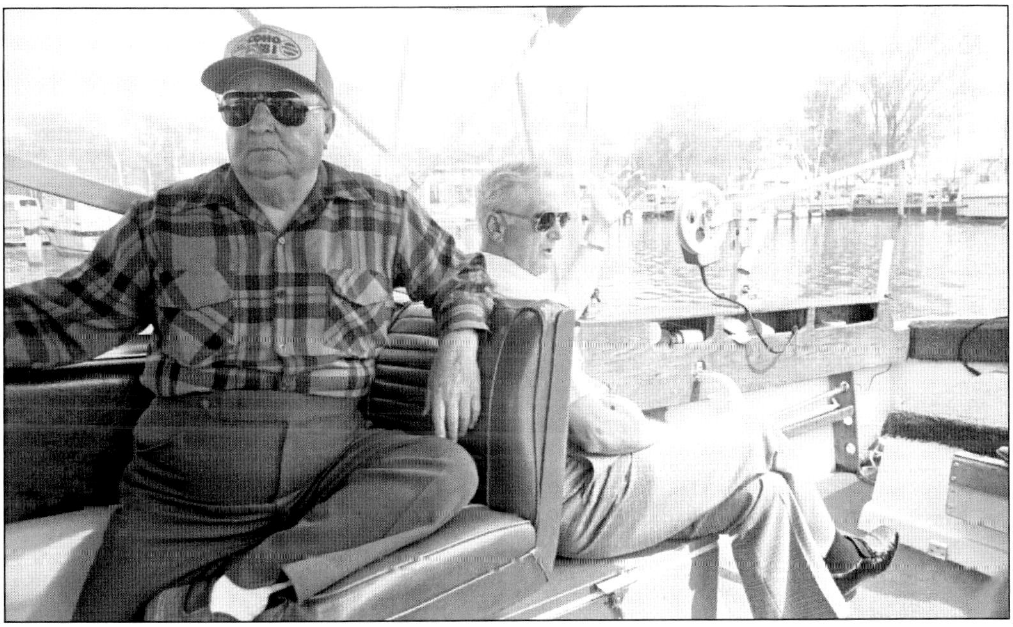

Arnold's skeptic's tour, renamed the See-It for Yourself Tour, attracted media from throughout northwest Indiana. Charter boats assisted in giving the tours as Spiers and others outlined the improvements made at the lakefront and those that needed to be made. They explained exactly what the CCM fund paid for and how the bond ordinances greatly affected the rest of the MCPA's spending. (Michigan City News Dispatch.)

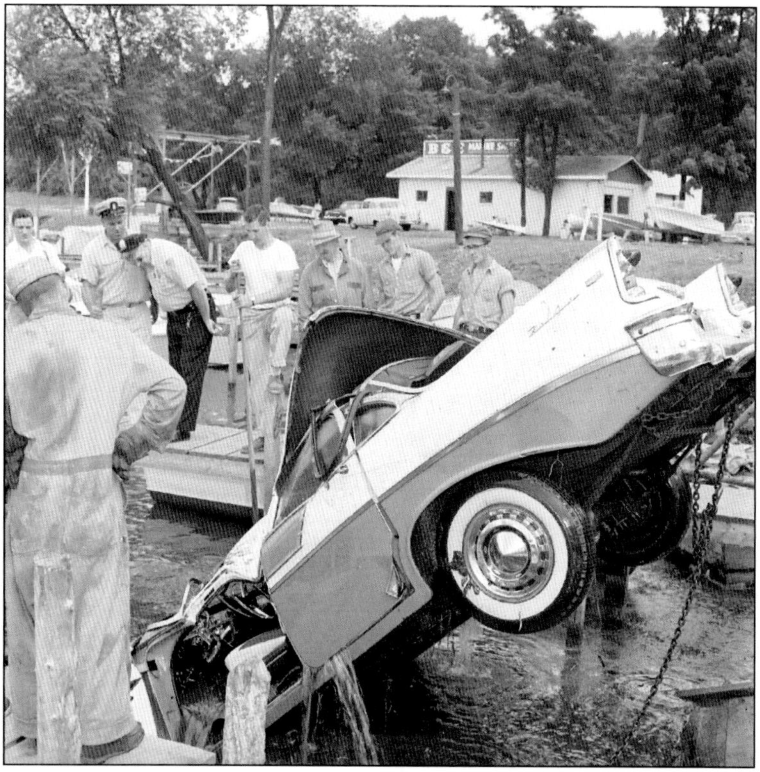

Although the tours were not as successful as the board wanted them to be, they did show that the public really was not informed on the happenings in the harbor. The board planned to change that. Meanwhile, like this 1958 photograph of a car being rescued from the basin, Al Spiers predicted that the fund would be empty in just a few years if the city council did not rescue it. (Michigan City News Dispatch.)

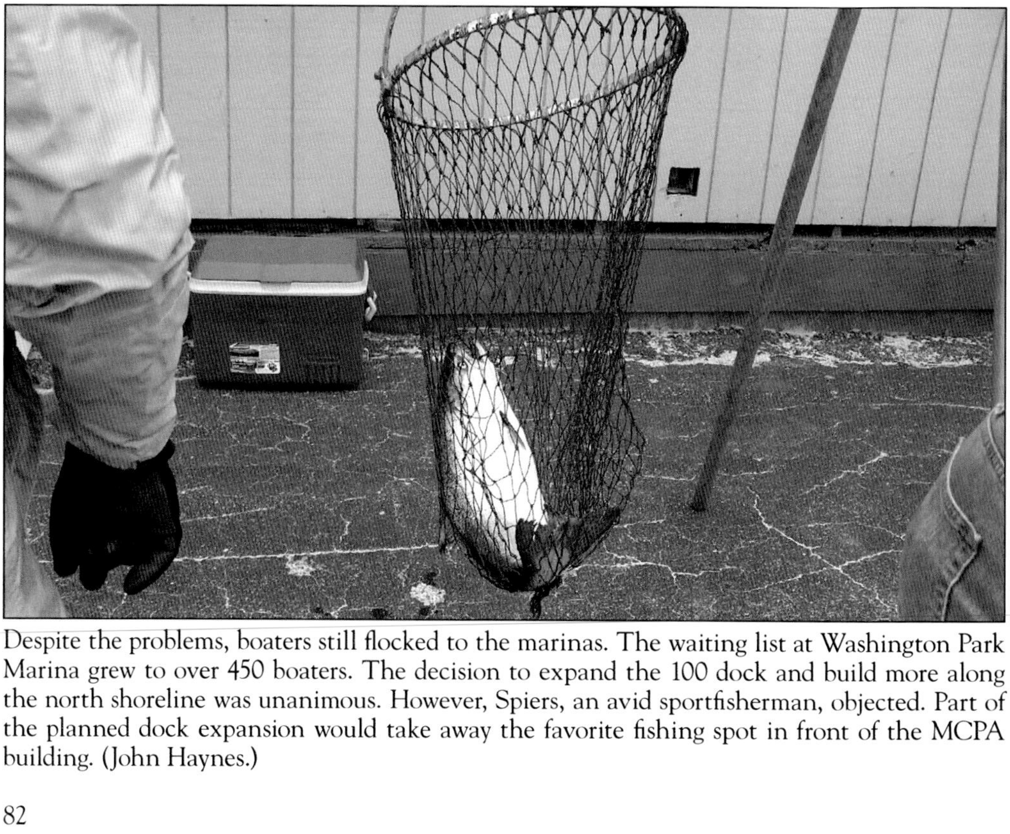

Despite the problems, boaters still flocked to the marinas. The waiting list at Washington Park Marina grew to over 450 boaters. The decision to expand the 100 dock and build more along the north shoreline was unanimous. However, Spiers, an avid sportfisherman, objected. Part of the planned dock expansion would take away the favorite fishing spot in front of the MCPA building. (John Haynes.)

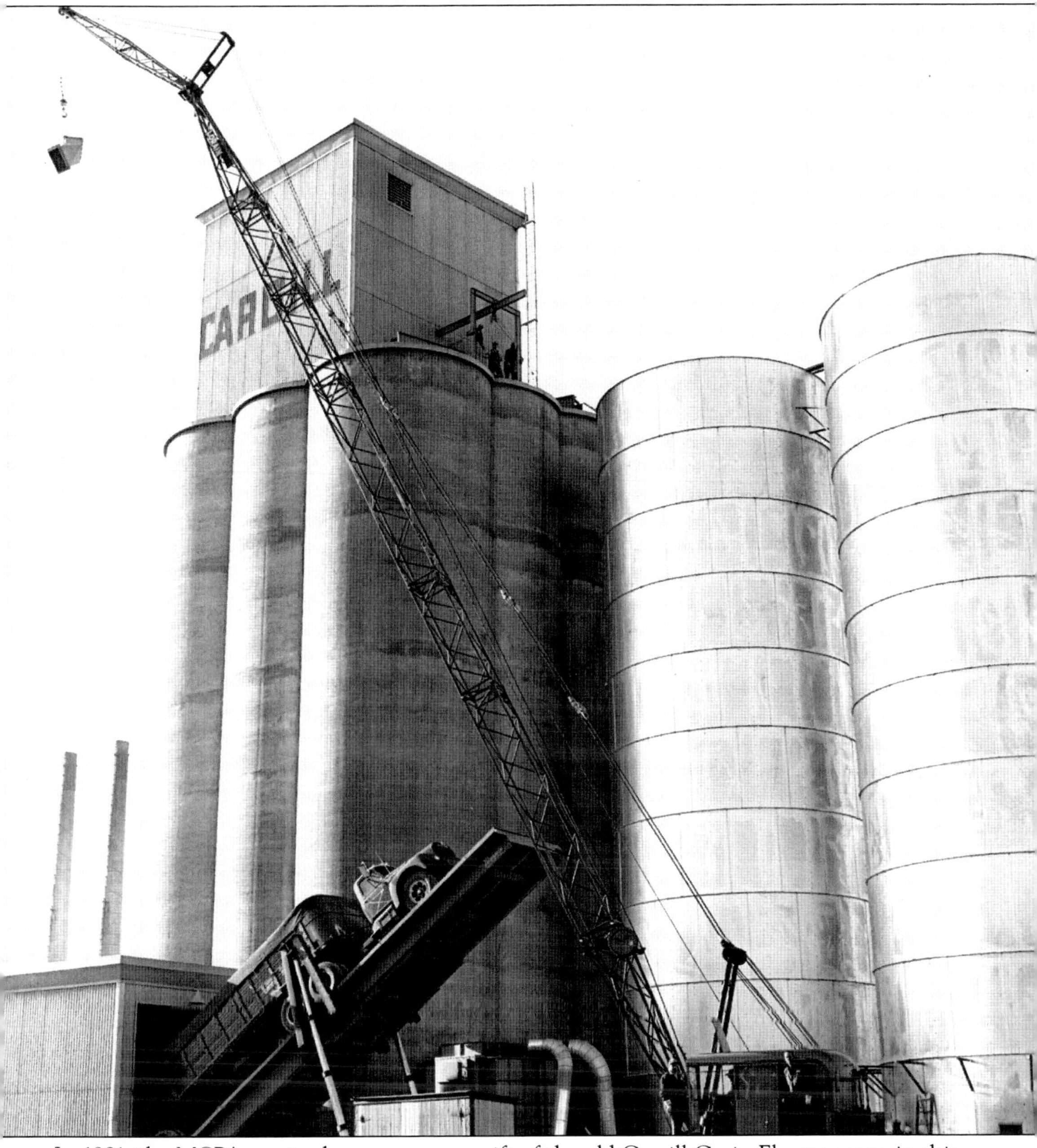

In 1981, the MCPA received an anonymous gift of the old Cargill Grain Elevator, seen in this 1957 photograph. Although happy to have the land, the board realized that it was another public property dependant on the stagnant CCM fund. The land needed to be landscaped and the remaining building cleared out—and then there was the giant grain elevator. The area sat unattended until the next year when the board needed a place for the walking fishermen. It was decided that part of the Cargill property could be used for that purpose. More land was needed on the shore, so the board struck a deal with NIPSCO. With his comrades taken care of, Spiers and the board began to plan for expansion of the marina. (Bill Swedenberg.)

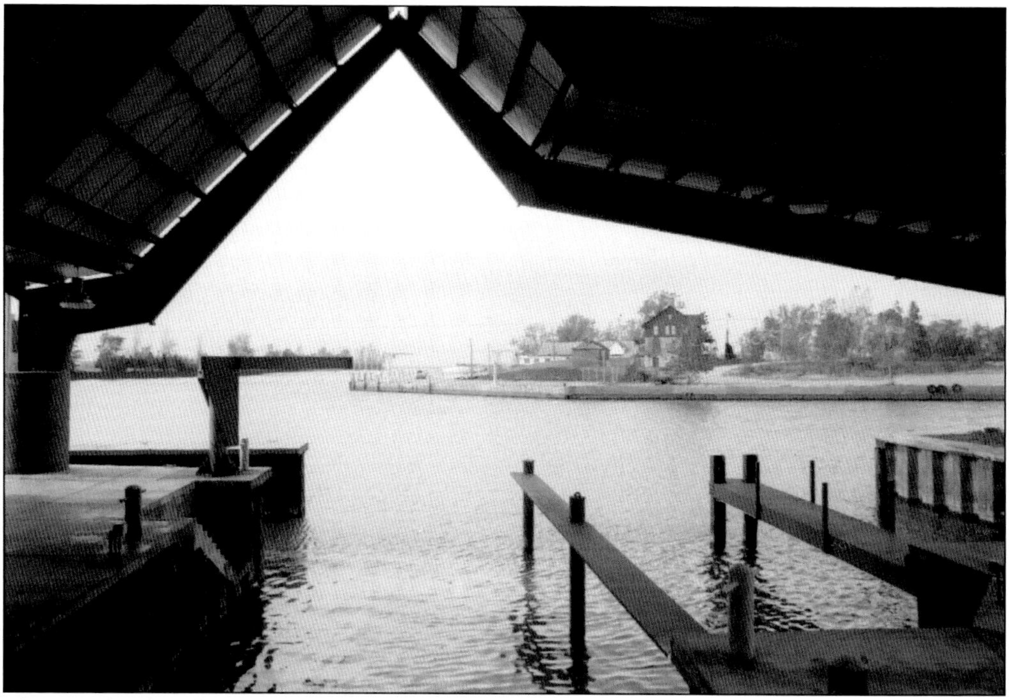

The west bank still was not suitable for use. The board had to tap into the waning CCM fund but with a little help. NIPSCO paid for some of the landscaping, and the rest was done with inexpensive prison labor lent by warden Jack Duckworth. The DNR announced plans to use the old grain elevator for an artificial fishing reef at the foot of Mount Baldy. In 1984, the board decided to deed the Cargill property to the DNR, which continued developing the property for a building of its own (pictured). Named Hoosier Slide Park, the property was officially opened to the public on August 10, 1984. (Michigan City News Dispatch.)

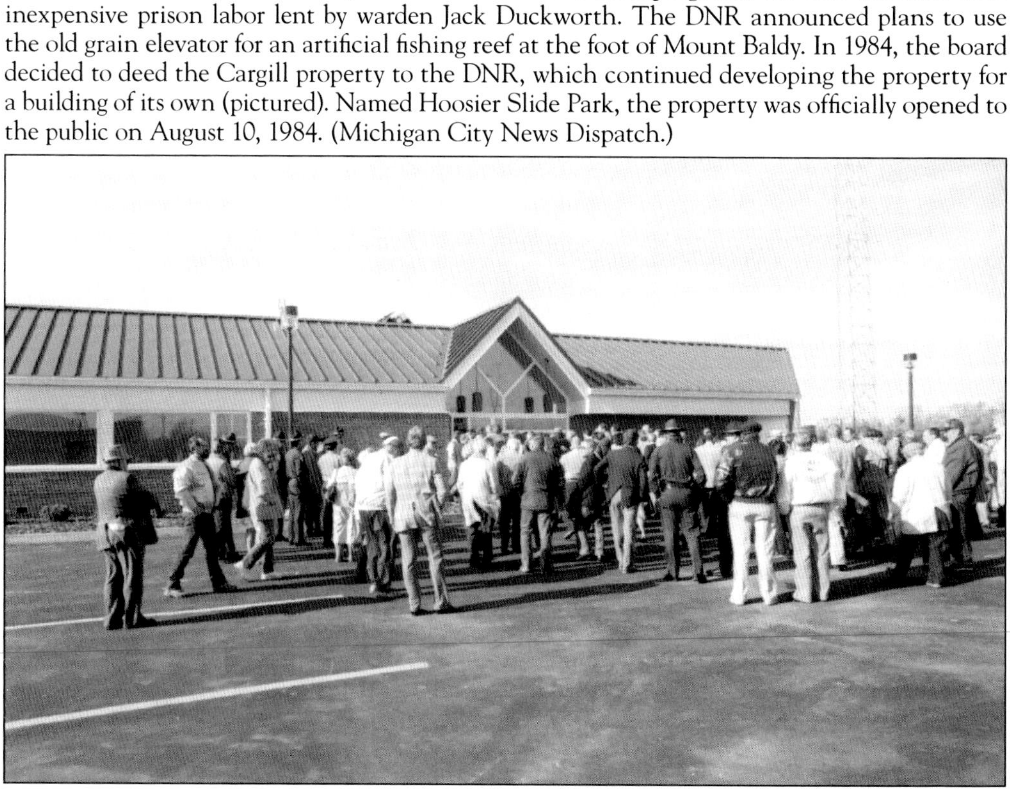

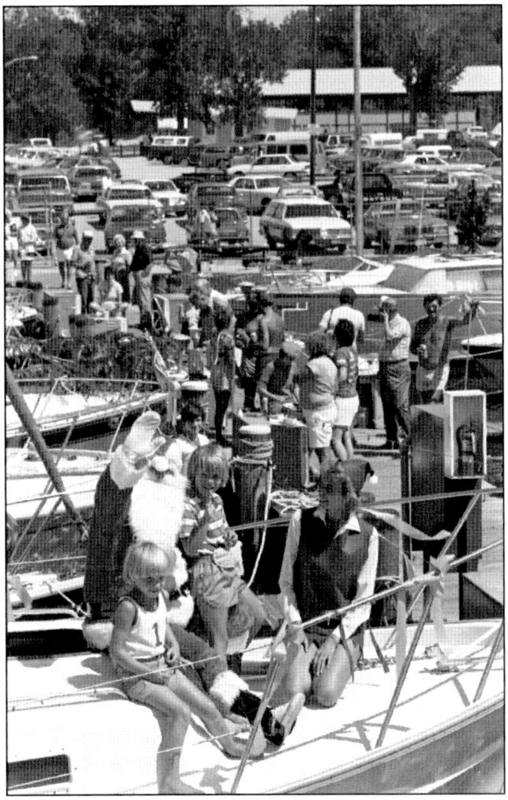

Other projects were contemplated and some even completed, to better serve marina patrons. One of these changes was for fishermen. It was a fish-cleaning station and was completed after years of research and contemplation. Another idea, charter row, was born during a 1982 meeting. However, the charter row project never made it out of development stages, although the idea has been resurrected many times over the years. (Right, Michigan City News Dispatch; below, Bill Swedenberg.)

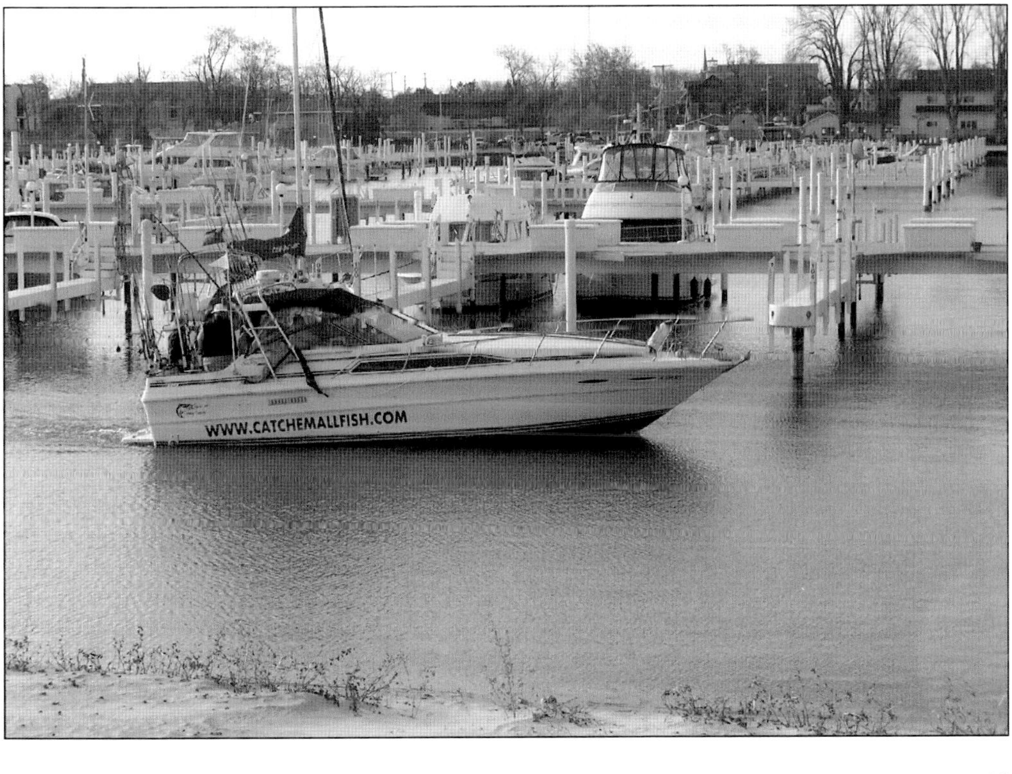

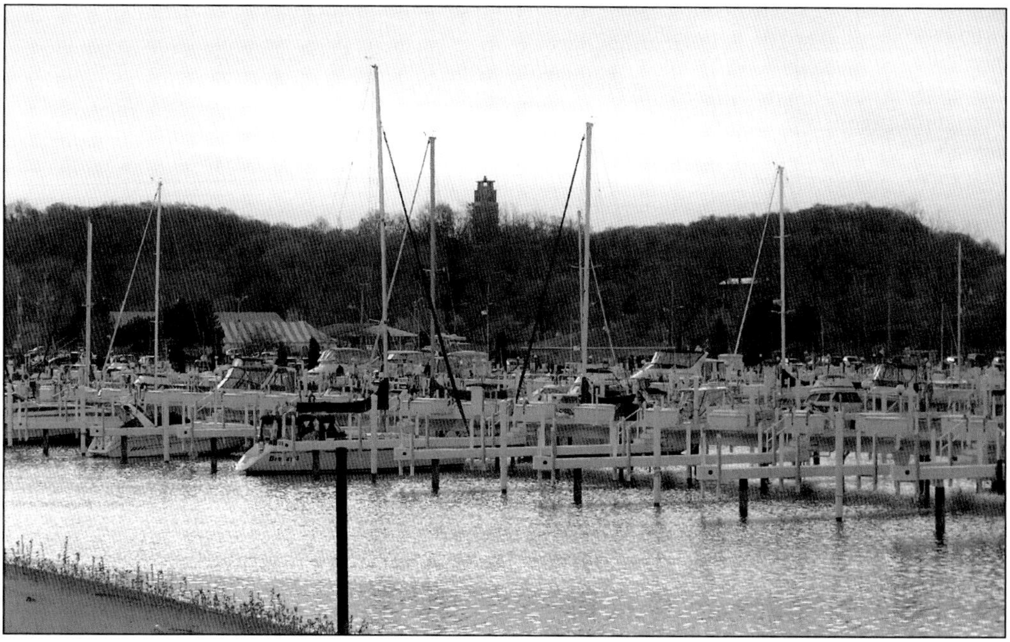

During this time, more docks were also built, some even moved. They were only a few swim strokes away from the beach, as seen in these photographs. The gas docks were replaced, and the MCPA building was expanded. The structure then more closely resembled the current administration building. A maintenance building was constructed. The growing popularity of the boat show required the purchase of more floating docks as well as more space for vendors. As chairman Warren Sherwood and the board took on more projects, they began to find more work that needed to be done. Washington Park needed an overhaul. In 1983, preparations began for phase three of the master plan. (Above, John Haynes; below, Bill Swedenberg.)

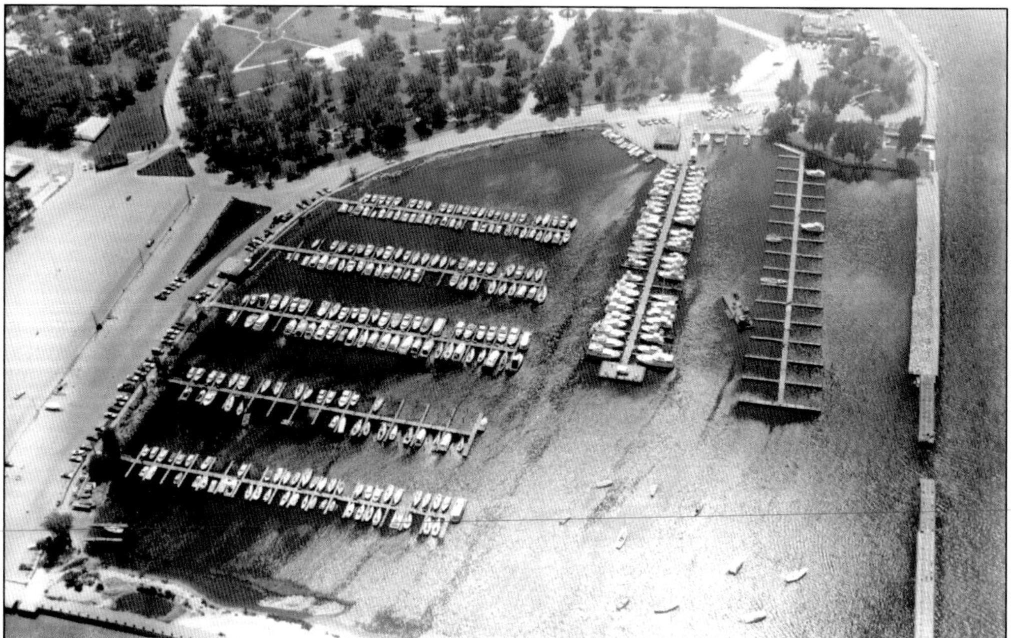

In its quest for funding improvements to city-owned harbor facilities, the board found Mayor Clifford Arnold to be the first since Francis Fedder to fight on its behalf. Mayor Arnold tried to get revenue-sharing funds to help the board with the construction of Hoosier Slide Park. He asked for $25,000 and got $3,000. Mayor Arnold thought the skeptic's tour would facilitate a CCM levy, but it did not. He believed the marina and the lakefront were the key to breathing life into Michigan City's dying north end. The city's mayors since Fedder in the 1950s did—and continue to—try to revitalize the area south of Trail Creek (seen to right in the aerial photograph). It was once a bustling area visible in the photograph below taken in the late 1940s or early 1950s. (Bill Swedenberg.)

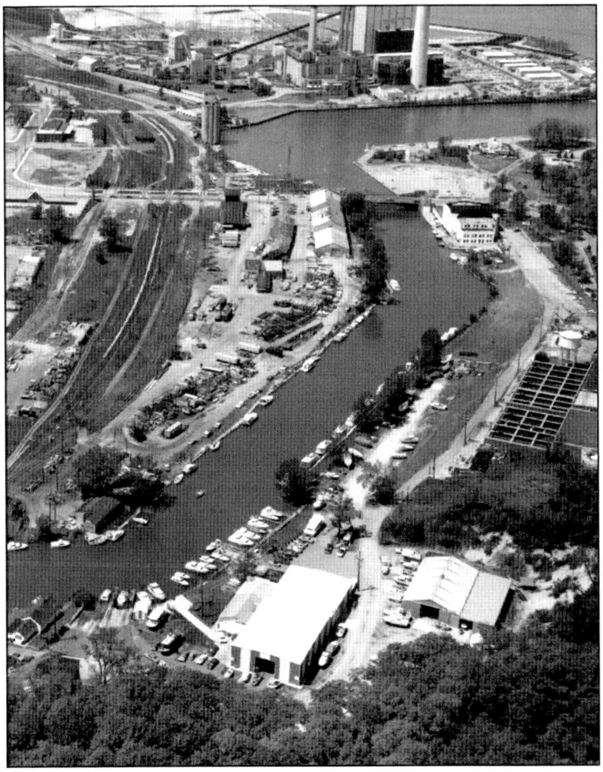

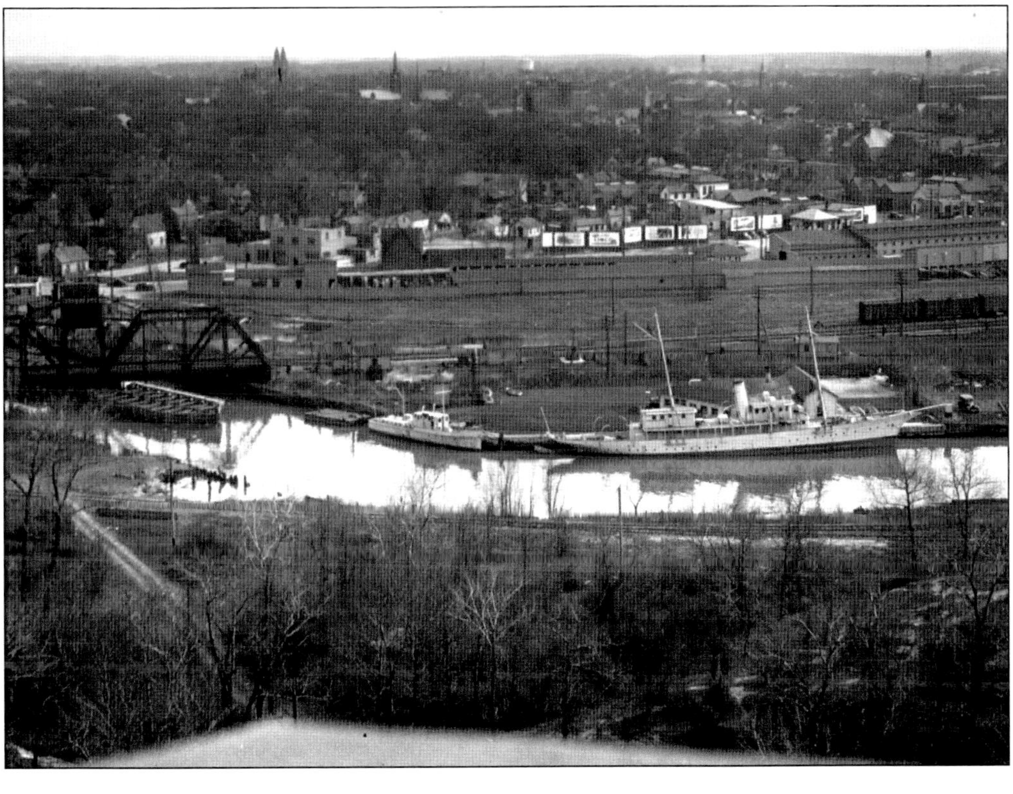

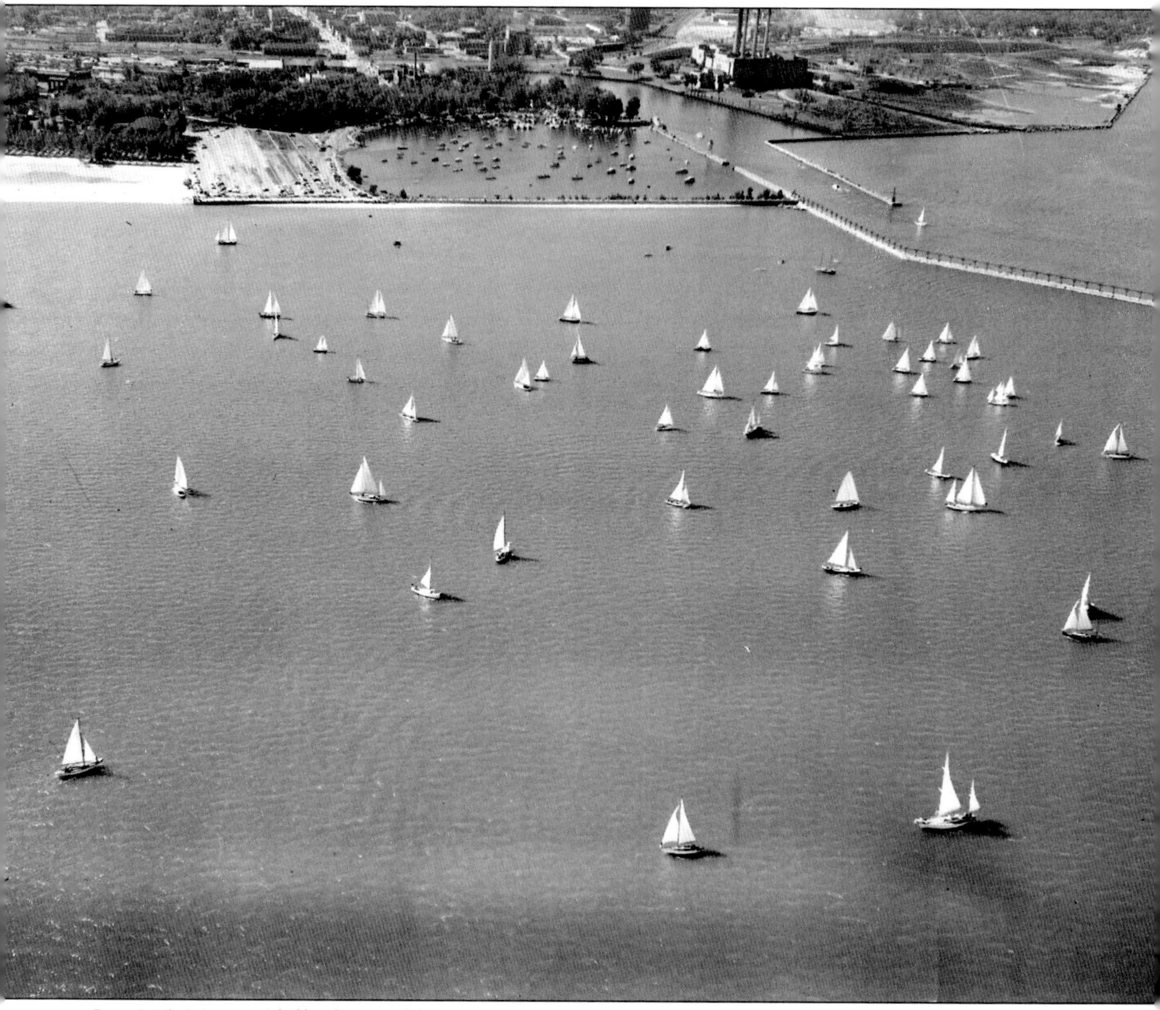

In 1985, Mayor Clifford Arnold and other mayors along Indiana's portion of Lake Michigan got together in the search for a solution to marine troubles. The group recounted its outrage at the funds Indianapolis received for a White River Park project. It contrasted its plight to that of Wisconsin and Michigan, whose state and local governments gladly give tax funds for harbor development projects and maintenance. To his companions, Mayor Arnold proposed a program that would provide state grants and loans for marina development. The men took this idea all the way to Indianapolis, where the Lake Michigan Marina Development Commission (LMMDC) was born. Composed of six members, the commission represented all five Indiana lakefront cities: Michigan City, Hammond, Gary, East Chicago, and Portage. A DNR representative occupied the sixth seat. The commission was granted $1.3 million to perform feasibility studies at each proposed site. Although it was only half the $2.6 million the mayors really wanted, they did not complain, and some of the burden on the city public harbor facilities (above) eased. (Michigan City News Dispatch.)

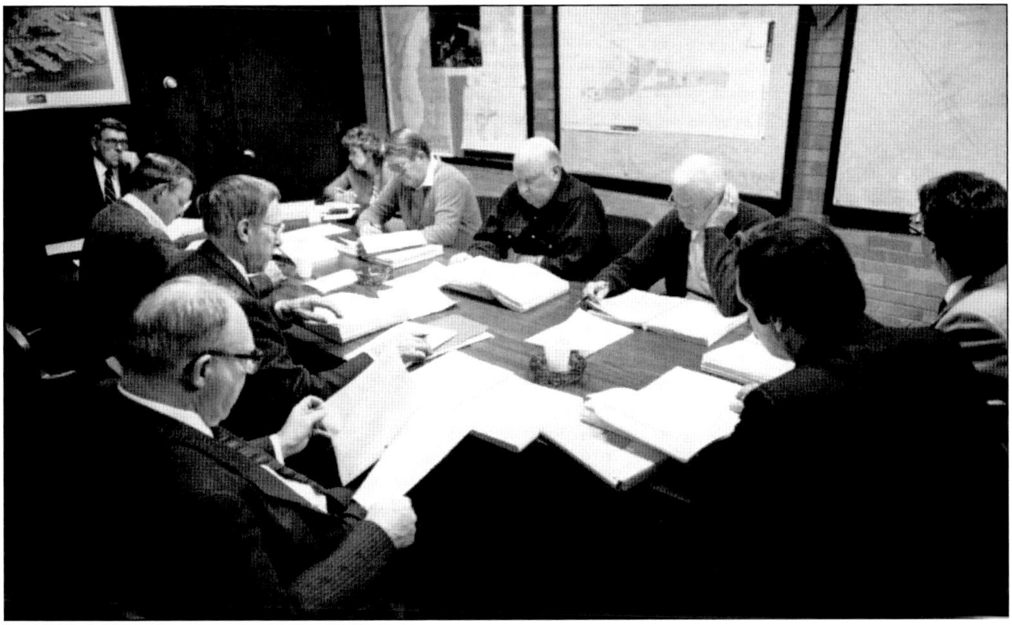

With the influx of LMMDC dollars for feasibility studies and for the later expansion of the marina, the board began to entertain several different proposals for the new addition. Ideas explored included an addition north of the marina that would have taken over the area immediately east of the catwalk. The ideas were only in the exploration stages at the MCPA; meanwhile, the city had made a decision on the marina expansion. (Michigan City News Dispatch.)

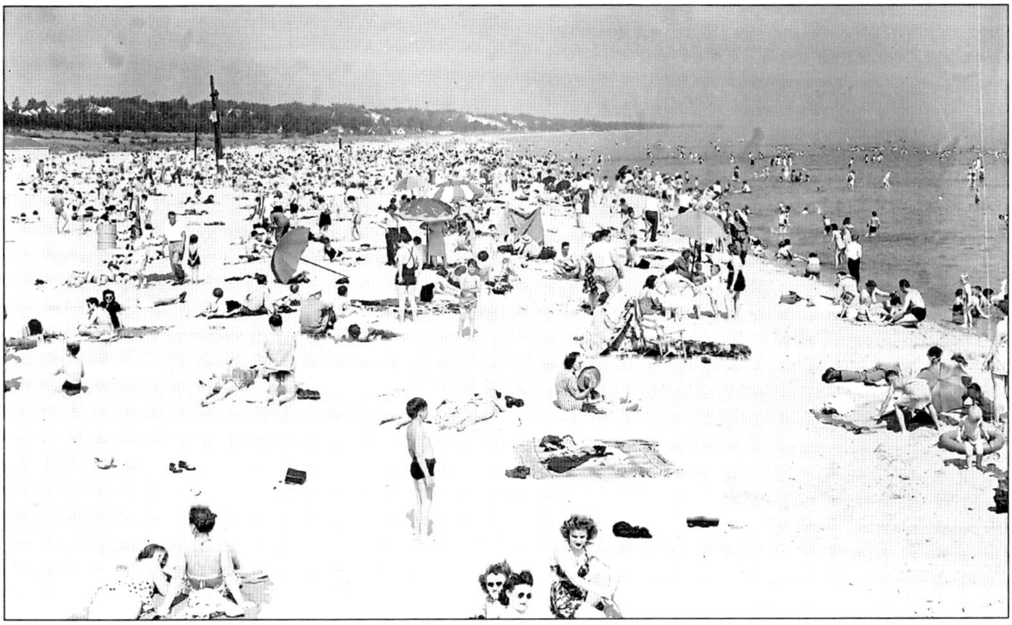

At the start of 1987, the grumblings from several citizens could be faintly heard, soon taking media attention away from the 1987 Pan American Games sailing events hosted by Michigan City. Led by former founding board member Roger McKee, the Concerned Citizens Group adamantly opposed development at the lakefront, especially on the city's historic Lake Michigan beach seen in this 1948 picture. (Michigan City News Dispatch.)

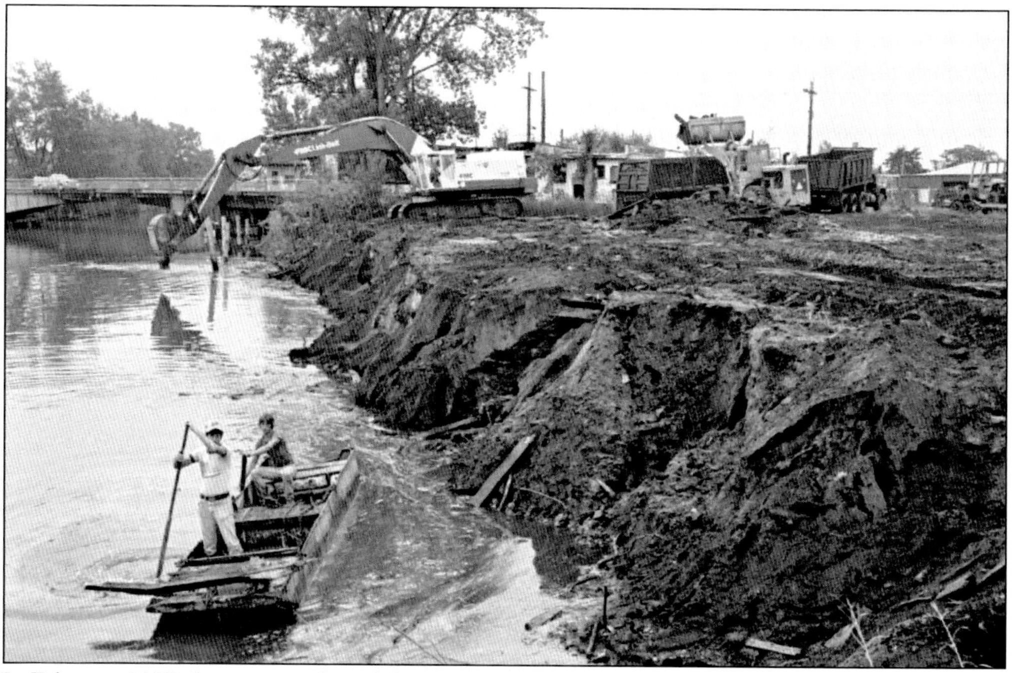

In February 1987, the group gathered 6,300 signatures on a petition to halt the MCPA's expansion plans, seen above. It pledged to fight for the preservation of the lakefront and its symbol, the lighthouse (below). Members of the group, including Lewis Hapke, dogged the board at meetings and hearings on the proposed projects. They wrote letters to the news media and rallied city officials to their aid. Later that year, 21 candidates for city office positions ran on a platform in tangent to the Concerned Citizens Group. According to the *Michigan City News Dispatch*, Roger McKee "declared war on the Port Authority" in June—just before the Pan American Games. (Michigan City News Dispatch.)

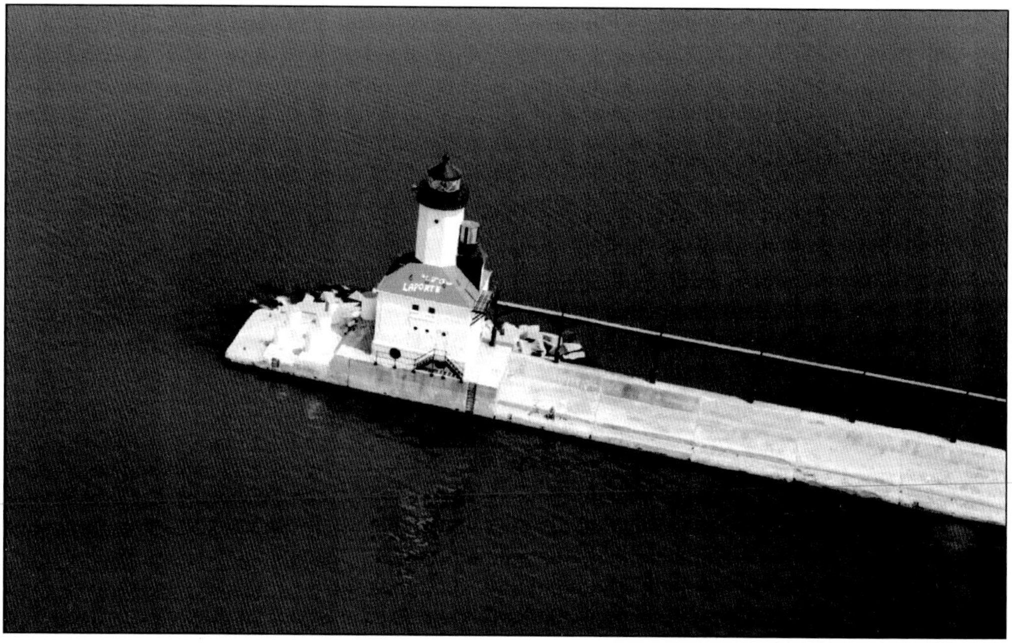

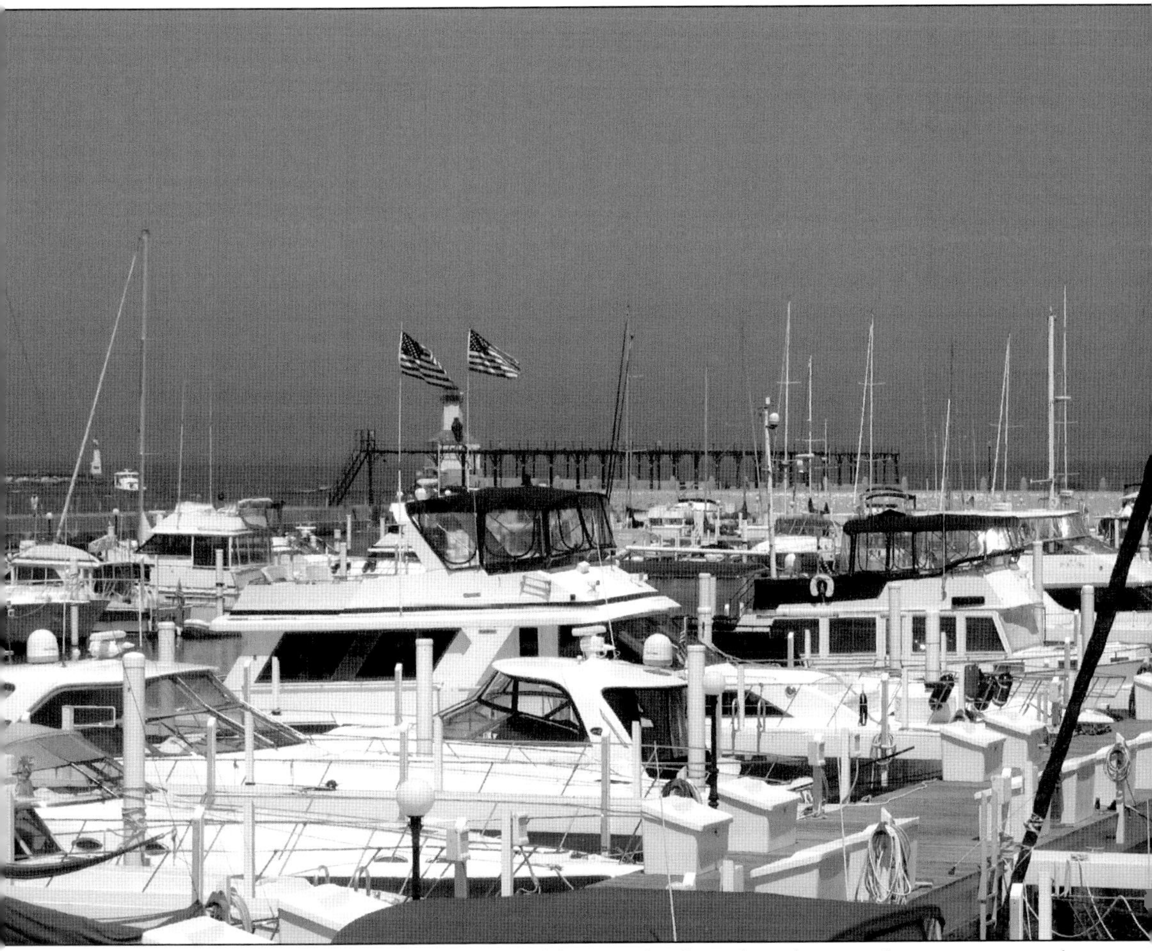

Eventually the board announced that it would set aside plans for a large-scale expansion and concentrate on adding slips to the basin to relieve congestion there. McKee's group opposed this too, citing traffic congestion in the harbor. Even the proposed charter row plans were assaulted in the media. The *Michigan City News Dispatch* reported that Al Spiers, in response to the backlash, admonished the board to "act or the idea will die." He also chastised it for not standing up for its projects, including charter row. Mayor Clifford Arnold urged the board to get going on a plan but for another reason. The funding offer from LMMDC would expire by 1989. The board and its engineer put their heads together to come up with a less-controversial project. (Rosemary Bunton.)

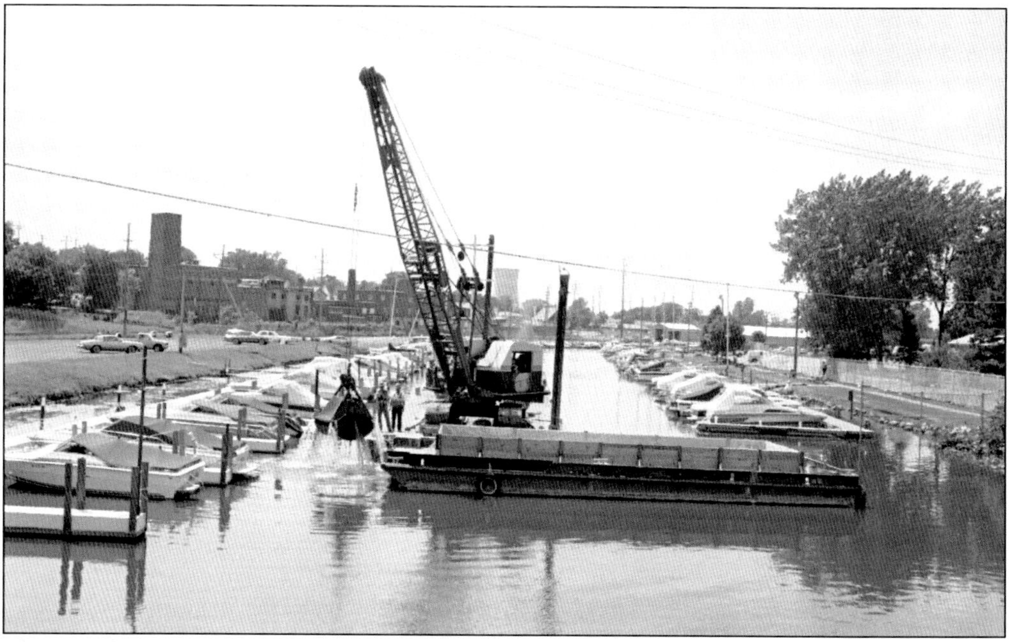

The air of conservation and environmental protection that was born in the gas shortages of the 1970s had grown tremendously during the 1980s. New rules evolved that threatened a 1987 dredge of Trail Creek. The federal Environmental Protection Agency, the Indiana Department of Environmental Management (IDEM), the LaPorte County Health Department (which stopped dredging while it investigated pollution charges), and the DNR all had to approve of both the dredge itself and the dump site for the spoil. In previous dredge projects, the spoil was dumped on land rented or purchased by the MCPA. (Above, Michigan City News Dispatch; below, John Haynes.)

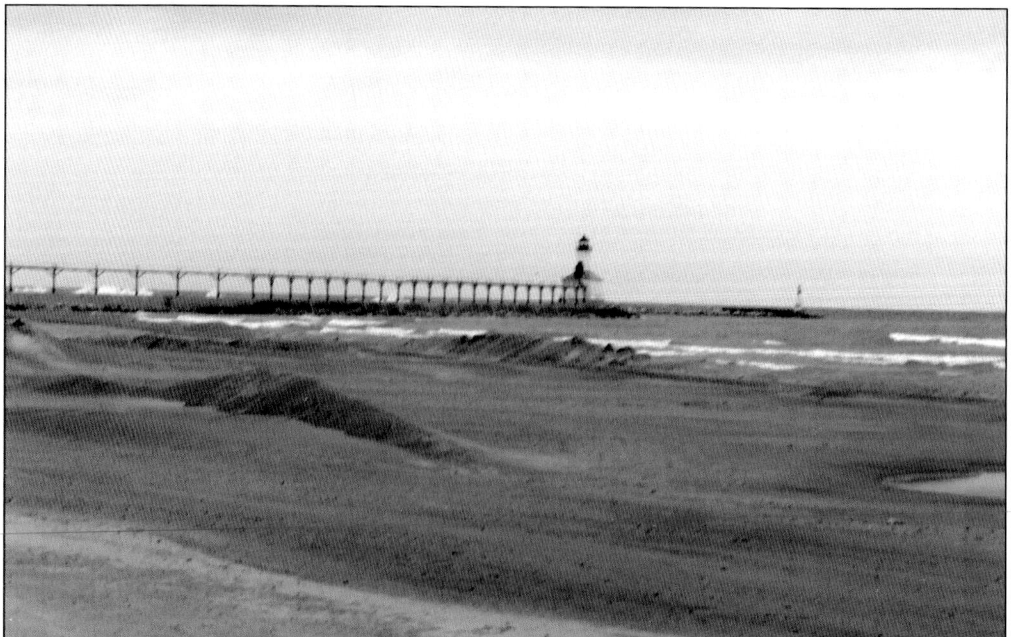

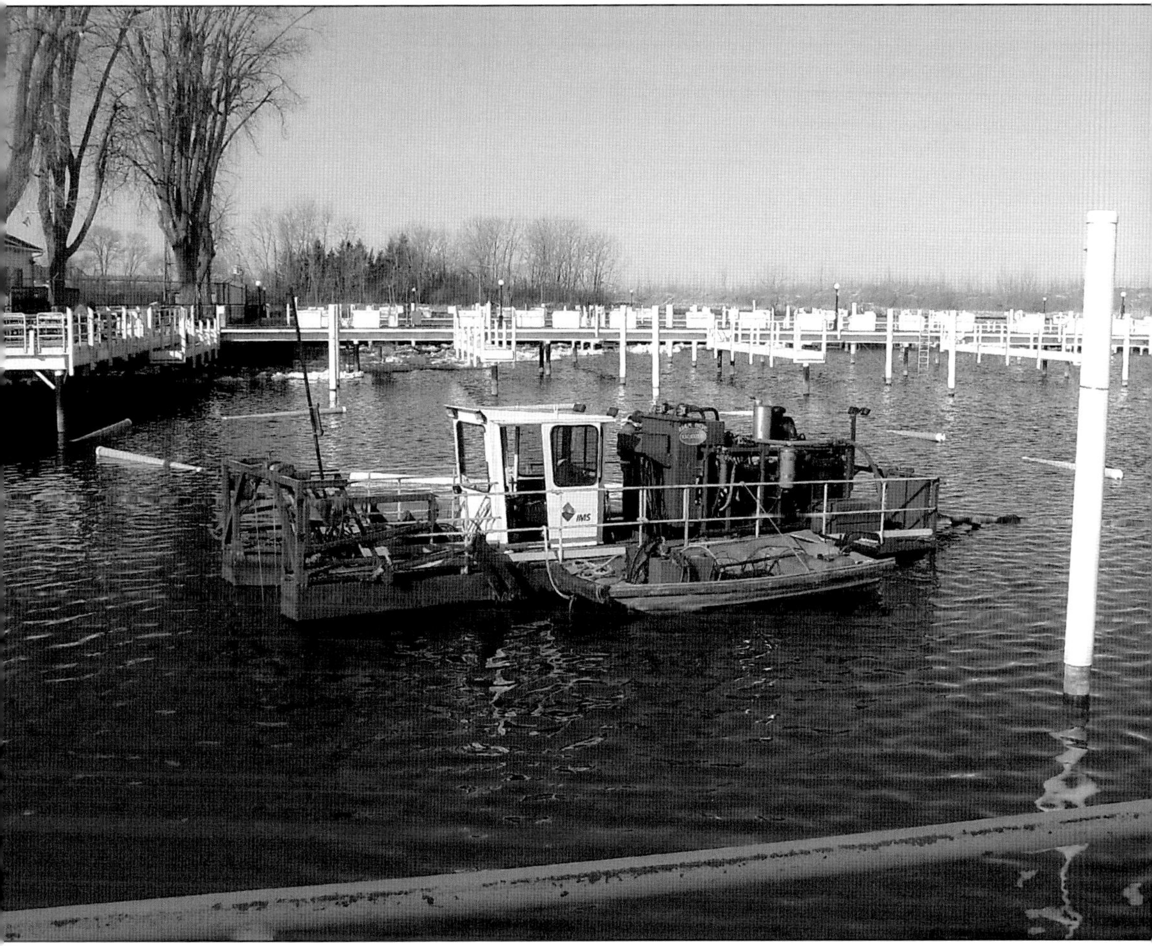

Now the dredged spoil had to be transported away from the harbor, dewatered, and then disposed. The practice that began in 1987 still persists today, as does the controversy that the MCPA met as a result of the new process. In 2008, the *Michigan City News Dispatch* was abuzz with residents' concern over spoil being pulled out of the basin (seen above) and dewatered on Washington Park beach.

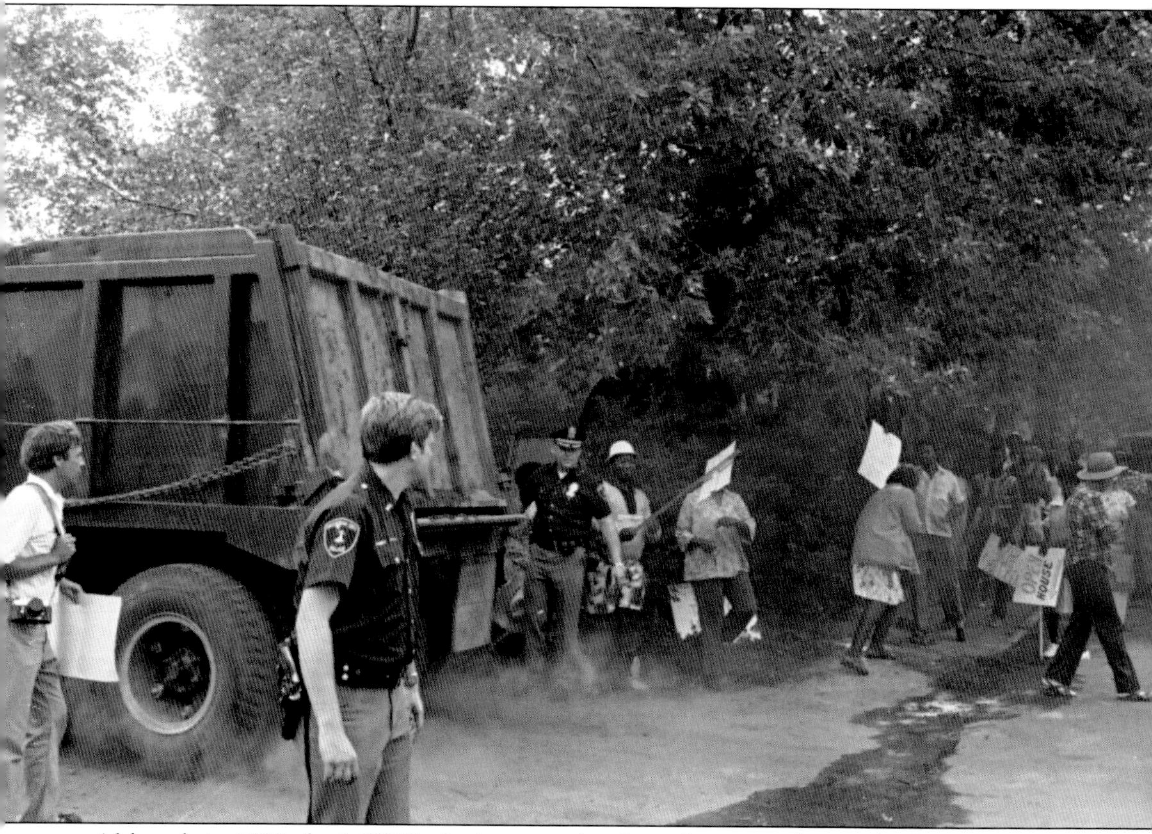

Although in 2008 the MCPA's dredge caused upheaval, no marches took place like the one seen in this 1987 photograph. Then, the dewatering practice was quite new and not much was known about the type of water being dredged from Trail Creek. Both issues raised red flags for the Concerned Citizens Group and Canada neighborhood residents as well. (Michigan City News Dispatch.)

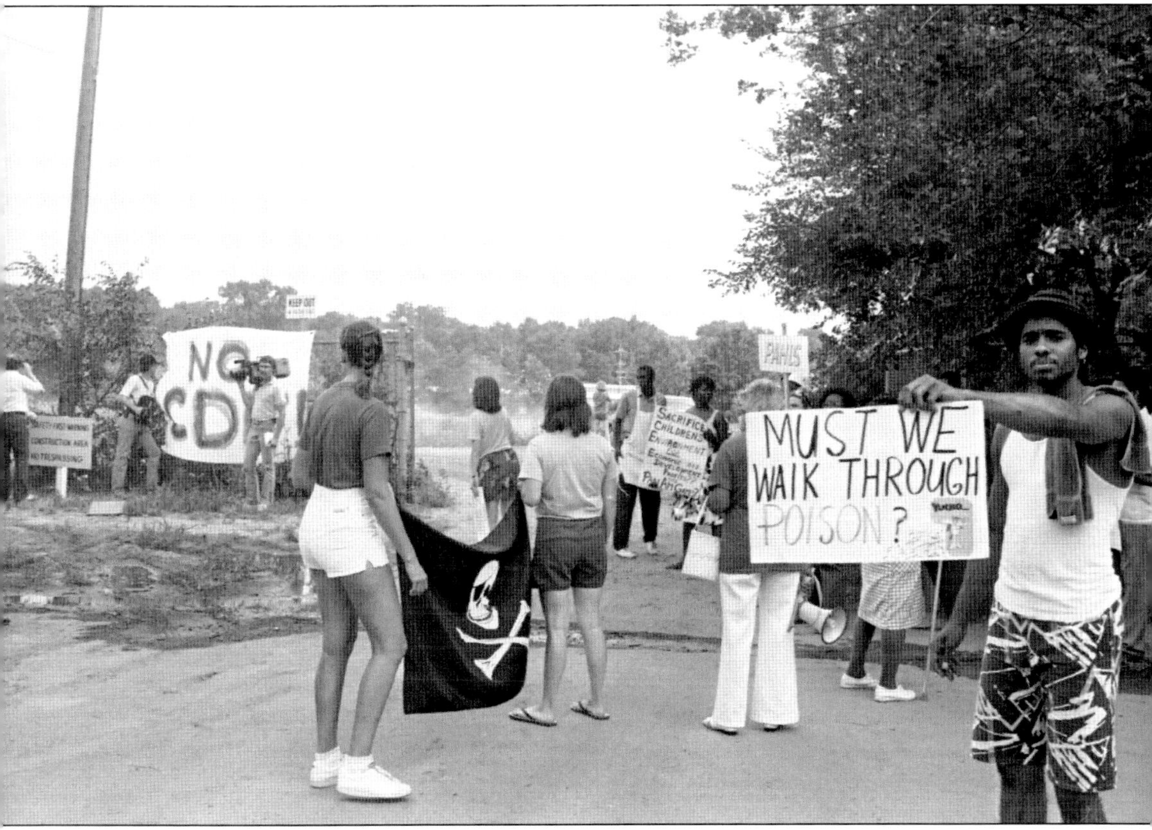

The U.S. Army Corps of Engineers and the board began in 1986 to get all the necessary permits and tests run. The dredge was halted in its preliminary stages and in mid-progress, when two groups sued for injunctions, citing the pollution issues. The place approved for dewatering of the spoil was previously owned by Waste Inc., a landfill situated along the banks of Trail Creek in the heart of the Canada community. The predominately black community heard the rumors of pollutants in the harbor and realized that those materials would be dumped in its backyard. Community members protested loudly in opposition of the U.S. Army Corps of Engineers and MCPA plans, attracting national attention. Their loudest voice was city councilman T. C. Falls and attorney Robert Blomquist, who also sought an injunction to stop the dumping. (Michigan City News Dispatch)

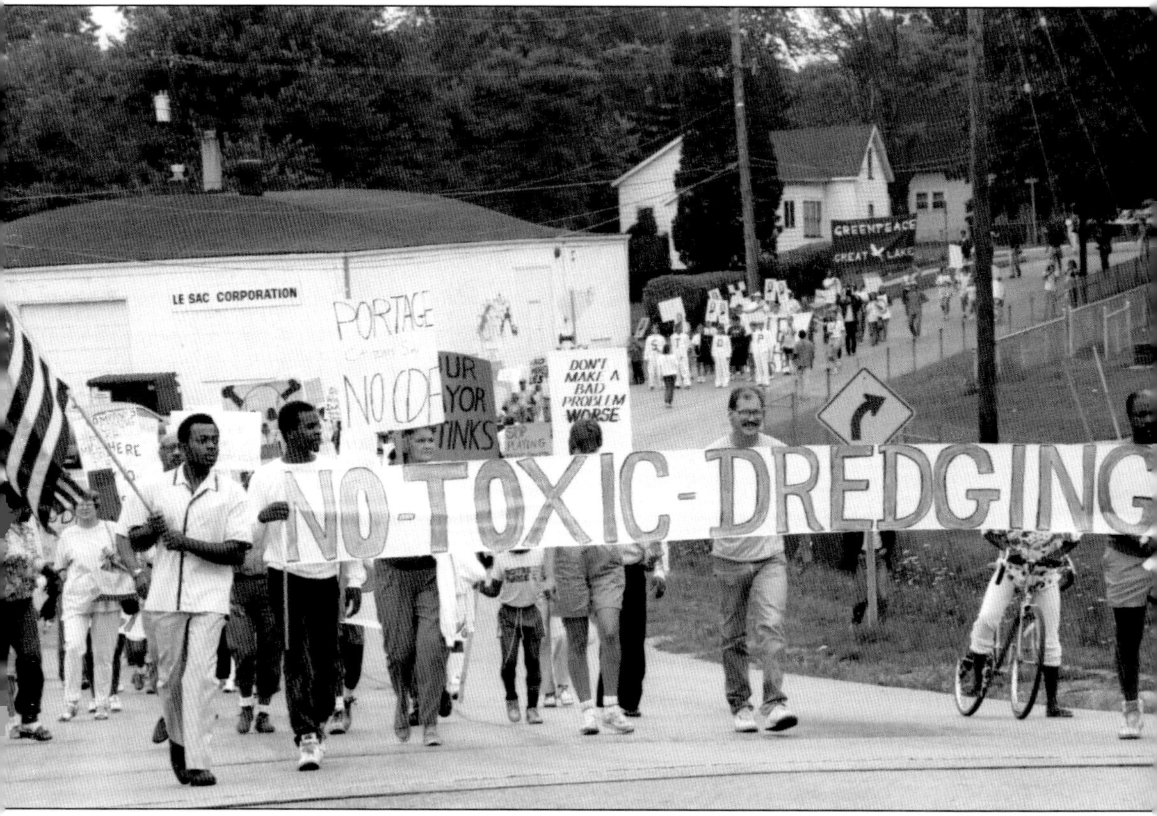

Rising tensions exploded on July 10, 1987. Thirty adults and several children stood in front of the gates of Waste Inc., refusing to allow the dump trucks through. They placed a scrap car in front of the gates as a second barrier. The crowds were dispersed, but they returned the next day, swarming the trucks entering the dump site. The Michigan City Police Department was called in, and eight protestors were arrested. The health department halted the dredge in late July, but the IDEM overruled it after rigorous negotiation with the U.S. Army Corps of Engineers. On the final day of dredging, the protesters returned to make a statement against what they saw as the degradation of their community. As they marched from the north end to the dump site, the Canada community was joined by Greenpeace, the National Organization for Women (NOW), PAHLS, U.S. representative Jim Jontz, city councilman Emery Whitlow, and of course T. C. Falls. In all, 250 marched. No arrests were made. Later a lawsuit was filed against Waste Inc., the MCPA, and the city on the community's behalf. (Michigan City News Dispatch.)

Seven

The Pan American Games

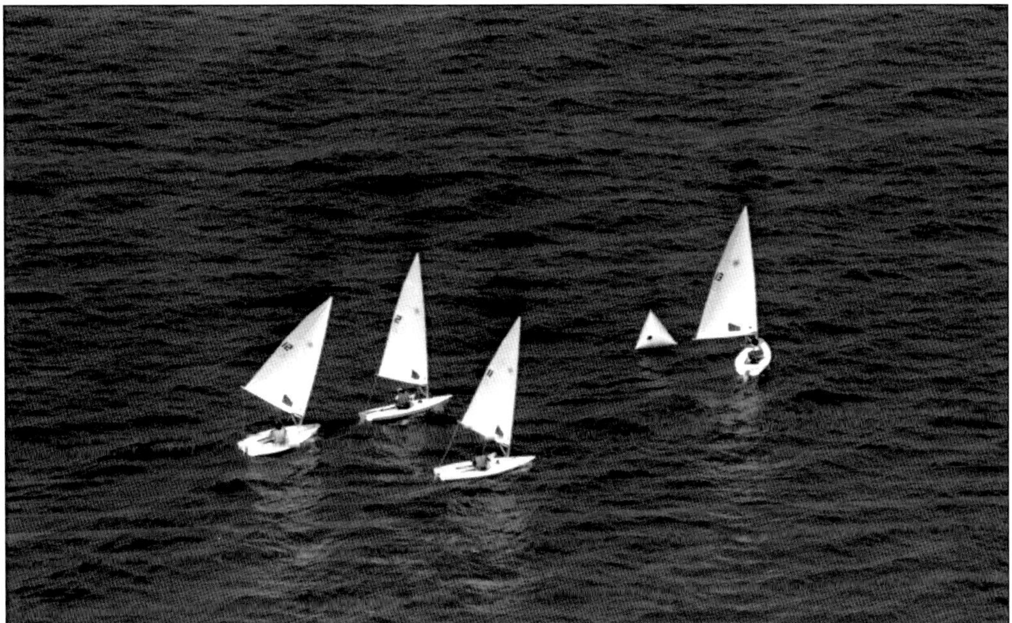

While the storm was brewing, in 1985 an announcement that the Pan American Games were coming to Indiana had everyone in a frenzy. During the 100th anniversary of the Colombia Races, the games committee visited Michigan City. Soon after, the city was officially given the honor of hosting the Pan American Games sailing event. Later that year, the city council reinstated the CCM of property taxes, collecting a levy of 3¢ per dollar. The MCPA began to spruce up the public facilities for the national event. (Michigan City News Dispatch.)

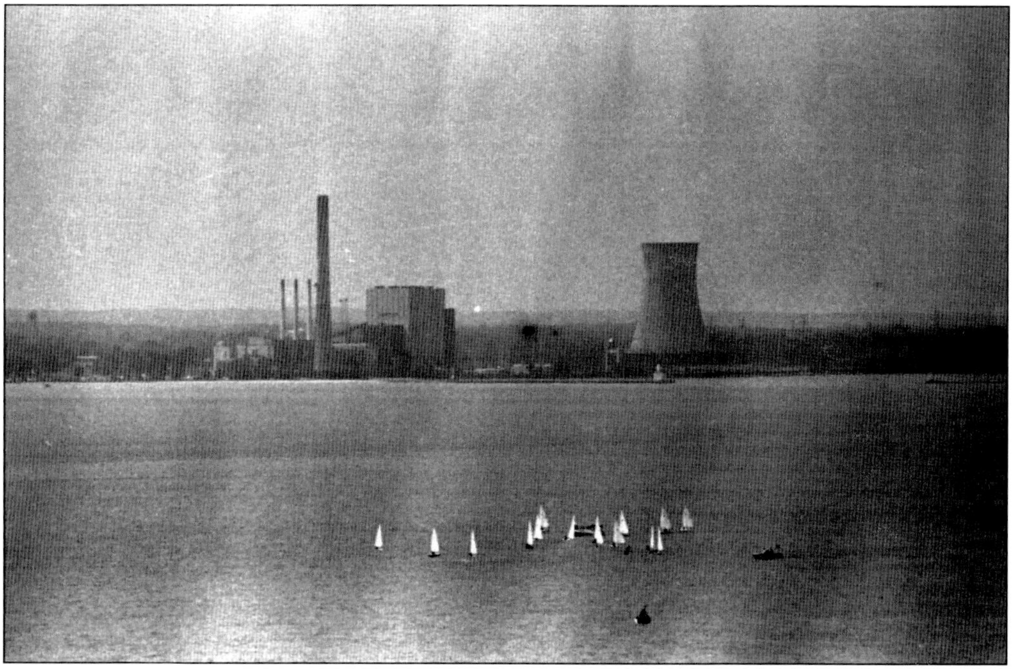

Everyone saw the games as a means to draw attention and revenue to the city, especially at the lakefront. The U.S. Army Corps of Engineers agreed to dredge because of the games. The tide of public opinion shifted in favor of the lake, for a moment. Talk of development produced suggestions and even drawings from the public—two were published in the *Michigan City News Dispatch*. The moment passed with the end of 1986. The next year began with the formation of the Concerned Citizens Group. (Michigan City News Dispatch.)

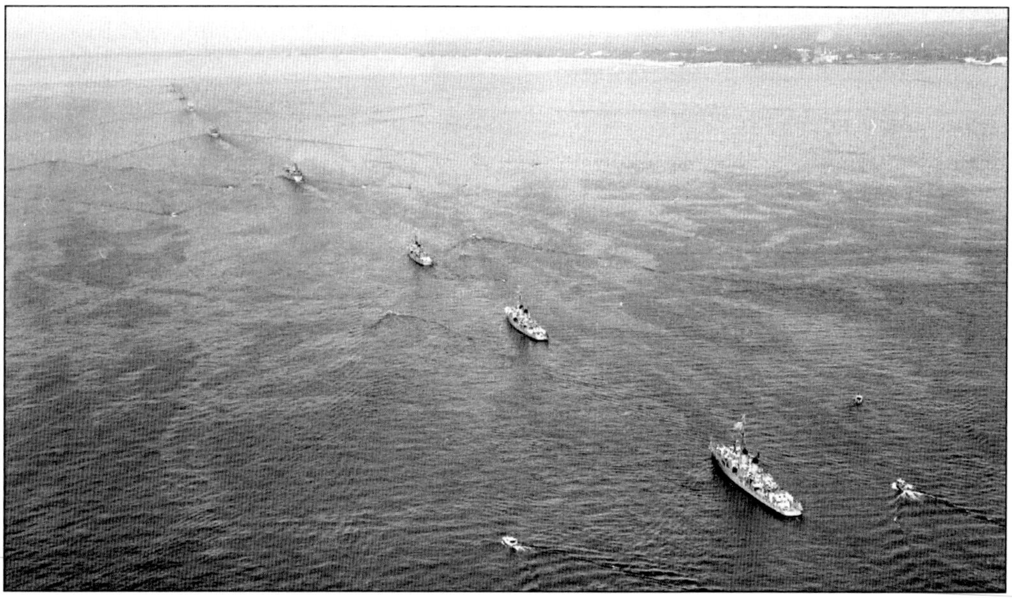

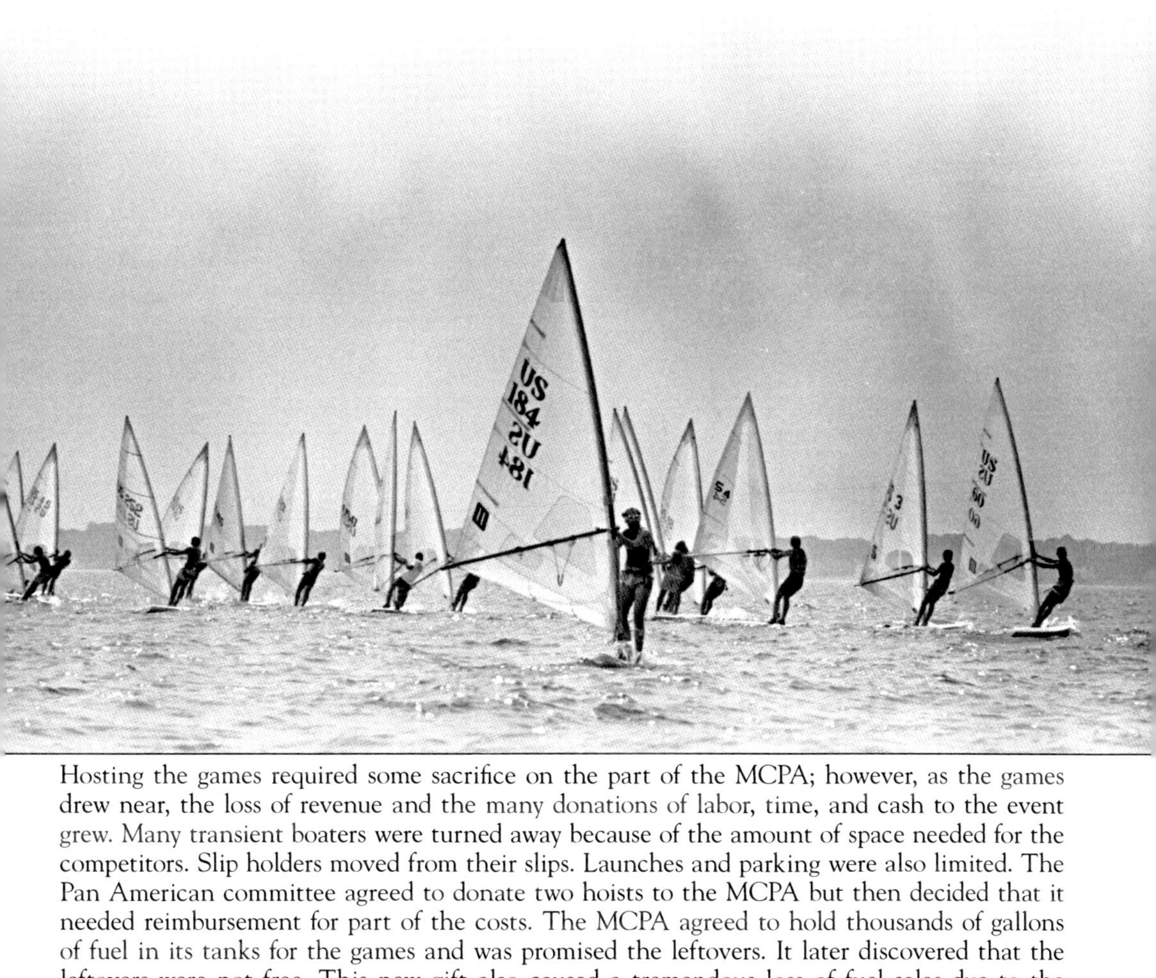

Hosting the games required some sacrifice on the part of the MCPA; however, as the games drew near, the loss of revenue and the many donations of labor, time, and cash to the event grew. Many transient boaters were turned away because of the amount of space needed for the competitors. Slip holders moved from their slips. Launches and parking were also limited. The Pan American committee agreed to donate two hoists to the MCPA but then decided that it needed reimbursement for part of the costs. The MCPA agreed to hold thousands of gallons of fuel in its tanks for the games and was promised the leftovers. It later discovered that the leftovers were not free. This new gift also caused a tremendous loss of fuel sales due to the amount of congestion. A month before the games, the mayor approached the board, requesting a $50,000 donation to the Pan American Games. He believed that the MCPA benefited most from the event, so it should be eager to make the donation. (Michigan City News Dispatch.)

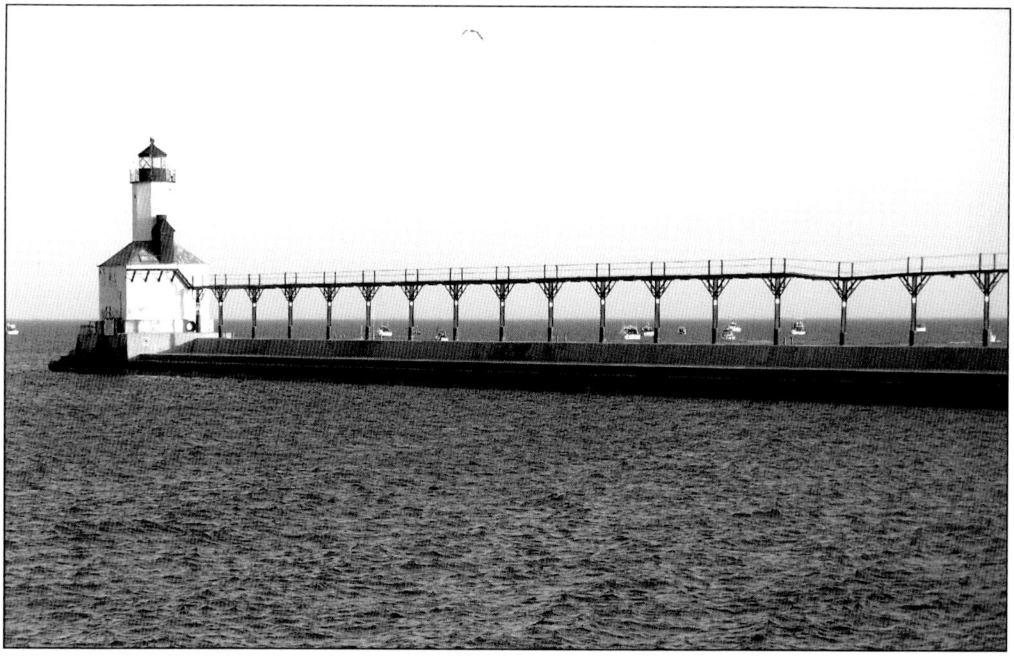

Al Spiers quickly outlined the $27,000 in estimated losses that the MCPA had already suffered because of the games. After the games, the board agreed they were exciting, though the turnout was much less than desired. Spiers proposed that the board consider its losses a donation to an event that greatly benefited the city. The motion was approved unanimously. (John Haynes.)

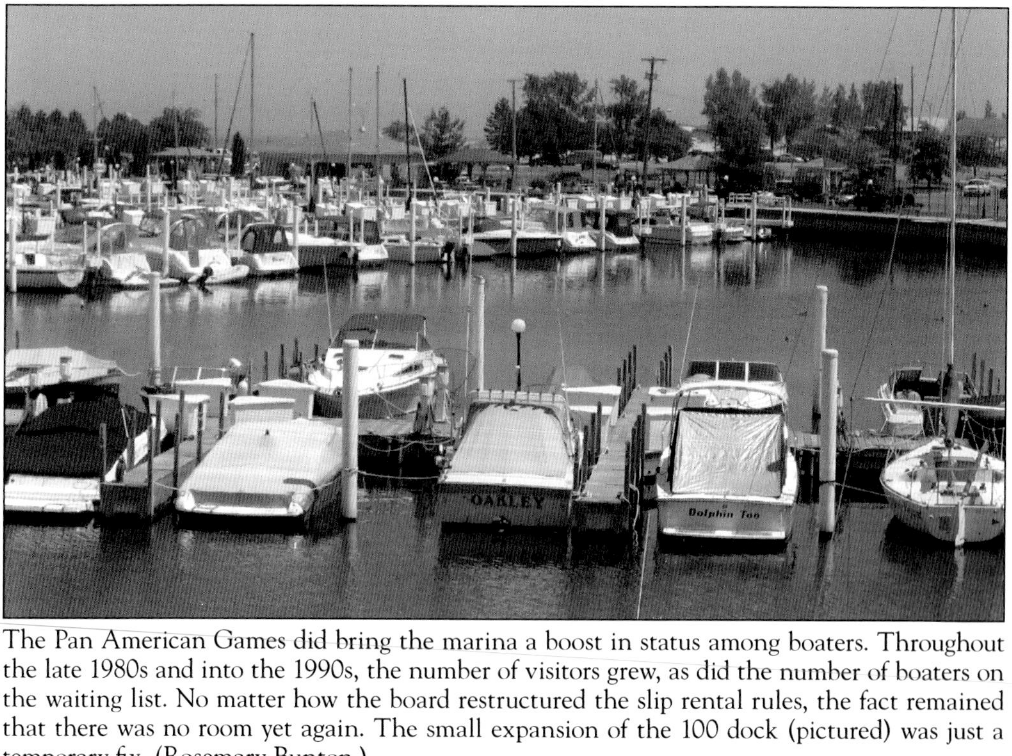

The Pan American Games did bring the marina a boost in status among boaters. Throughout the late 1980s and into the 1990s, the number of visitors grew, as did the number of boaters on the waiting list. No matter how the board restructured the slip rental rules, the fact remained that there was no room yet again. The small expansion of the 100 dock (pictured) was just a temporary fix. (Rosemary Bunton.)

Eight

CHANGING OF THE GUARD

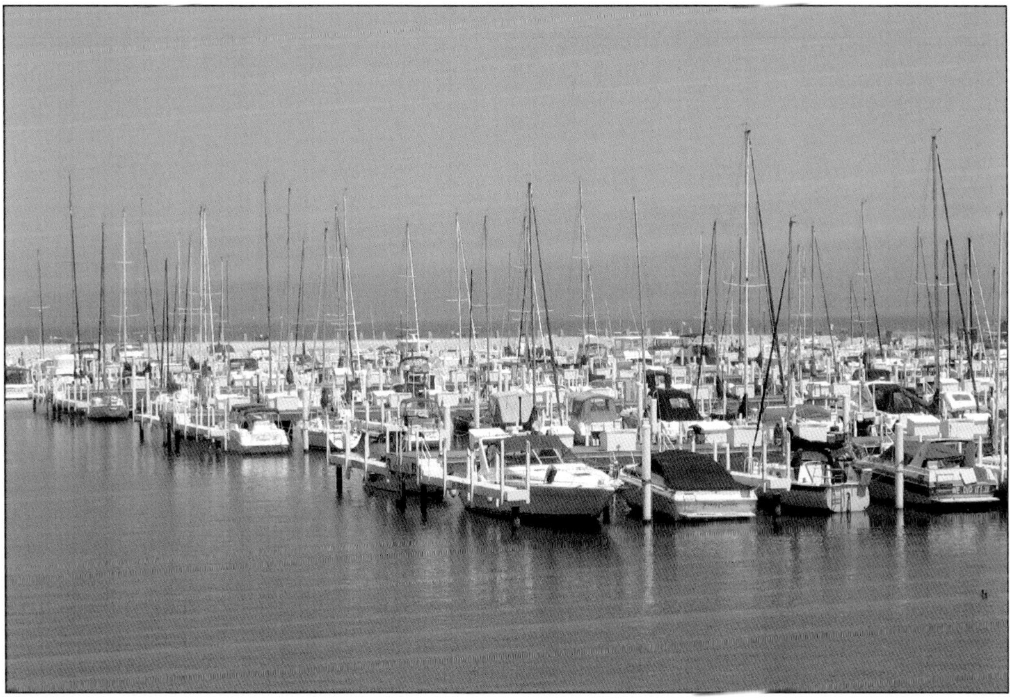

In spite of the controversy, the board proceeded in planning expansion. As necessary as the harbor dredge was, expansion had to occur despite public outcry. First, the board and harbormaster Lewis (Lew) Timberlake needed relief. Timberlake was fielding the mass questions, requests, complaints, and concerns of the boaters as well as the angered public. At Timberlake's urging, the board created the position of dockmaster, and Gary Waltz was hired. Board chairman Richard Kruse later granted Timberlake more autonomy that gradually increased. Meanwhile, the dockmaster oversaw the marinas' operations, including slip assignments and dock committee meetings. (Rosemary Bunton.)

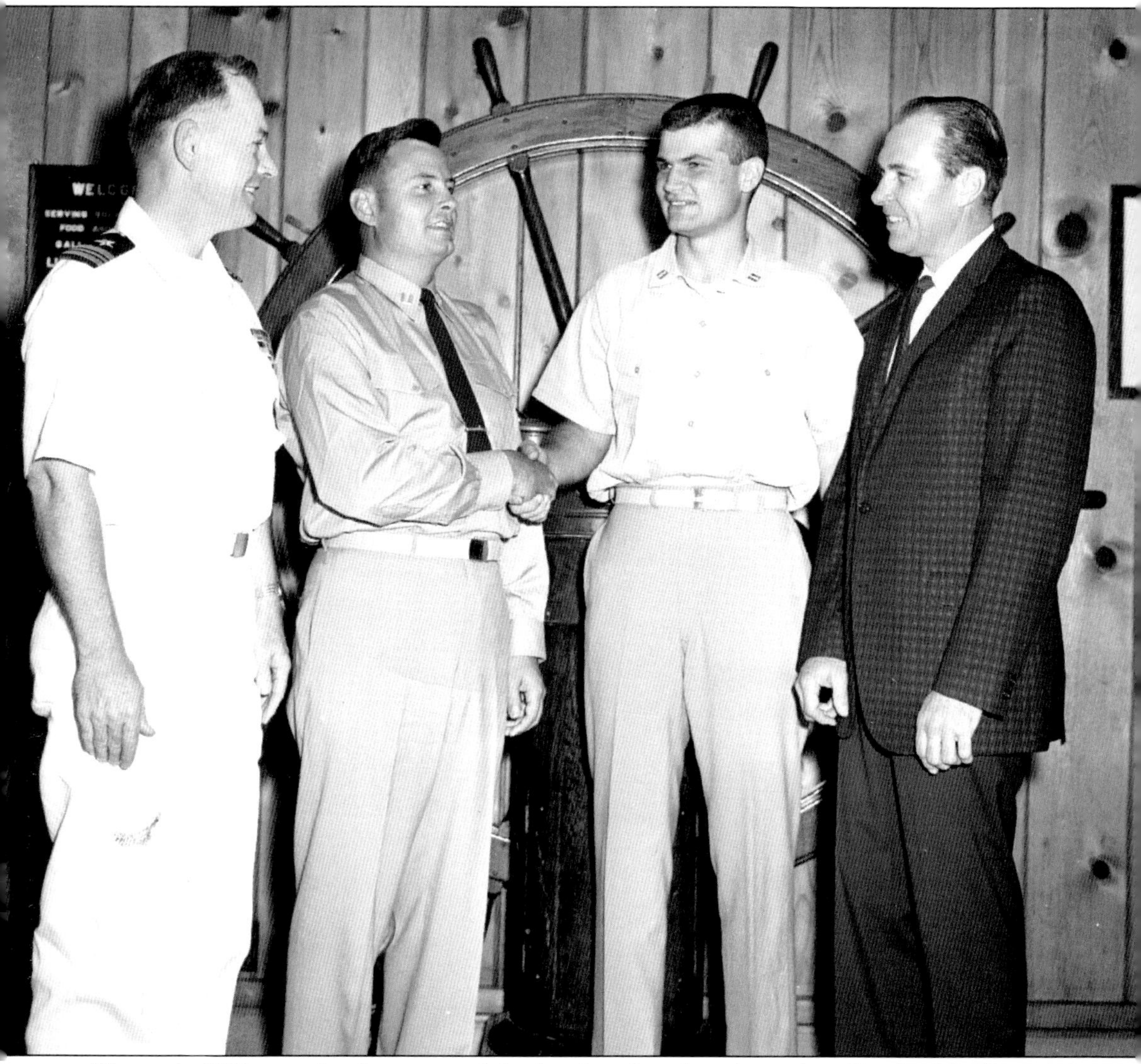

The early 1990s saw the departure of the last founding board member. Hartley Job (far right) had seen the marina as a puddle with a few boats become a world-class boating facility with an extension on Trail Creek. Job left the board in what he felt were capable hands, citing that he had reached a plateau in his career as a board member. He told a *Michigan City News Dispatch* reporter that it was time for fresh minds to effect progress in order to prevent the MCPA from a pattern toward regression.

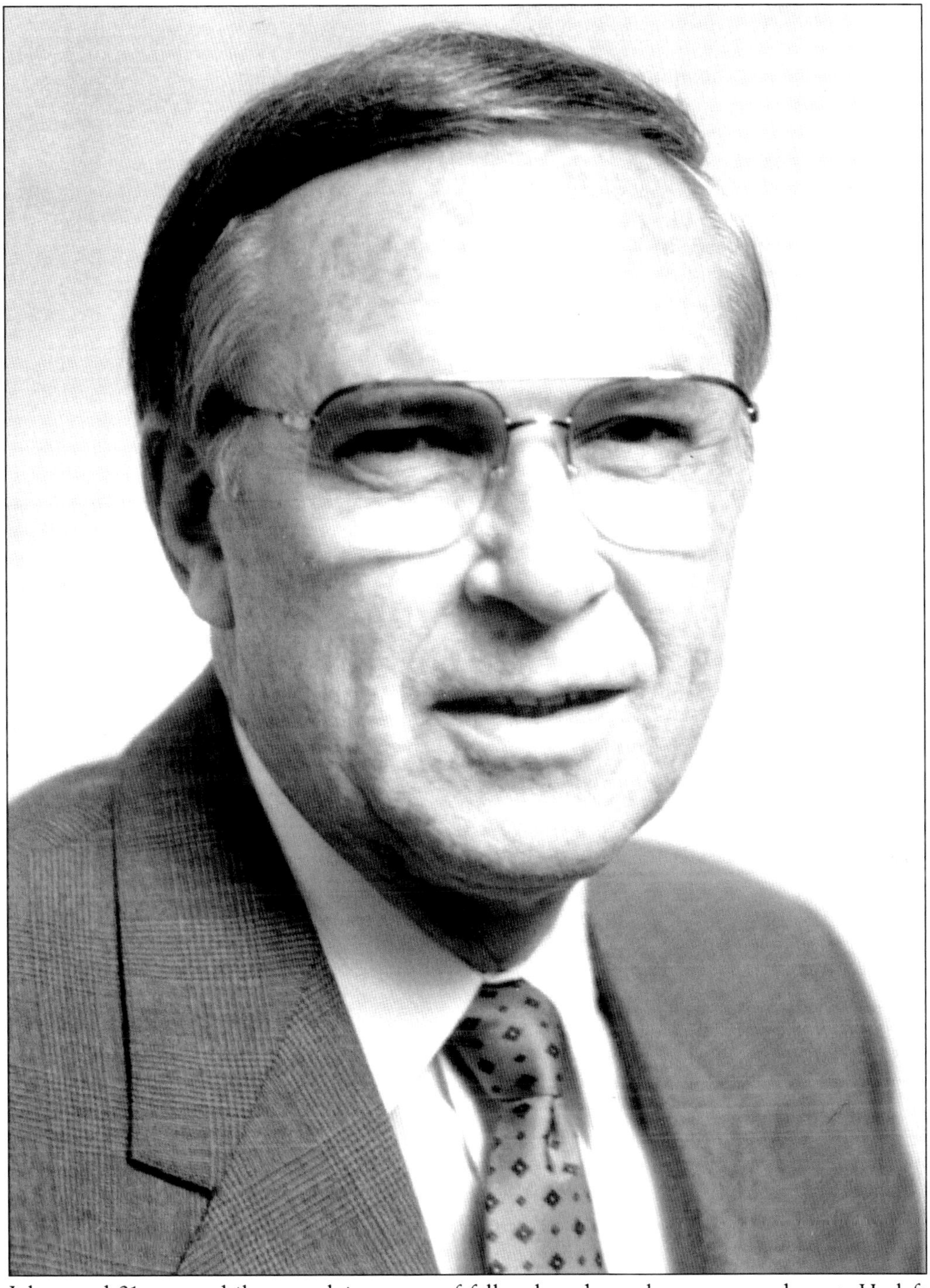

Job served 31 years while a revolving array of fellow board members came and went. He left reminiscing about what the MCPA had been through, looking forward to what it could become. Job was responsible for helping the MCPA along its way to the marina it is now. He also documented the journey, leaving evidence of the agency's tumultuous history, one that stays accustomed to controversy to this day. (Bill Swedenberg.)

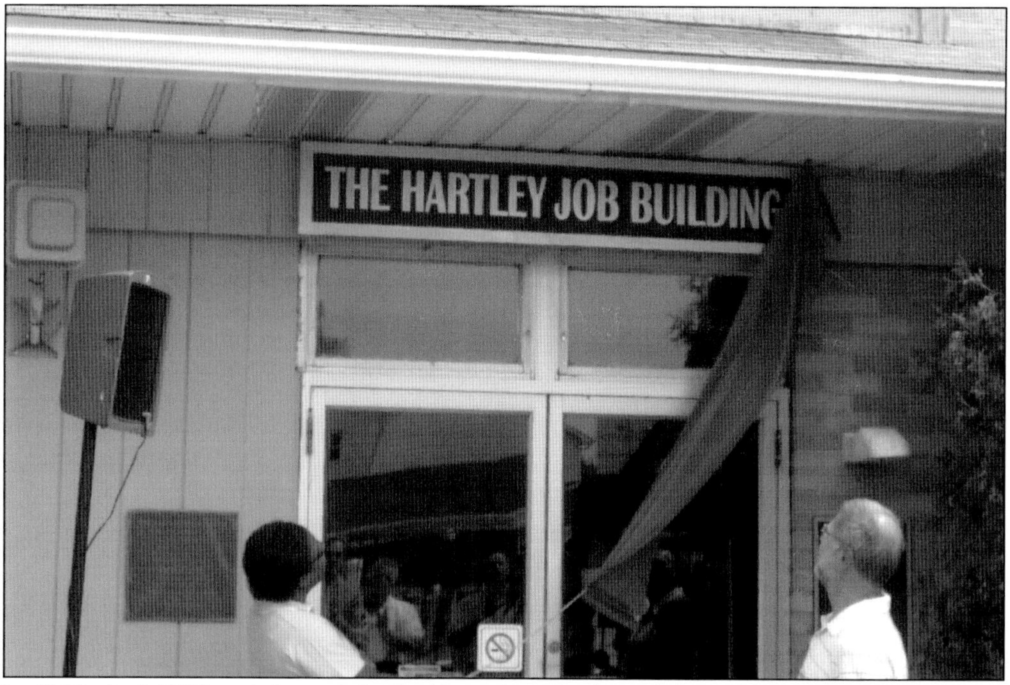

In 2008, the MCPA rededicated the building that Hartley Job helped build (and that his wife Phyllis helped christen in 1965) as the Hartley Job Building. The dedication was the kickoff for the 29th annual Michigan City In-Water Boat Show. (Rosemary Bunton.)

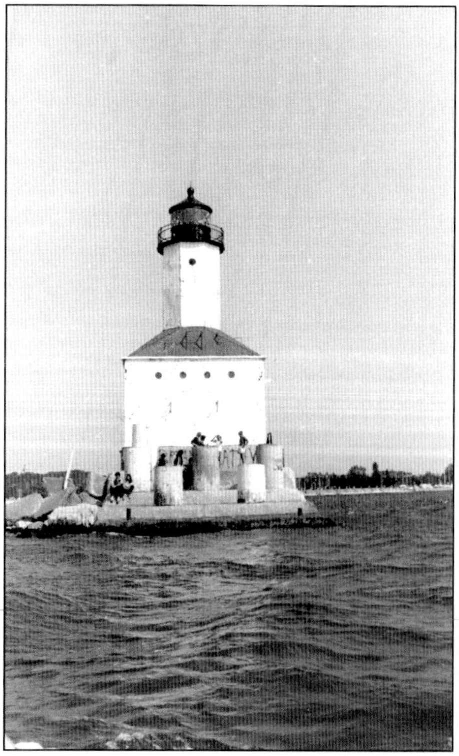

The MCPA honored Job because of his commitment to Michigan City's marinas. He was a part of their creation from the beginning. Michigan City's lighthouse, the symbol for the town, also benefitted during Job's term on the board. (Bill Swedenberg.)

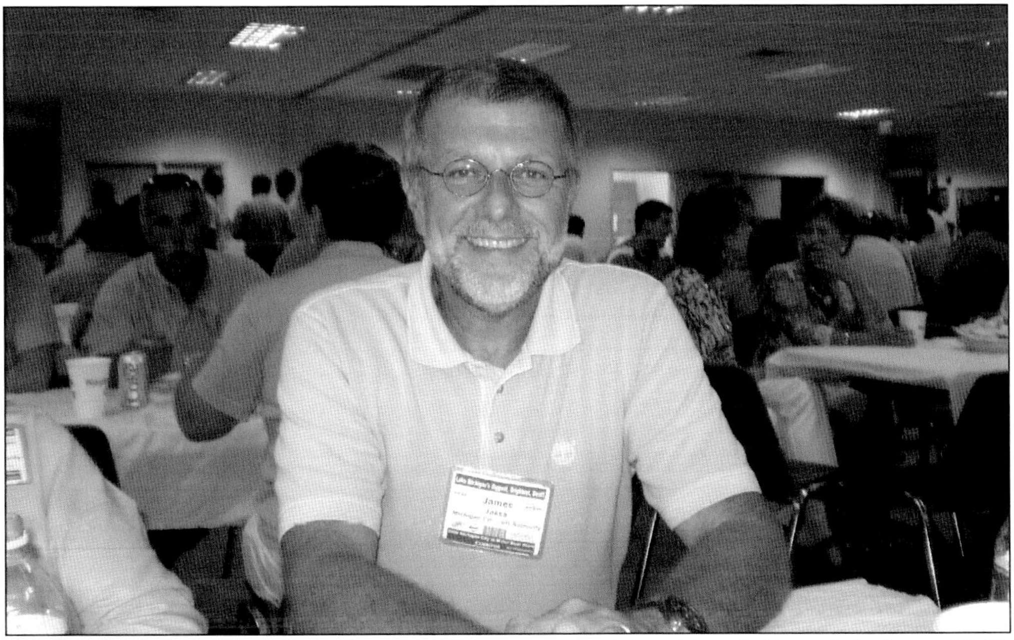

Speaking at the dedication was then board chairman Jim Jaksa (above), Norm Schultz, and Job's son Larry (below). Jaksa spoke on Job's accomplishments during his term with the MCPA Board of Directors and then presented Phyllis Job with the official proclamation that dedicated the building to her late husband. The *Michigan City News Dispatch* reported that Larry Job revealed to the audience that his father was not always so enthusiastic about the marina. "My dad one day came to a crossroads that many of us cross [that] changes our life; he bought a boat. From then on all of his civic activities quickly became waterlogged." (Above, Mary Ann Pawlicke; below, Rosemary Bunton.)

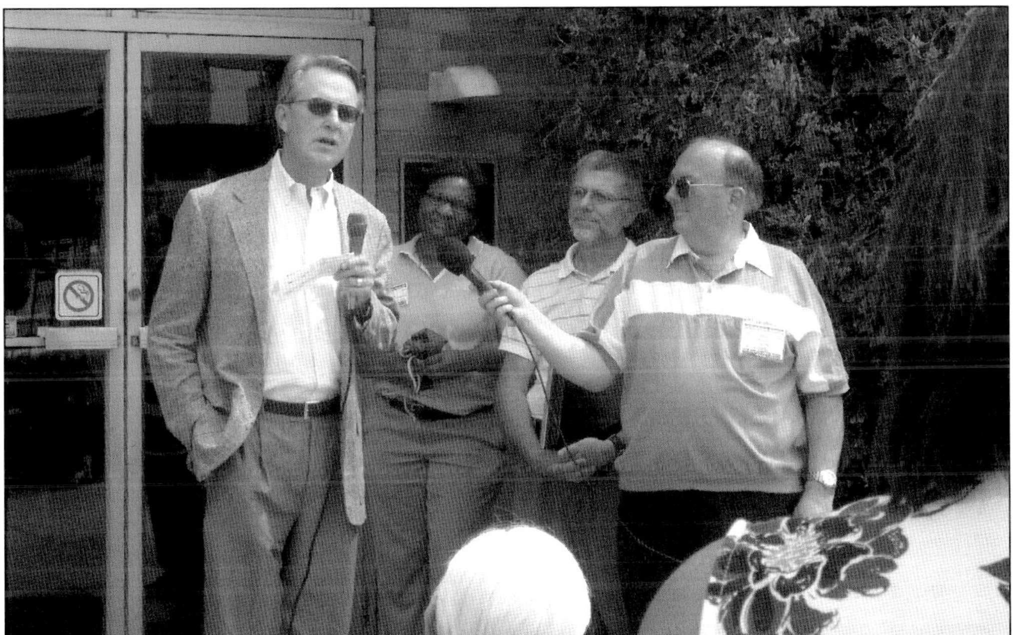

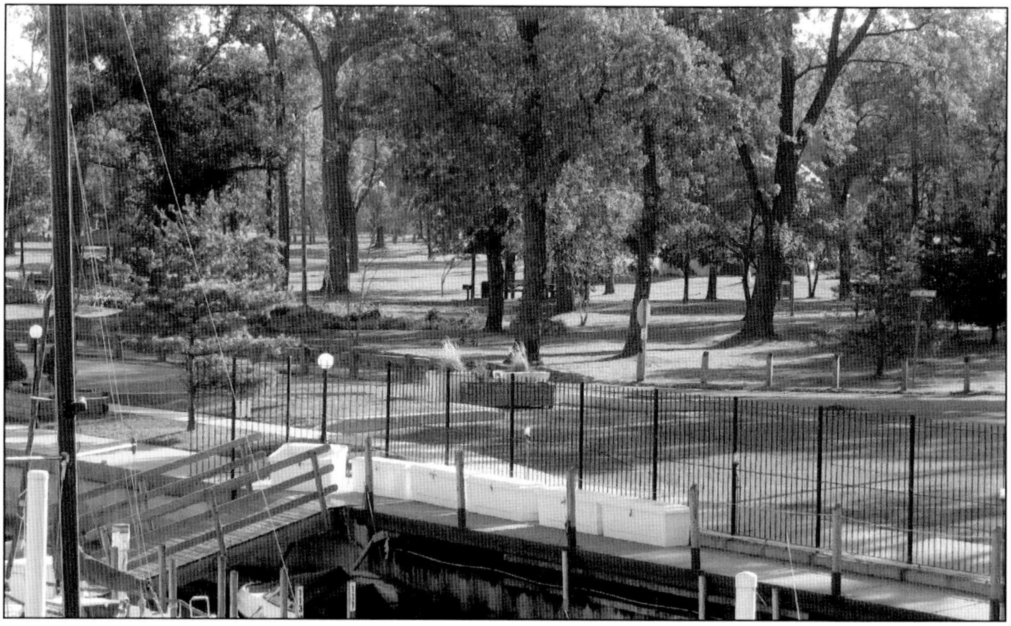

Bruce Gilbert, Hartley Job's replacement, began effecting the change Job mentioned. His term as chairman saw the initiation of CCM changes as well as restructuring of the board meetings. His goal was to make the meetings and eventually the meeting minutes more efficient. Gilbert did use some of Job's old tricks, pushing for a private loan to reconstruct the fishing pier project (situated just beyond the launch ramp in the picture). (Rosemary Bunton.)

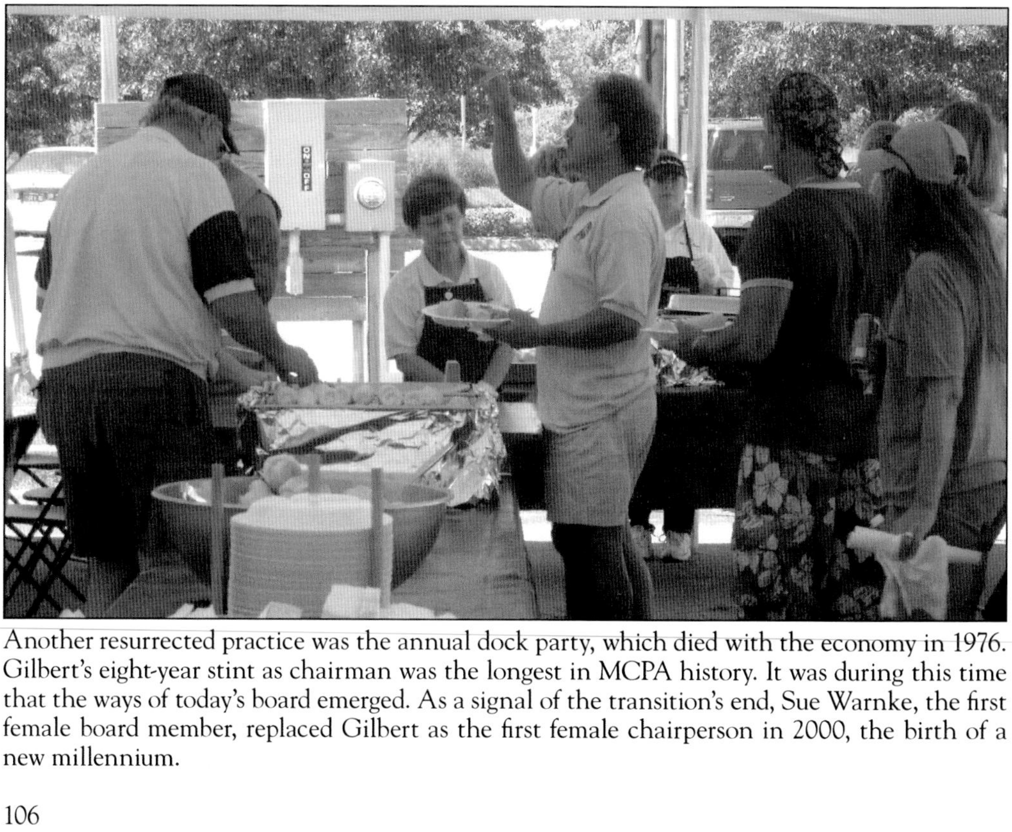

Another resurrected practice was the annual dock party, which died with the economy in 1976. Gilbert's eight-year stint as chairman was the longest in MCPA history. It was during this time that the ways of today's board emerged. As a signal of the transition's end, Sue Warnke, the first female board member, replaced Gilbert as the first female chairperson in 2000, the birth of a new millennium.

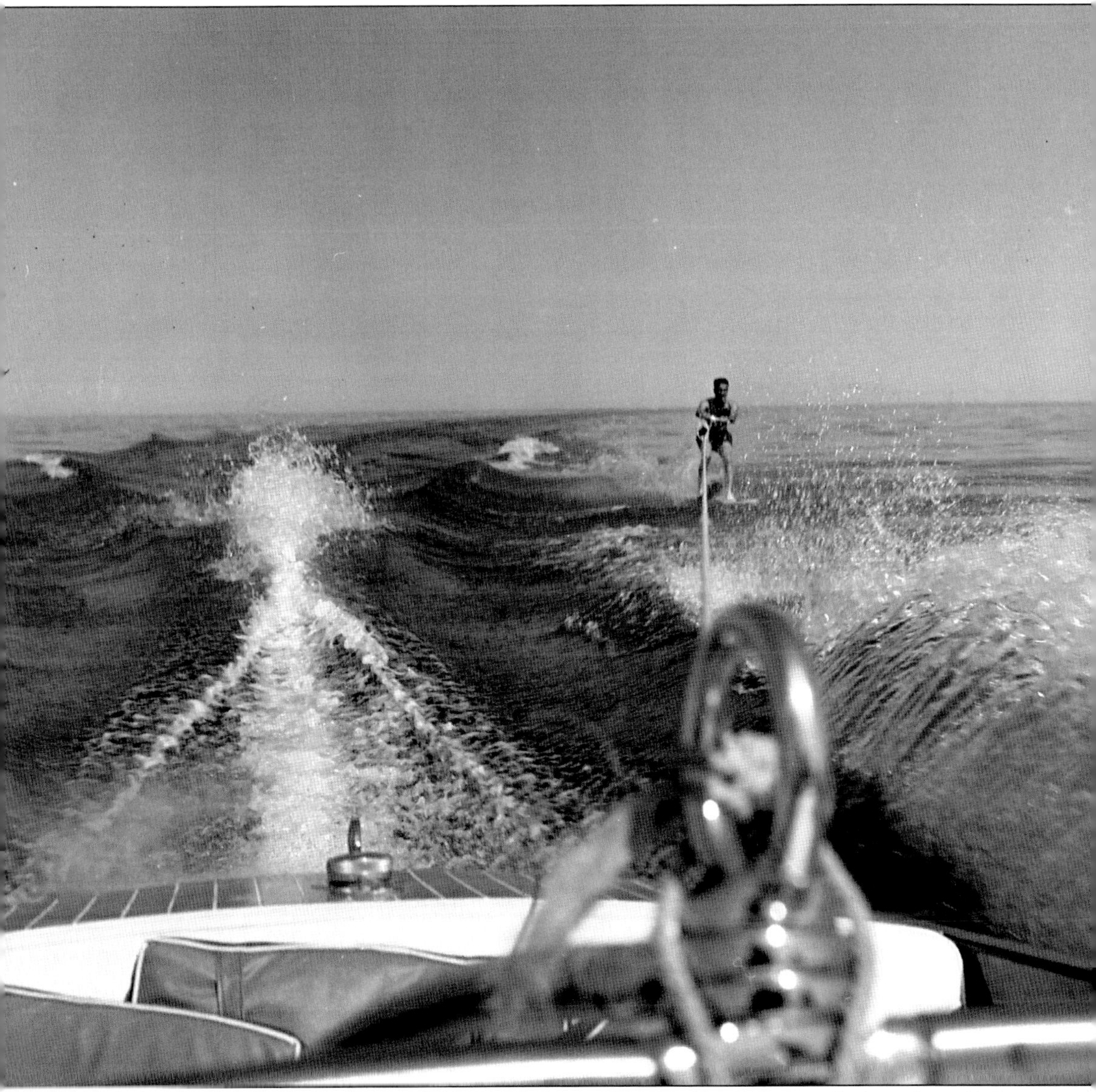

Another major change was that of the MCPA attorney. Marcellus Meyer took the job in 1963. After 30 years of fighting the MCPA's legal battles, Meyer retired on January 19, 1993. He was replaced by attorney Jeffrey Katz, who holds the position today. Katz picked up where Meyer left off, being the legal mind behind all the board's activities. (Michigan City News Dispatch.)

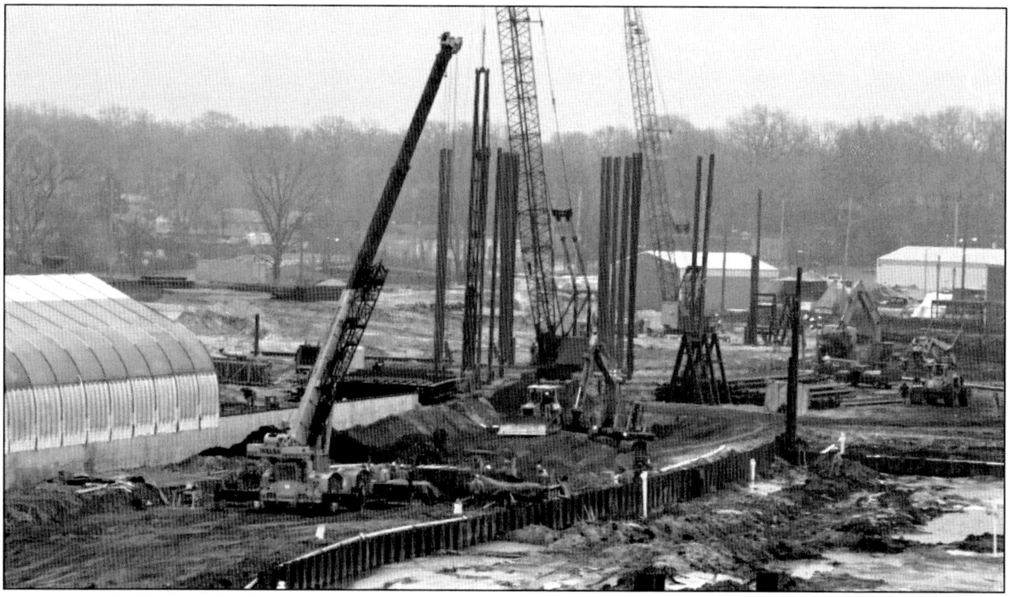

Riverboat gambling was sweeping the waterways. May 1996 brought the announcement that Blue Chip Casino Inc., a riverboat gambling facility, was coming to dock in Trail Creek. Soon after, Blue Chip wanted the deteriorating Sprague Municipal Marina. The facility was in the direct path of construction. A deal was brokered that netted the MCPA a newly built marina that was much better than the old one, and Trail Creek Marina was christened. (Michigan City News Dispatch.)

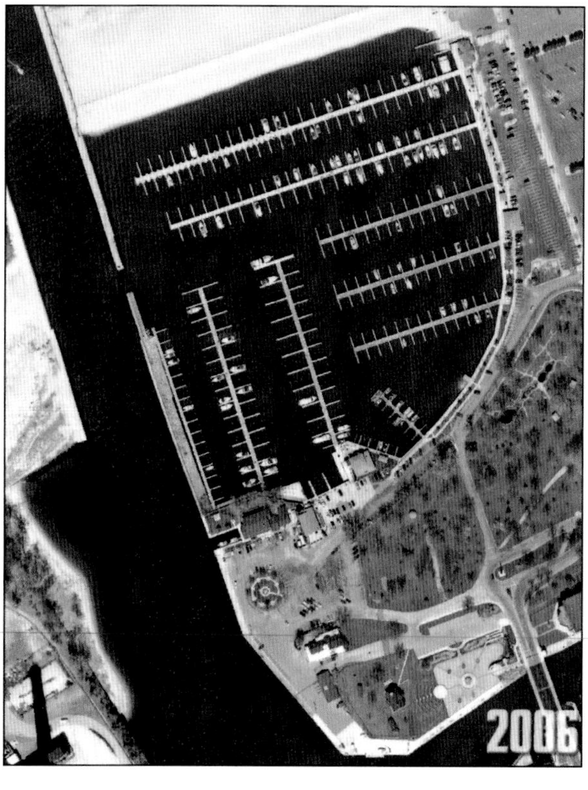

The new facility made the aging Washington Park Marina look worse by comparison. The board decided to undertake a complete overhaul. Jeffrey Katz attacked the bond issue, advising that the board acquire funds to refinance old bonds and underwrite new construction. A $5.5 million price tag seemed steep but necessary. Reconstruction of the 100, 200, and 300 docks began immediately. The next year, another bond was issued to complete the makeover, including landscaping, Jet Ski docks, and a dock extension. Washington Park Marina was rededicated in 1999. These bonds were later repaid, partially, with some of the $4.45 million received when Blue Chip expanded and needed part of the area that was Sprague Pointe.

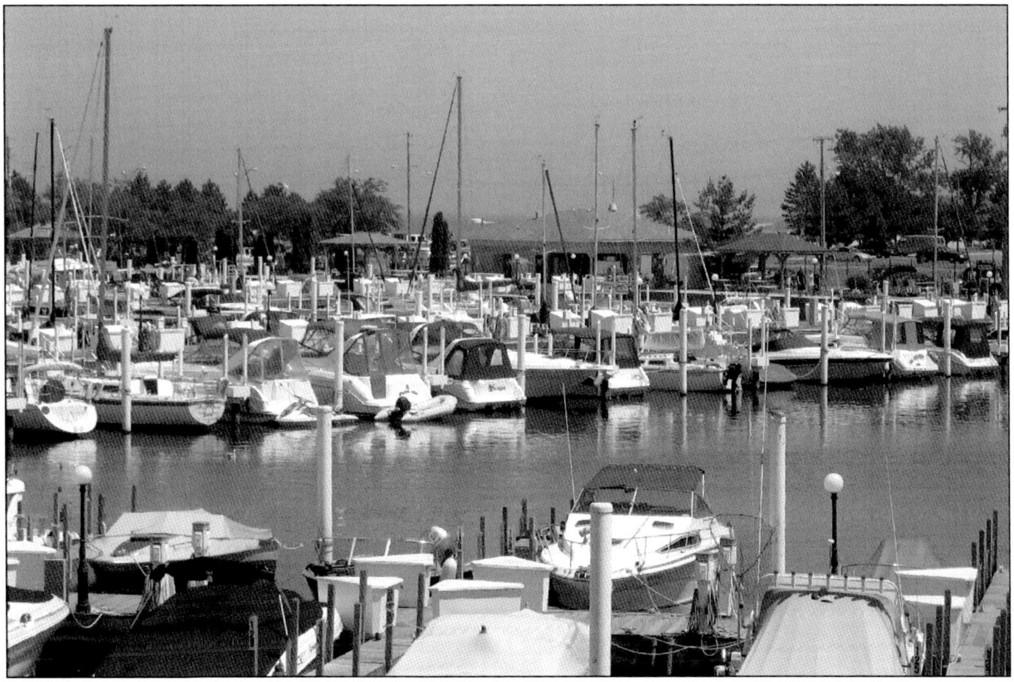

Despite the new facilities, the MCPA found its waiting list growing for both marinas during the boating season. A boater newsletter was created to effectively communicate with slip holders. (Rosemary Bunton.)

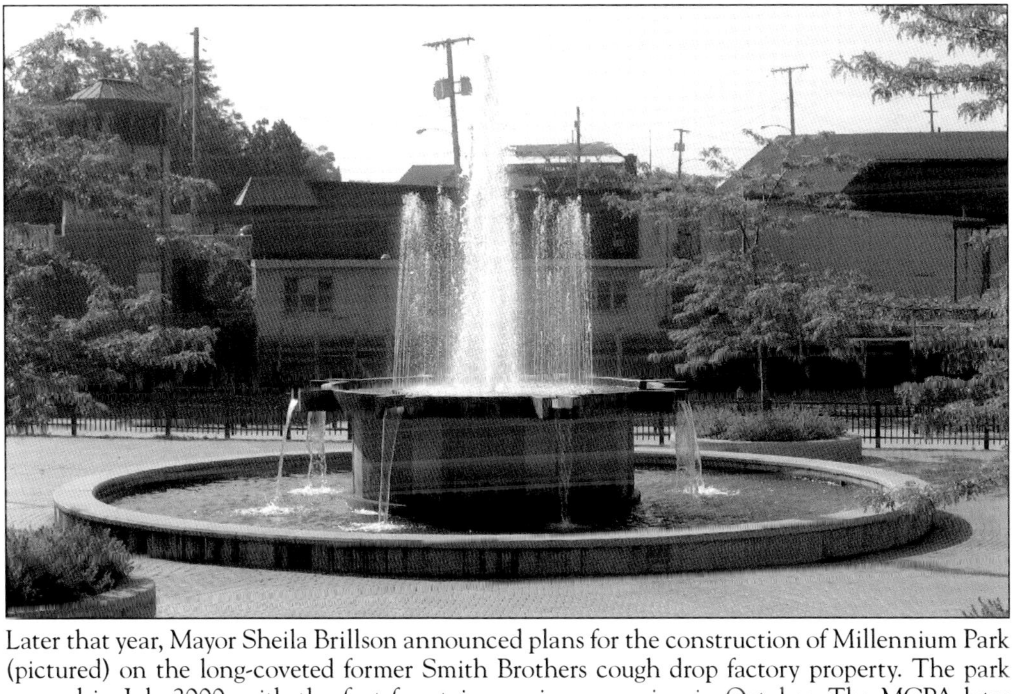

Later that year, Mayor Sheila Brillson announced plans for the construction of Millennium Park (pictured) on the long-coveted former Smith Brothers cough drop factory property. The park opened in July 2000, with the first fountain soaping occurring in October. The MCPA later relinquished responsibility for the park due to the added duties and costs that were associated with the property. (Michigan City News Dispatch.)

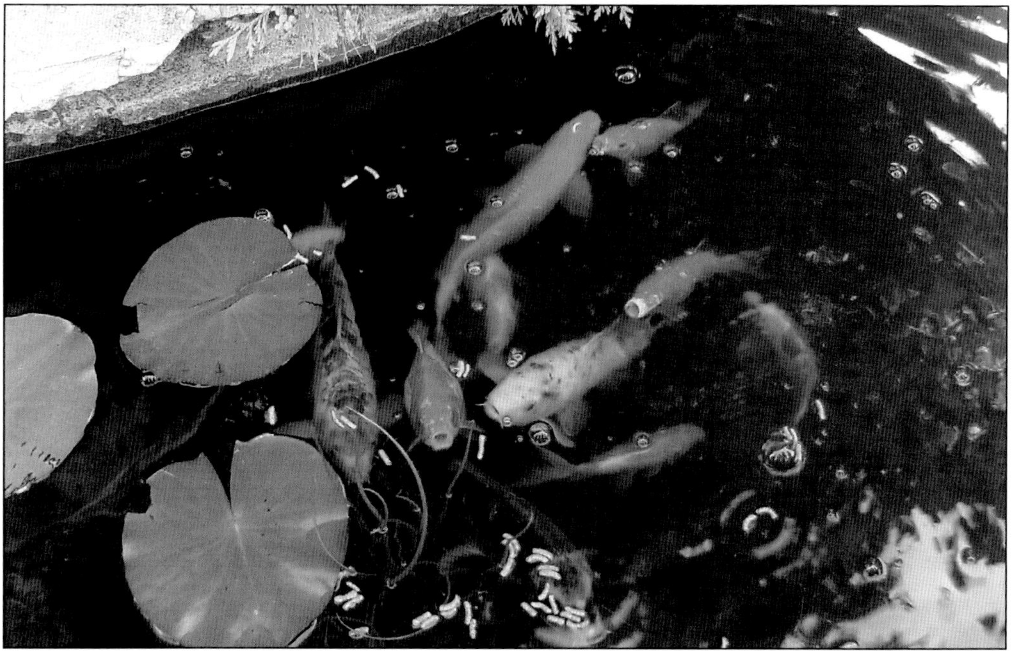

The year 2000 brought in changes throughout the MCPA. Trail Creek Marina got a complete face-lift. A new fence and landscaping transformed the area. Acquisitions from a separate improvement project, these koi now occupy a brick pond outside the Washington Park Marina.

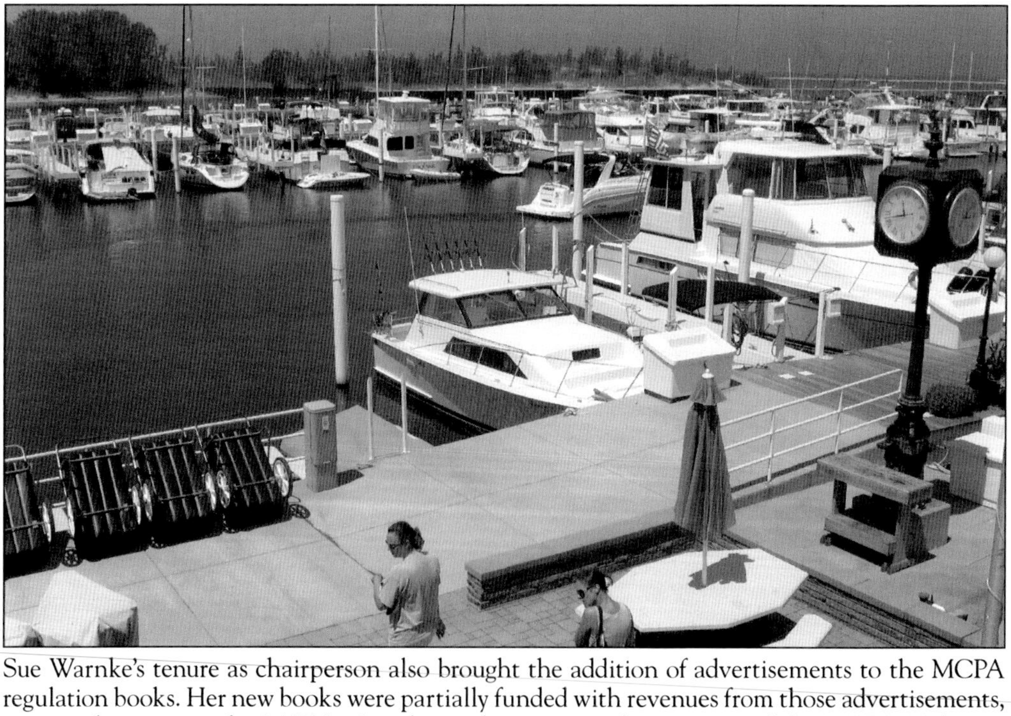

Sue Warnke's tenure as chairperson also brought the addition of advertisements to the MCPA regulation books. Her new books were partially funded with revenues from those advertisements, cutting the costs to the MCPA. Another milestone was the creation of the MCPA Web site. Thus, under Warnke's tenure, the MCPA and marina (seen here) were updated and ready to compete for boating business in the new millennium. (Rosemary Bunton.)

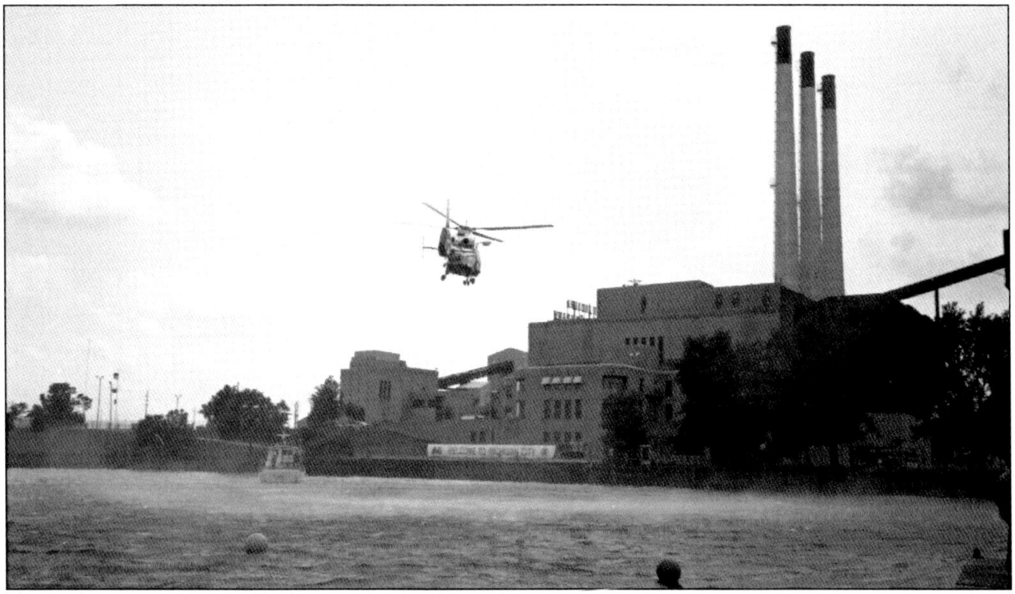

In November 2000, the news of heinous indiscretions heralded the MCPA's first scandal. The accusations centered on the MCPA's harbormaster John Rudisell. Mayor Sheila Brillson opted to suspend Rudisell, the first and only suspension in MCPA history. Two months later, as the accusations mounted and charges were filed, Brillson fired Rudisell with the endorsement of the board. Assistant harbormaster Scott Westphal took over the duties of harbormaster. (Michigan City News Dispatch.)

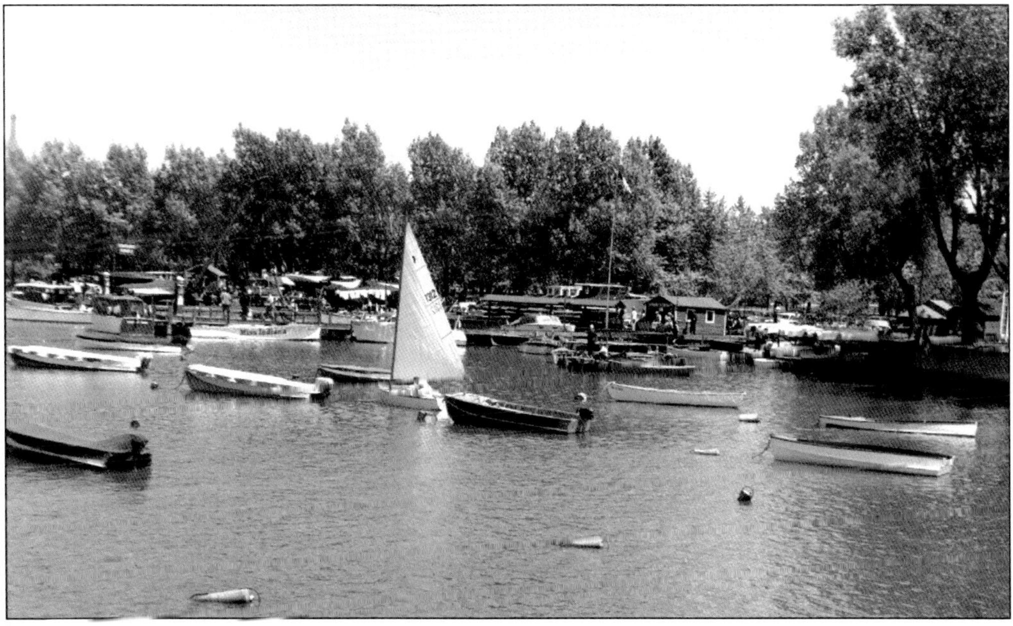

The media soon assaulted the MCPA with rumors of Rudisell's misdoings at the marinas. Although an investigation into the MCPA's files disproved the rumors that arose, Warnke and the board felt that it was time for reorganization. The MCPA was on a cash system since its incorporation. Now all MCPA checks and new employees would be processed by the city. (Bill Swedenberg.)

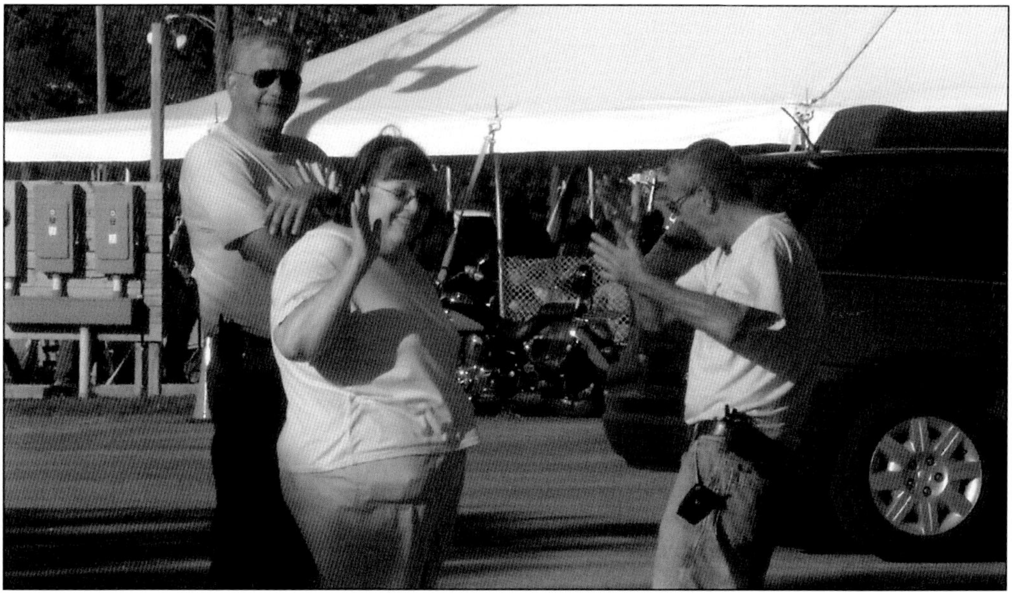

The chairman's seat changed hands in the year after Sue Warnke left from Robert Kavenuagh (far right) to Bruce Gilbert and then to John Quinn, who saw to the completion of the reorganization. According to the February 26, 2002, meeting minutes, Gilbert's first act, to make the harbormaster akin to the "CEO of the Port Authority," was the ending to Richard Kruse's 1989 plan to give the harbormaster more autonomy. Tim Frame, the current harbormaster, is pictured at left, and assistant harbormaster of operations Mary Ann Pawlicke is in the center.

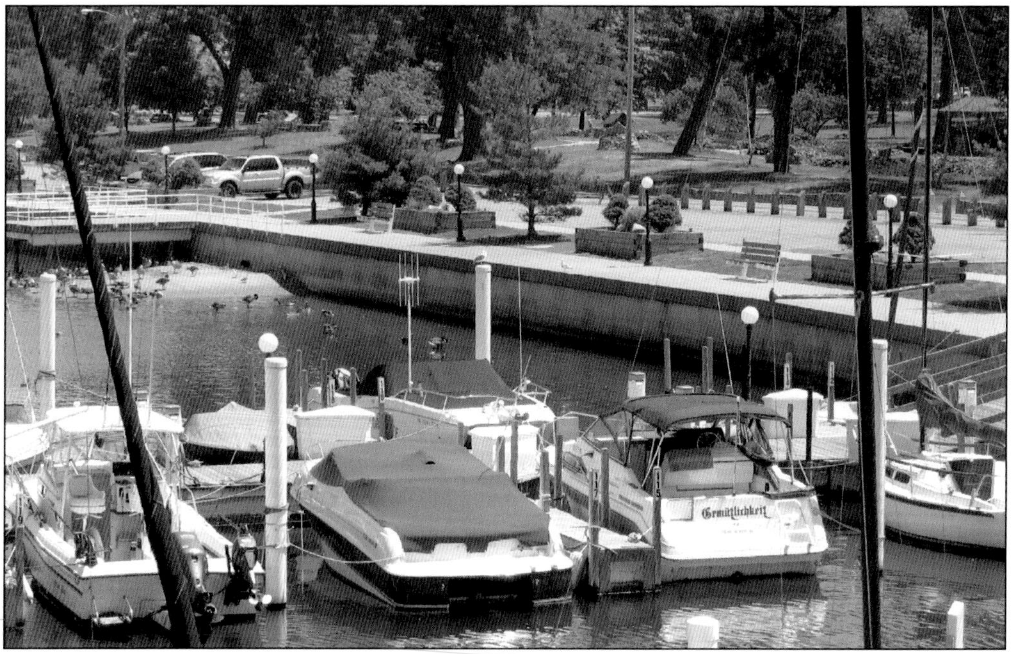

Another unlikely alliance came a few years later when the park board and the MCPA agreed to cooperate over parking fee collection. The pictured dock sits adjacent to the parking lot. This seemingly small arrangement is a tremendous step for the two boards that began their relationship in court suing each other. (Rosemary Bunton.)

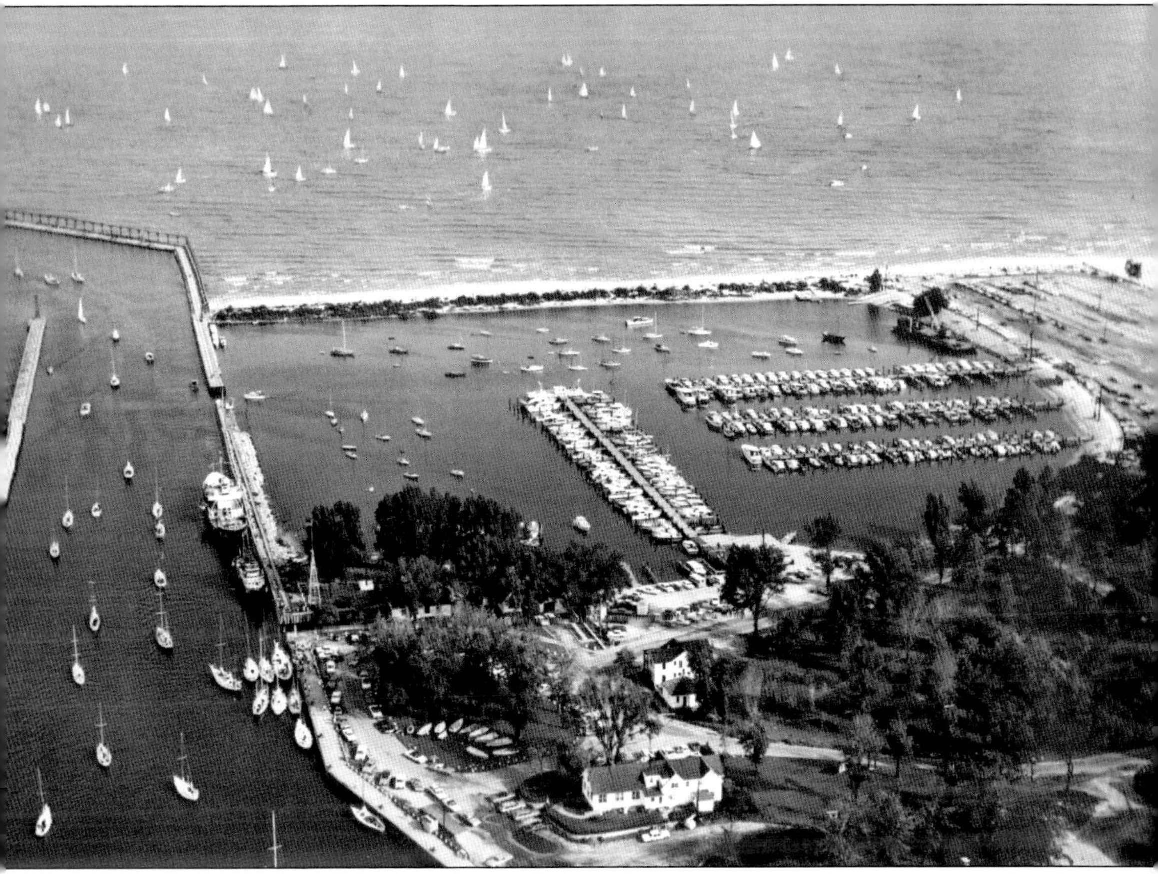

By the end of 2002, the once-independent MCPA was becoming more and more intertwined with the city. The process required a level of cooperation that took 40 years to achieve.

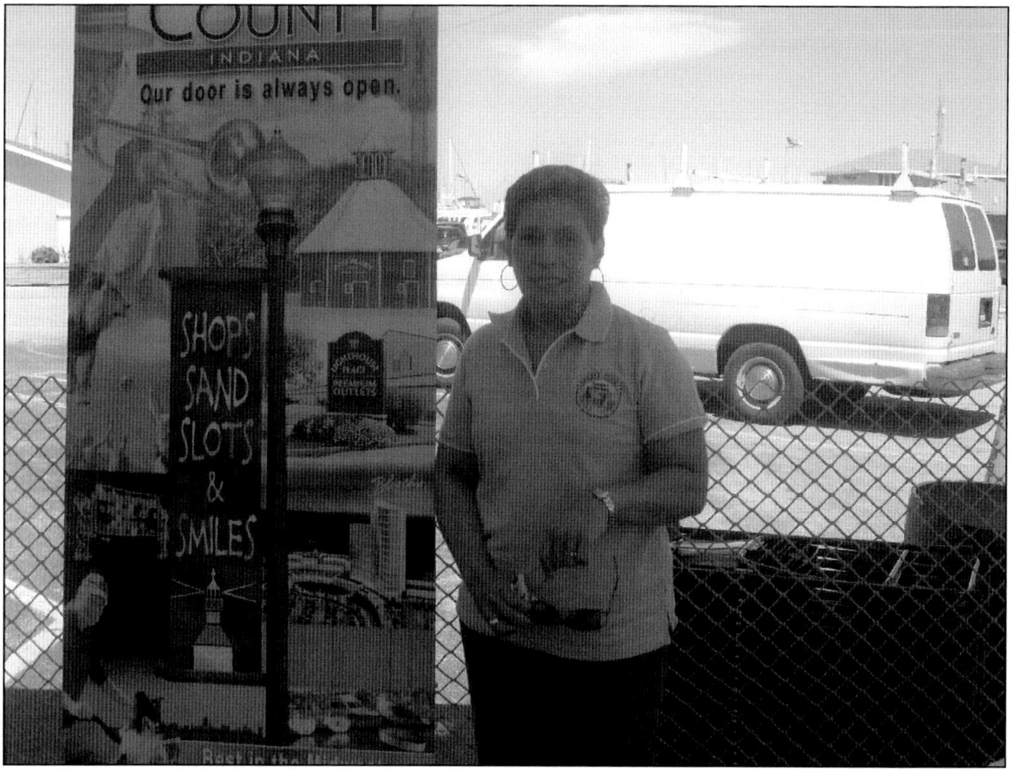

Linda Simmons (pictured) joined the board in 2002 and brought about another long-overdue partnership between the MCPA and the LaPorte Convention and Visitor's Bureau. The partnership has resulted in an increased awareness of activities at the marinas.

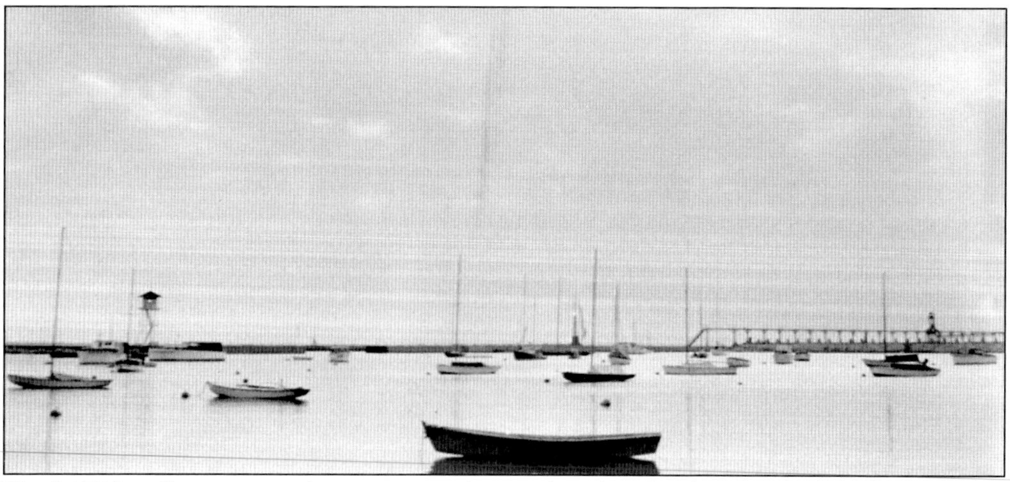

The MCPA still maintains the autonomy that its founders fought to protect. It also operates without tax funds—the marina is maintained through slip fees and revenues. Although it has outsourced certain aspects of its operations like hiring and check distribution, the MCPA is and will remain self-sufficient. (Michigan City Public Library.)

Nine

The Next Chapter

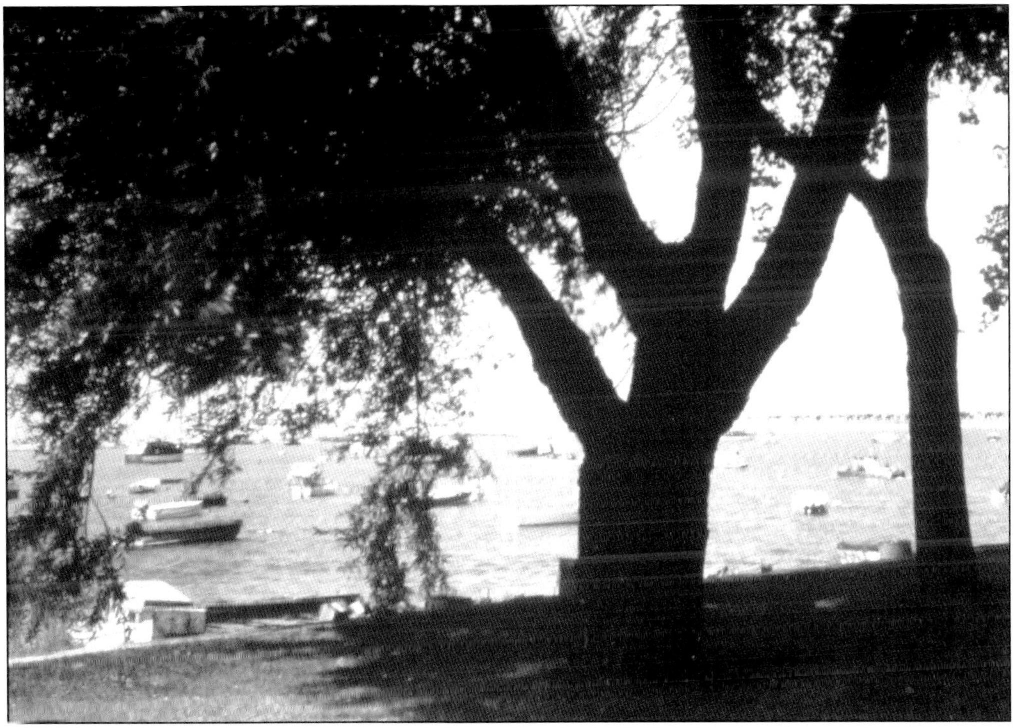

The ways of the world have seeped into the walls of the marina. In 2004, Airbaud Communications brought WiFi to the marina. The fear of terrorism brought bomb threat protocols and multiplied the importance of insurance, which now warrants it own committee. As the changes blow in, the MCPA still maintains the tradition of superior service to boaters, no matter if they are local or from abroad. (Bill Swedenberg.)

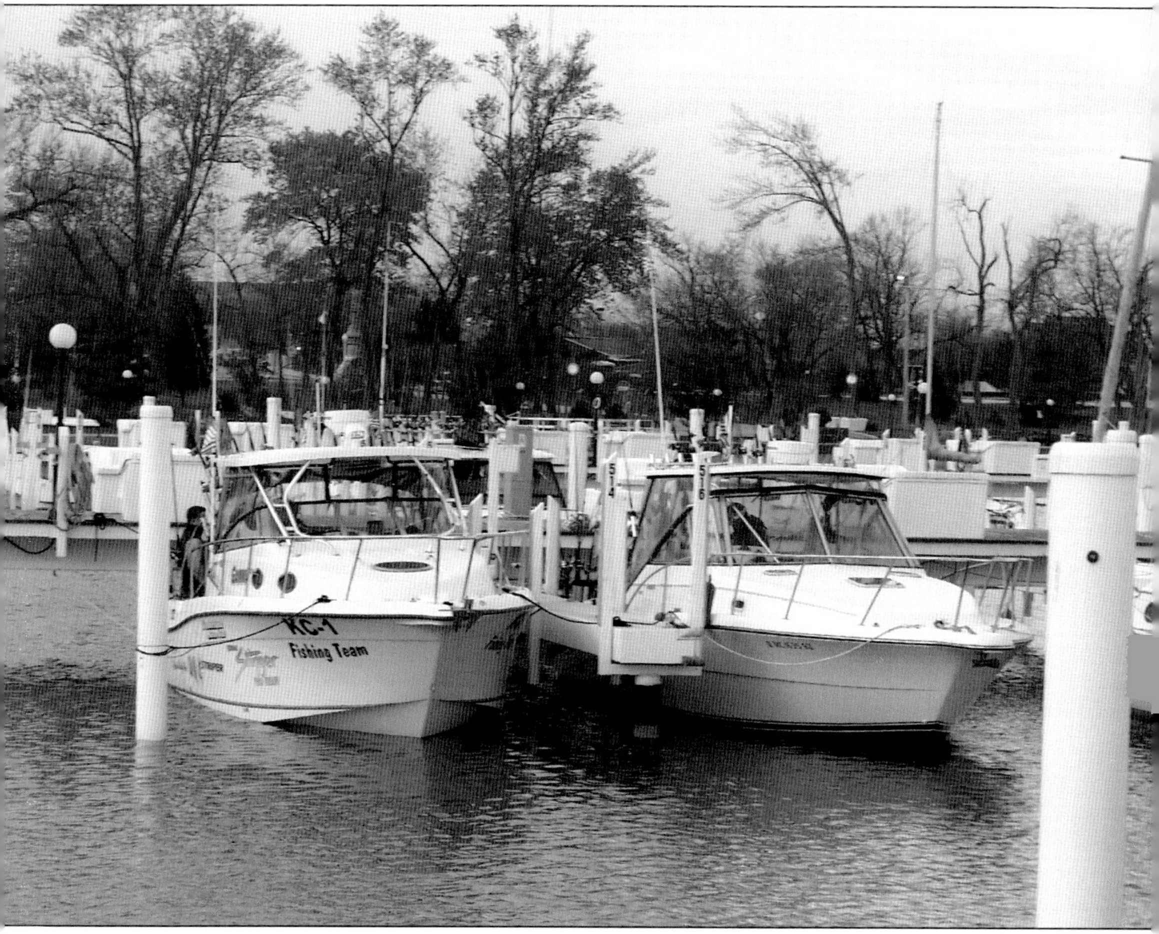

The MCPA now barely resembles the one that began 50 years ago—those five men huddled into the cramped space of the city engineer's office, with no money and a vision for turning the muddy, shallow basin that was entangled in vegetation near Trail Creek and so shallow one could walk across it into what it is today.

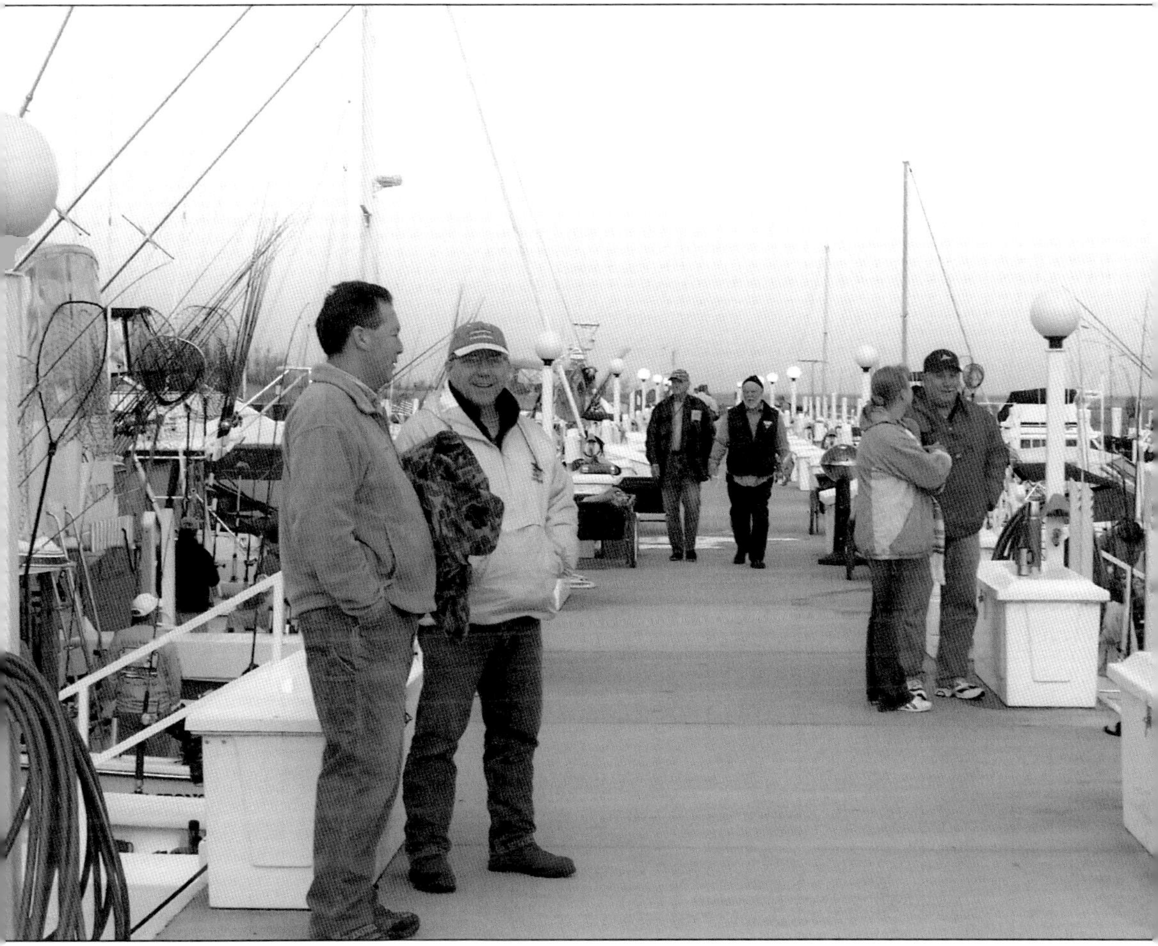

Today the slips are full and the docks are places that boaters spend time not just docking their boats. There are gas docks, a fish-cleaning station, and plenty of places to bathe, entertain, or just relax. (John Haynes.)

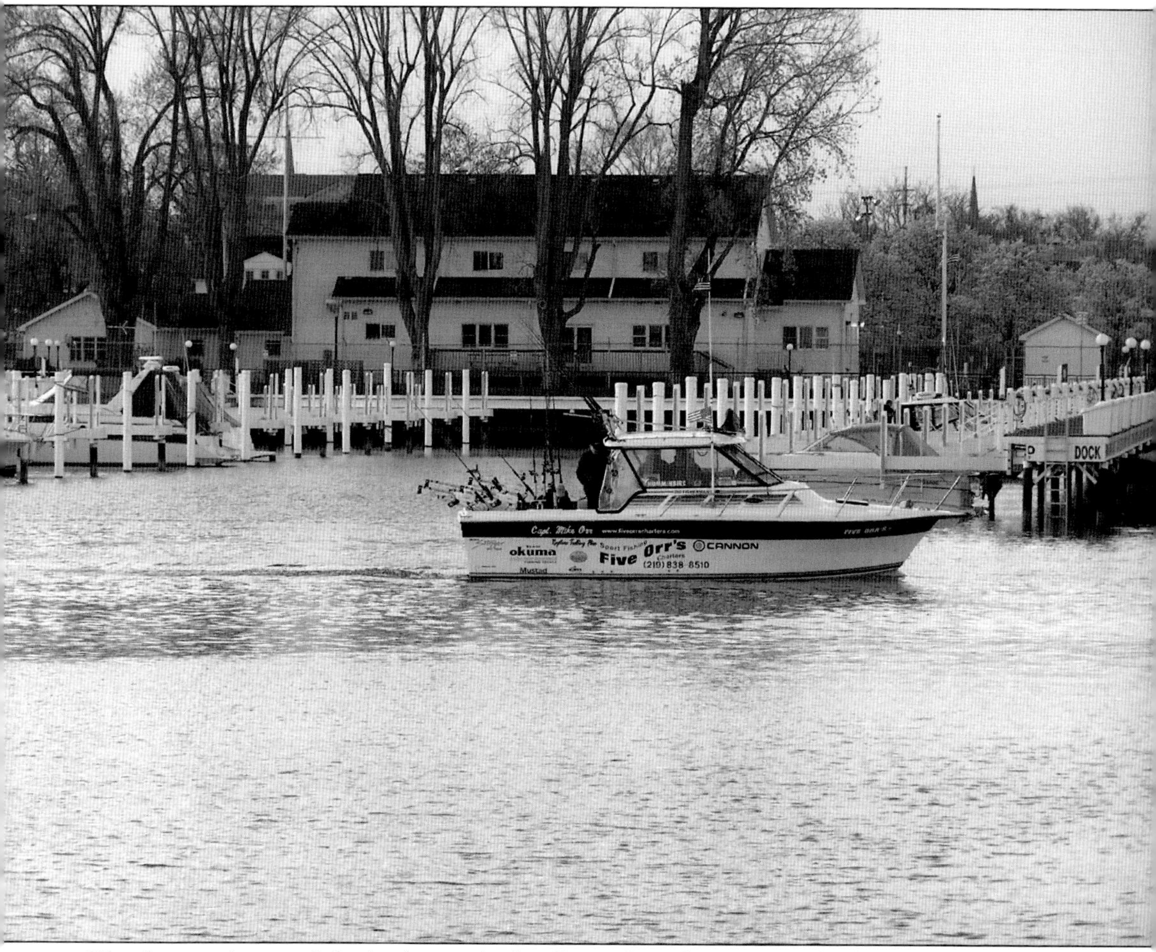

This boat sails out of the harbor with the Coast Guard station in the background. The U.S. Coast Guard is another one of the MCPA's neighbors and partners. (John Haynes.)

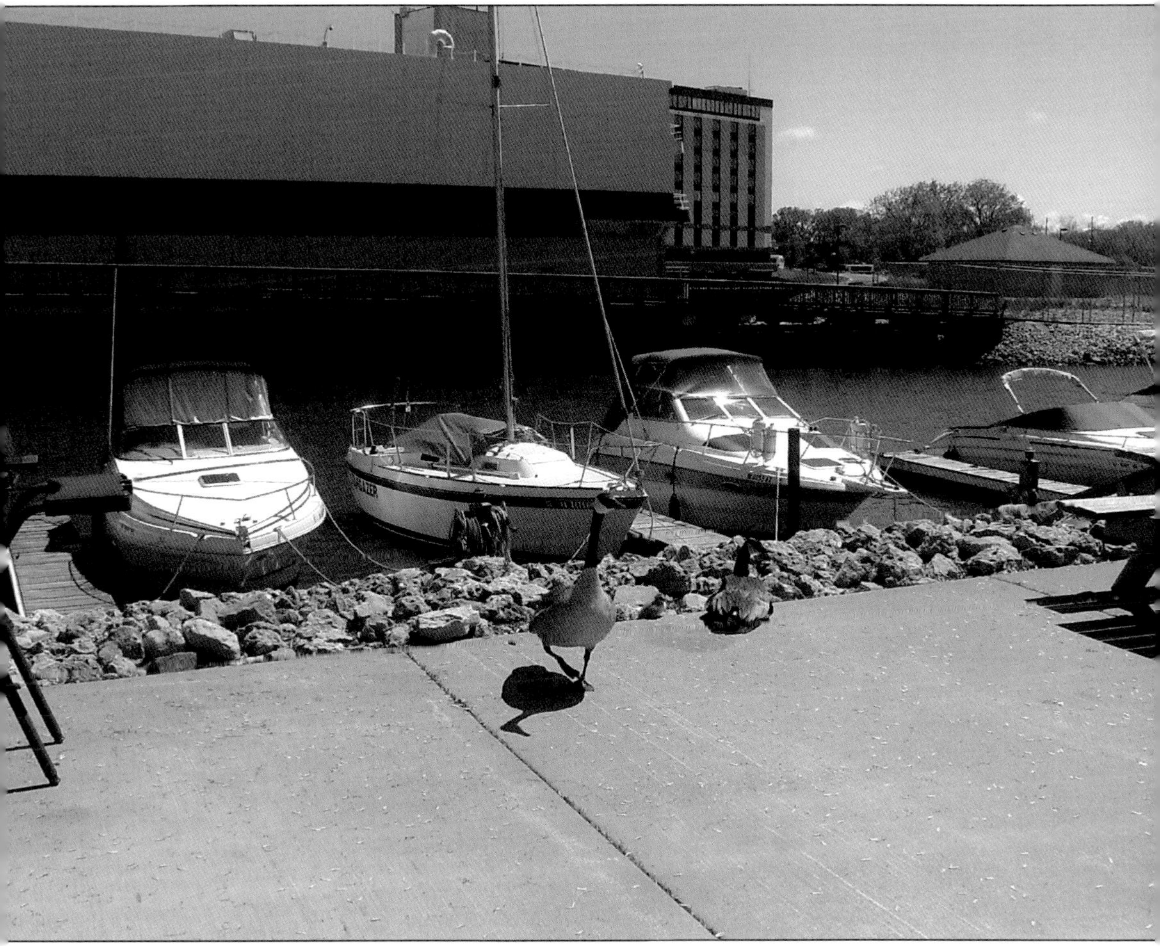

Today board members sit in a spacious boardroom with a view of the luxurious yacht harbor that on any given day during the season is packed with boaters from Michigan City and beyond. Today's MCPA also includes an upstream marina and Trail Creek Marina (pictured), which mirrors the one in the basin.

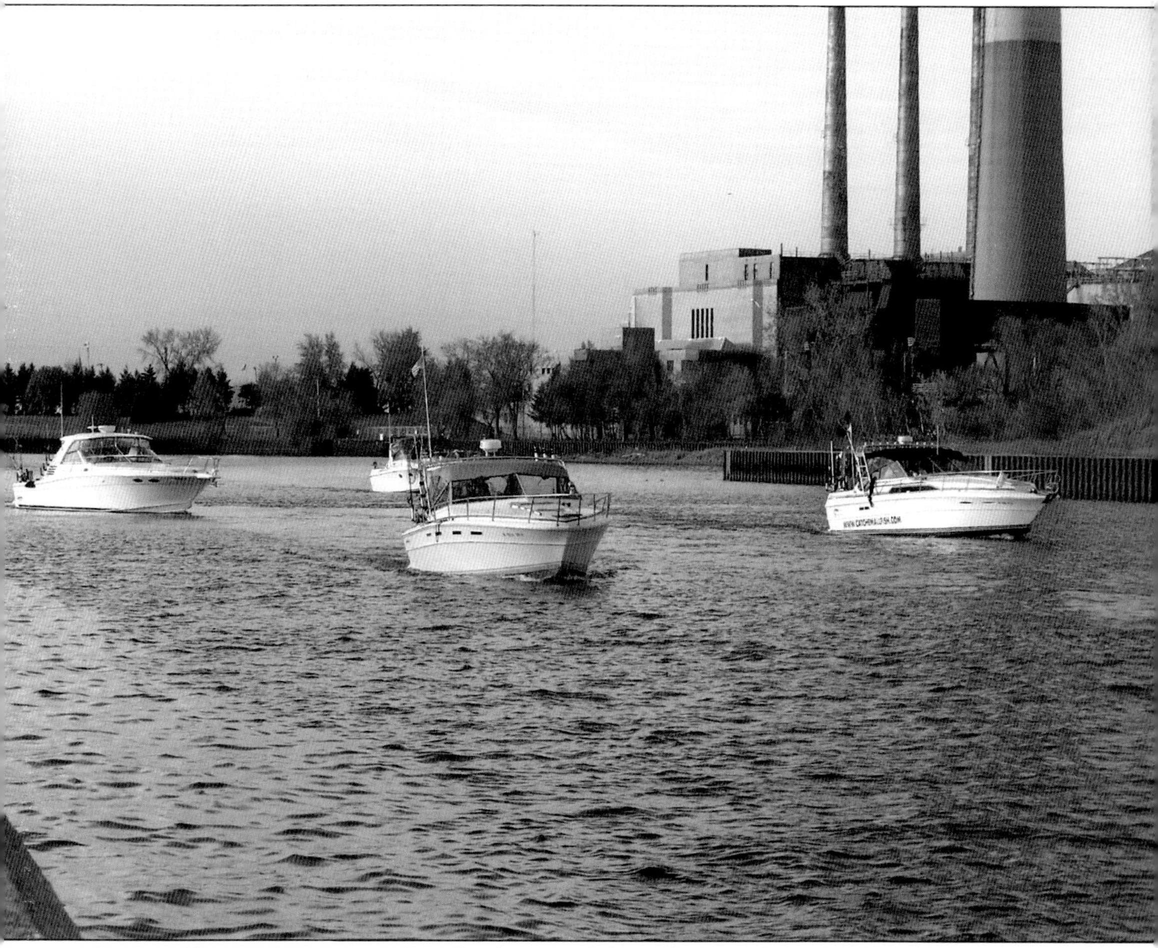

One could go so far as to say that the dreams of those five men have been realized. Others may say that the MCPA has improvements yet to be made. Whatever the opinion, all would agree that the MCPA is first class and may be even in a higher class all its own. (John Haynes.)

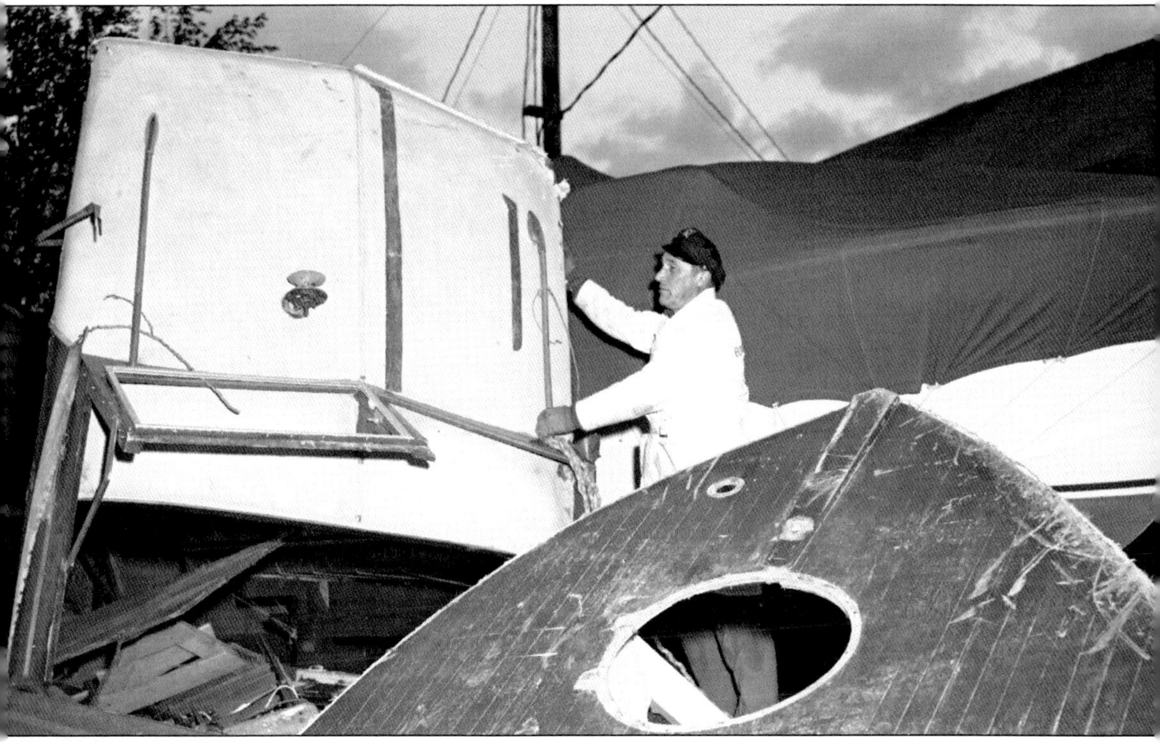

The people of Michigan City have wanted a harbor of their own since the early 1800s. Grassroots efforts have sprung up throughout history to build that harbor. From the Michigan City Harbor Company's faulty bonds to the incorporation of the MCYC, individuals tried their hands at building a port. This photograph shows some of the items (boat and automobile parts) retrieved from the basin during construction in 1961. Although many would not believe it today, the basin was used as a dumping ground in the early 1900s. (Michigan City News Dispatch.)

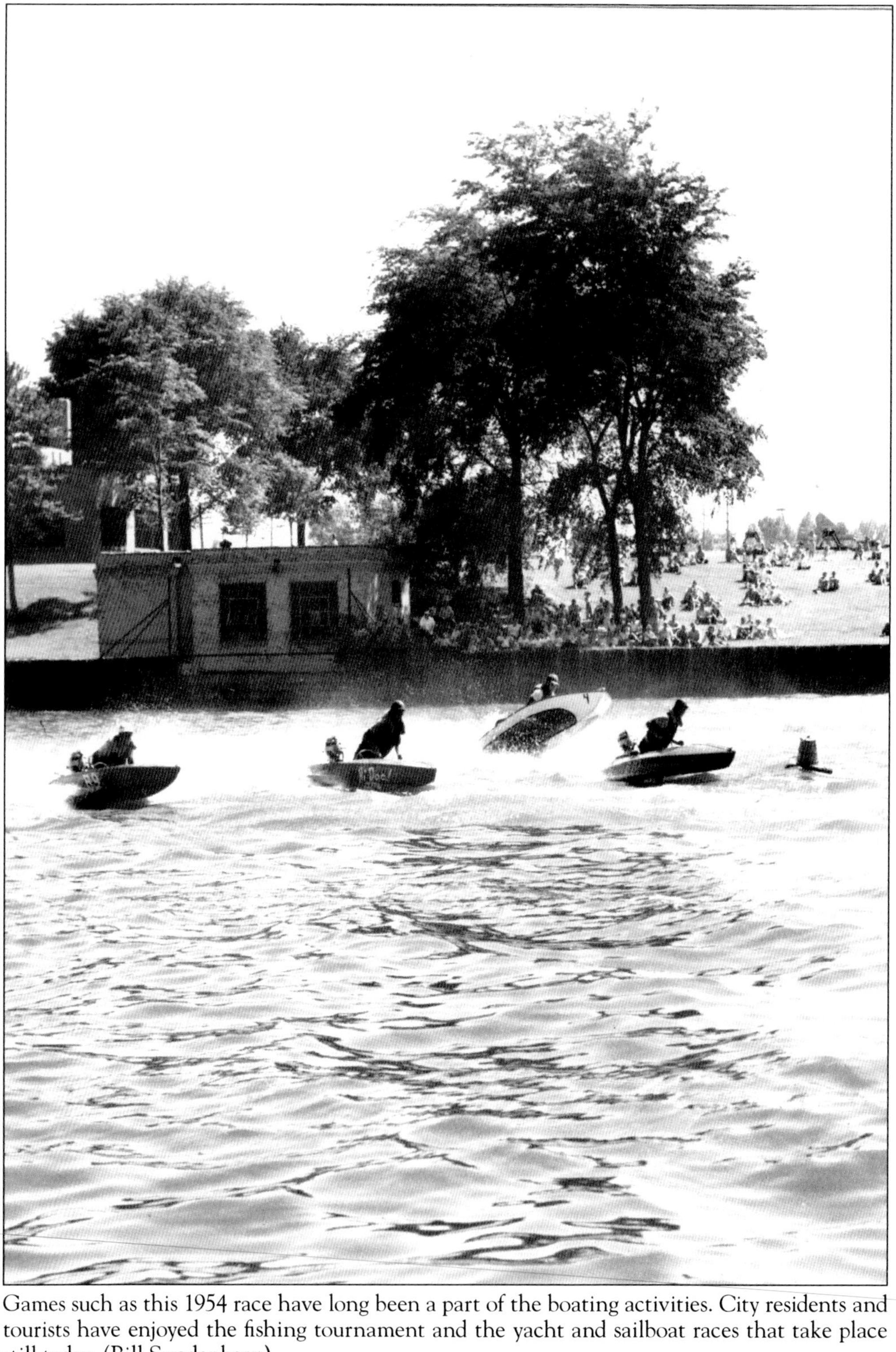

Games such as this 1954 race have long been a part of the boating activities. City residents and tourists have enjoyed the fishing tournament and the yacht and sailboat races that take place still today. (Bill Swedenberg.)

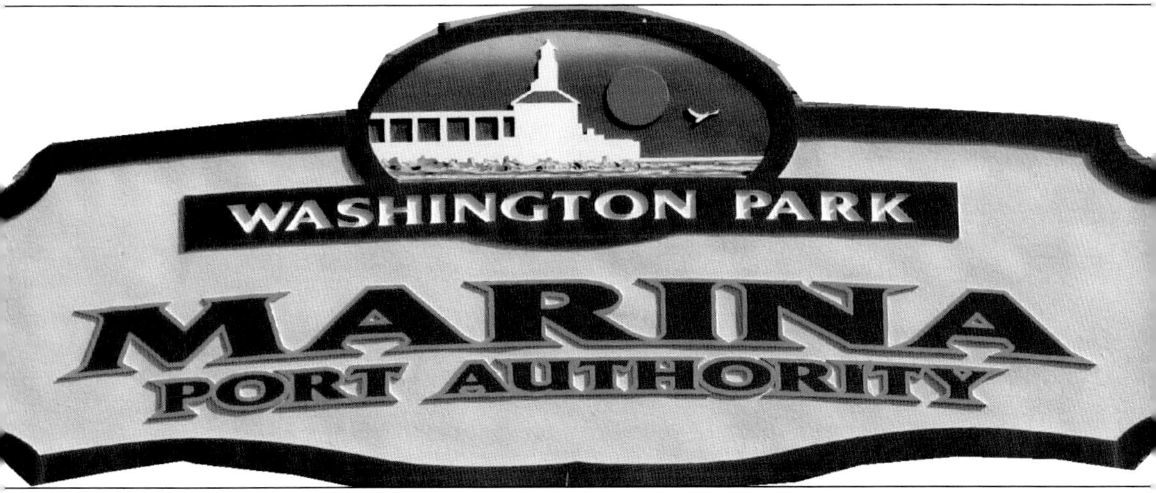

It was not until everyone unified in 1958 to create the MCPA in 1959 that real progress began. Most expected that the work was done. They had an agency to handle improving and maintaining the harbor; the people of Michigan City sometimes forgot that their support was still needed. There were even times when the MCPA and its boaters were considered separate from the rest of the city. A brutal relationship resulted. (Rosemary Bunton.)

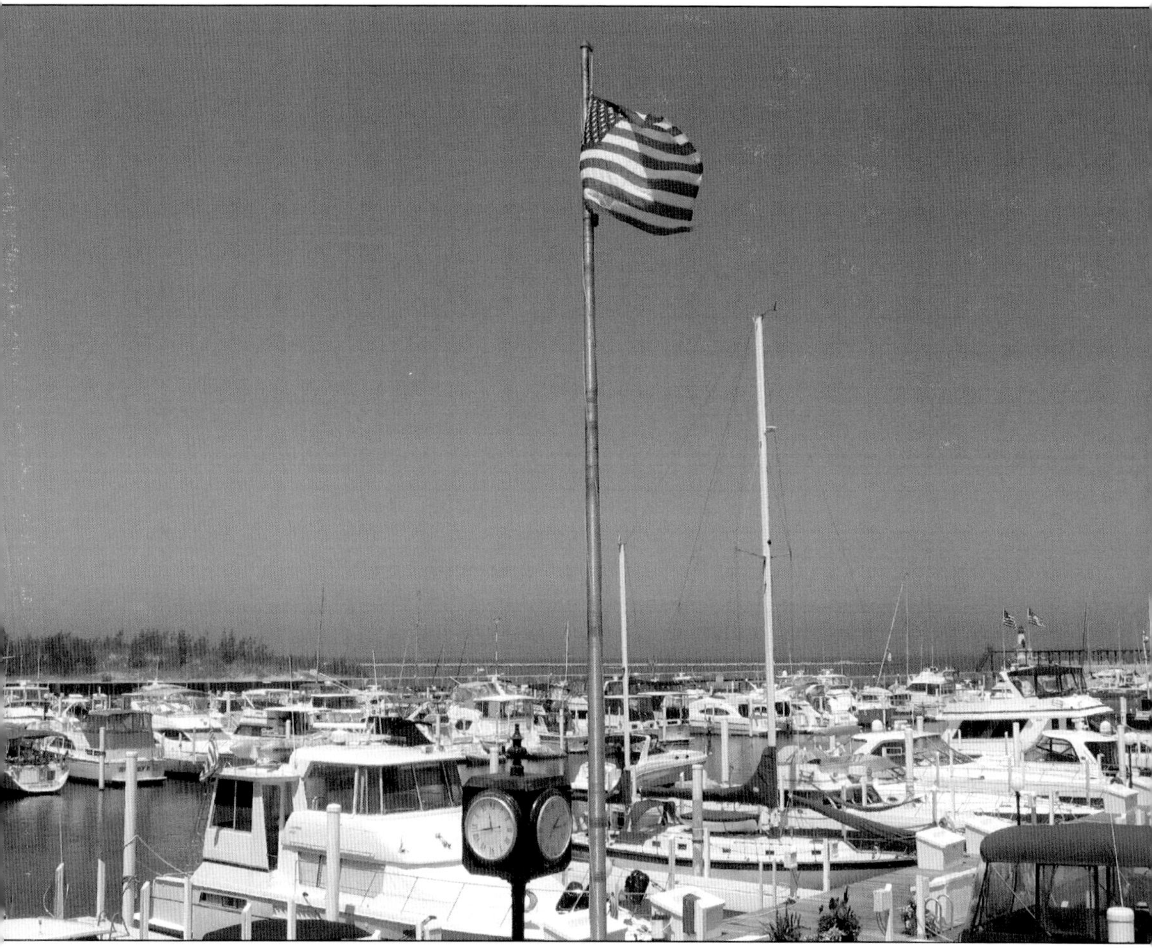

This photograph of the boats docked in Washington Park Marina was taken during the boating season. Despite the issues that have risen over the years, boaters continued to make Michigan City's marinas their destination every summer. (Rosemary Bunton.)

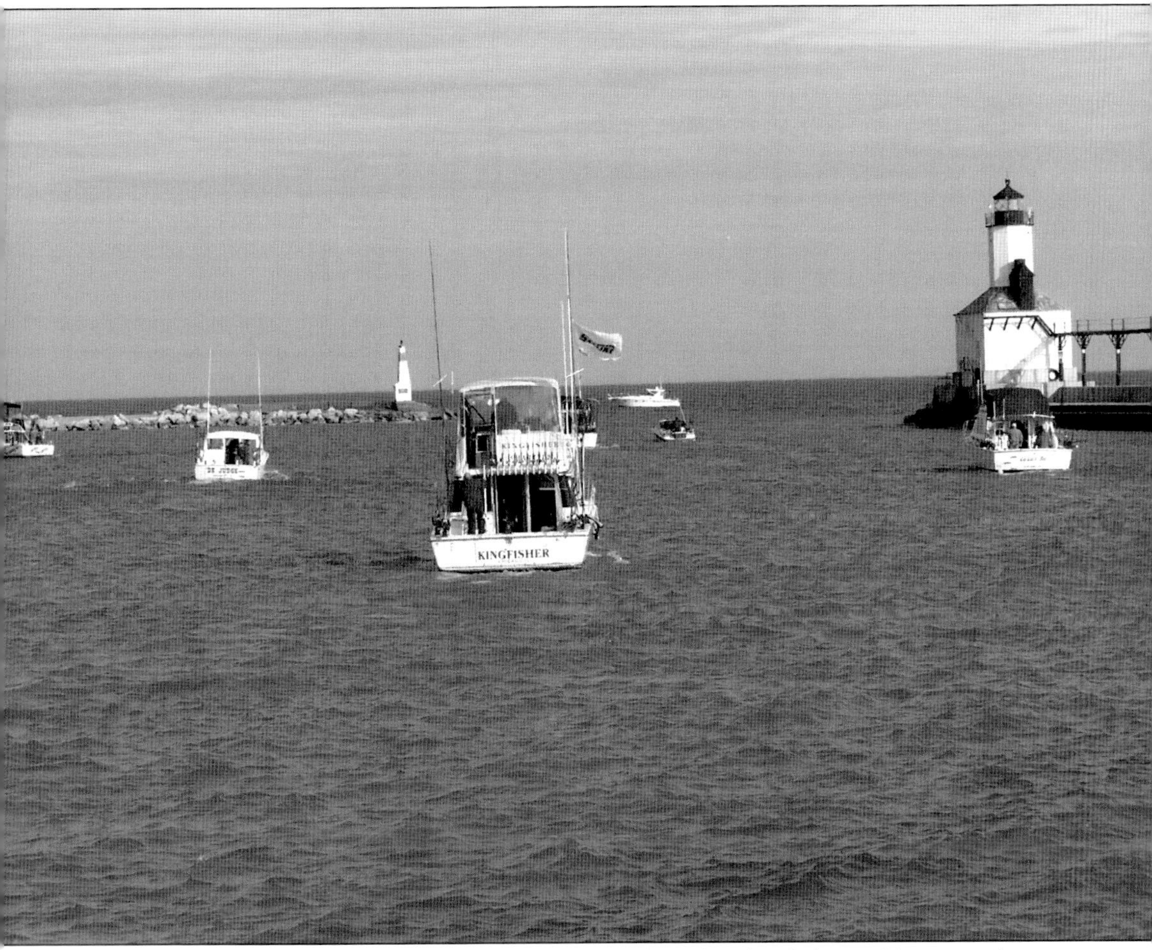

However, times change, and so do people. When the board realized the problem was that no one knew who or what the MCPA was, an effort began to educate the public. Starting with the skeptic's tours of 1982, the board tried to change its public perception. Over 20 years later and after financially binding itself to the city, the MCPA's relationship with Michigan City has healed. (John Haynes.)

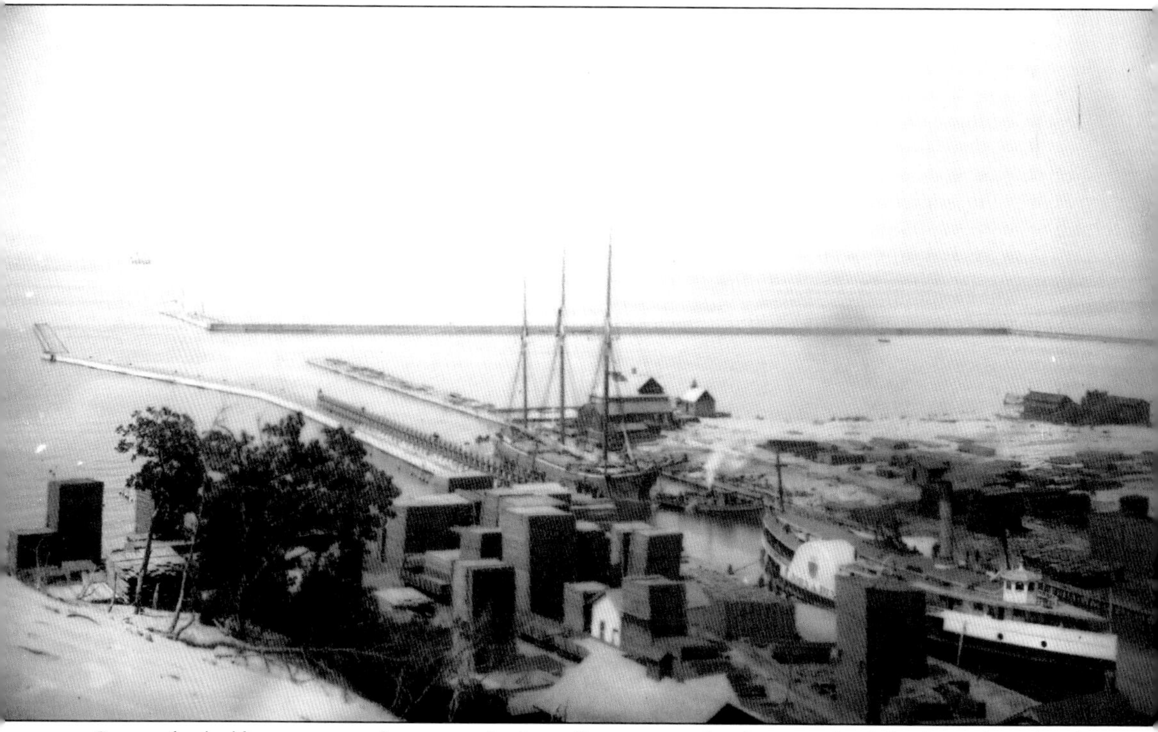

So, as the half-century mark passes, the board's eye is to the future, which looks to be a bright one. With the city behind it, the marina will continue to grow and change, but it will be a community effort, as the founding fathers intended. (Bill Swedenberg.)

Bibliography

Haverstick, Amanda. "Building Named for Hartley Job." *Michigan City News Dispatch*, August 22, 2008, A1.
Kaser, Bob. "Basin Expansion Offers Harbor Help." *Michigan City News Dispatch*, February 26, 1959, A1.
———. "City's Sinking Harbor Level Raises Problems." *Michigan City News Dispatch*, February 24, 1959, A1.
———. :200 Pleasure Boaters Form Association Here." *Michigan City News Dispatch*, March 28, 1959, A4.
Michigan City News Dispatch. "Lakeland Postpones Port Action." July 7, 1959, A2.
———. "Park Board to Hire Expert on Development of Basin." March 6, 1959, A1.
———. "Port Authority Hires Butler for Court Fight." September 24, 1959, A1.
Minutes of the Michigan City Port Authority I. Michigan City, IN: Michigan City Port Authority, 1959, 4–5.
Minutes of the Michigan City Port Authority II. Michigan City, IN: Michigan City Port Authority, 1990, 432.
Minutes of the Michigan City Port Authority FY 2002. Michigan City, IN: Michigan City Port Authority, 2002.
Nicewarner, Gladys Bull. *Michigan City, Indiana: The Life of a Town*. Michigan City, IN: Self-published, 1980.
Oglesbee, Rollo, and Albert Hale. *History of Michigan City, Indiana*. LaPorte, IN: Edward J. Widdell Publishing, 1908.
Our Heritage: Michigan City, IN. Michigan City, IN: Michigan City News Dispatch, 1976.